CHRISTIAN WORLDVIEW  INTEGRATION SERIES

EDUCATION *for Human Flourishing*

A Christian Perspective

PAUL D. SPEARS &
STEVEN R. LOOMIS

IVP Academic

An imprint of InterVarsity Press
Downers Grove, Illinois

InterVarsity Press
P.O. Box 1400, Downers Grove, IL 60515-1426
World Wide Web: www.ivpress.com
E-mail: email@ivpress.com

InterVarsity Press® is the book-publishing division of InterVarsity Christian Fellowship/USA®, a movement of students and faculty active on campus at hundreds of universities, colleges and schools of nursing in the United States of America, and a member movement of the International Fellowship of Evangelical Students. For information about local and regional activities, write Public Relations Dept., InterVarsity Christian Fellowship/USA, 6400 Schroeder Rd., P.O. Box 7895, Madison, WI 53707-7895, or visit the IVCF website at <www.intervarsity.org>.

Scripture quotations, unless otherwise noted, are from The Holy Bible, English Standard Version, *copyright © 2001 by Crossway Bibles, a division of Good News Publishers. Used by permission. All rights reserved.*

Figure 5.1 is adapted from Jerald Hage and Charles H. Powers, Post-Industrial Lives: Roles and Relationships in the 21st Century, *and used by permission of Sage Publications Inc. Books, Newbury Park, Calif.*

Design: Cindy Kiple

ISBN 978-0-8308-2812-8

Printed in the United States of America ∞

 InterVarsity Press is committed to protecting the environment and to the responsible use of natural resources. As a member of Green Press Initiative we use recycled paper whenever possible. To learn more about the Green Press Initiative, visit <www.greenpressinitiative.org>.

Library of Congress Cataloging-in-Publication Data

Spears, Paul D.
 Education for human flourishing: a Christian perspective/Paul D.
Spears and Steven R. Loomis.
  p. cm.—(A call to integration and the Christian worldview
  integration series)
Includes bibliographical references and indexes.
ISBN 978-0-8308-2812-8 (pbk.: alk. paper)
1. Education (Christian theology) I. Loomis, Steven R. II. Title.
BT738.17.S64 2009
 371.10201—dc22
                  2009021599

P	20	19	18	17	16	15	14	13	12	11	10	9	8	7	6	5	4	3	2	1
Y	25	24	23	22	21	20	19	18	17	16	15	14	13	12	11	10	09			

For June Hetzel:
educator, leader and saint
Steven R. Loomis

For my wife, whom I cherish,
and my children, Ian and Alexis,
because they make my life special,
and are the reason I care about education
Paul D. Spears

CONTENTS

A Call to Integration and the
Christian Worldview Integration Series

Life's short and we're all busy. If you're a college student, you're *really* busy. There's your part-time job (which seems full time), your social life (hopefully) and church. On top of that you're expected to go to class, do some reading, take tests and write papers. Now, while you are minding your own business, you hear about something called "integration," trying to relate your major with your Christianity. Several questions may come to mind: What is integration, anyway? Is it just a fad? Why should I care about it? And even if I do care about it, I don't have a clue as to how to go about doing it. How do I do this? These are good questions, and in this introduction we're going to address them in order. We are passionate about helping you learn about and become good at integrating your Christian convictions with the issues and ideas in your college major or your career.

What Is Integration?

The word *integrate* means "to form or blend into a whole," "to unite." We humans naturally seek to find the unity that is behind diversity, and in fact coherence is an important mark of rationality. There are two kinds of integration: conceptual and personal. In conceptual integration, *our theological beliefs, especially those derived from careful study of the Bible, are blended and unified with important, reasonable ideas from our profession or college major into a coherent, intellectually satisfying Christian worldview.* As Augustine wisely advised, "We must show our Scriptures not to be in conflict with whatever [our critics] can demonstrate about the nature of things from reliable sources."[1] In personal integration we seek to live a unified life, a life in which we are the same in public as we are in private, a life in which the various aspects of our personality are consistent with each other and conducive to a life of human flourishing as a disciple of Jesus.

The two kinds of integration are deeply intertwined. All things being equal, the more authentic we are, the more integrity we have, the more we should be able to do conceptual integration with fidelity to Jesus and Scripture, and with intellectual honesty. All things being equal the more conceptual integration we accomplish, the more coherent will be our set of beliefs and the more confidence we will have in the truth of our Christian worldview. In fact, conceptual integration is so important that it is worth thinking some more about why it matters.

SEVEN REASONS WHY INTEGRATION MATTERS

1. *The Bible's teachings are true.* The first justification for integration is pretty obvious, but often overlooked. *Christians hold that, when properly interpreted, the teachings of Holy Scripture are true.* This means two things. If the Bible teaches something relevant to an issue in an academic field, the Bible's view on that topic is true and thus provides an incredibly rich resource for doing work in that academic field. It would be irresponsible to set aside an important source of relevant truth in thinking through issues in our field of study or vocation. Further, if it looks like a claim on our field tends to make a biblical claim false, this tension needs to be resolved. Maybe our interpretation of Scripture is mistaken, maybe the Bible is not even talking about the issue, maybe the claim in our field is false. Whatever the case, the Christian's commitment to the truth of Scripture makes integration inevitable.

Adolfo Lopez-Otero, a Stanford engineering professor and a self-described secular humanist, offers advice to thinking Christians who

---

[1]Augustine *De genesi ad litteram* 1.21, cited in Ernan McMullin, "How Should Cosmology Relate to Theology?" in *The Sciences and Theology in the Twentieth Century*, ed. Arthur R. Peacocke (Notre Dame, Ind.: University of Notre Dame Press, 1981), p. 20.

want to have an impact on the world: "When a Christian professor approaches a non-believing faculty member . . . they can expect to face a polite but condescending person [with a belief that they possess] superior metaphysics who can't understand how such an intelligent person [as yourself] still believes in things which have been discredited eons ago."[2] He goes on to say that "[Christian professors] cannot afford to give excuses . . . if they are honest about wanting to open spiritual and truthful dialogue with their non-believing colleagues—that is the price they must pay for having declared themselves Christians."[3] While Lopez-Otero's remarks are directed to Christian professors, his point applies to all thinking Christians: If we claim that our Christian views are true, we need to back that up by interacting with the various ideas that come from different academic disciplines. In short, we must integrate Christianity and our major or vocation.

   2. *Our vocation and the holistic character of discipleship demand integration.* As disciples grow, they learn to see, feel, think, desire, believe and behave the way Jesus does in a manner fitting to the kingdom of God and their own station in life. With God's help we seek to live as Jesus would if he were a philosophy professor at Biola University married to Hope and father of Ashley and Allison, or as a political philosopher at Baylor University married to Frankie.

   Two important implications flow from the nature of discipleship. For one thing the lordship of Christ is holistic. The religious life is not a special compartment in an otherwise secular life. Rather, the religious life is an entire way of life. To live Christianly is to allow Jesus Christ to be the Lord of every aspect of our life. There is no room for a secular-sacred separation in the life of Jesus' followers. Jesus Christ should be every bit as much at home in our thinking and behavior when we are developing our views in our area of study or work as he is when we are in a small group fellowship.

   Further, as disciples of Jesus we do not merely have a job. We have a vocation as a Christian teacher. A job is a means for supporting our-

---

[2]Adolfo Lopez-Otero, "Be Humble, but Daring," *The Real Issue* 16 (September-October 1997): 10.
[3]Ibid., p. 11.

selves and those for whom we are responsible. For the Christian a vocation (from the Latin *vocare*, which means "to call") is an overall calling
from God. Harry Blamires correctly draws a distinction between a general and a special vocation:

> The general vocation of all Christians—indeed of all men and women—
> is the same. We are called to live as children of God, obeying his will in
> all things. But obedience to God's will must inevitably take many dif-
> ferent forms. The wife's mode of obedience is not the same as the nun's;
> the farmer's is not the same as the priest's. By "special vocation," there-
> fore, we designate God's call to a [person] to serve him in a particular
> sphere of activity.[4]

As Christians seek to discover and become excellent in their special
vocation, they must ask: How would Jesus approach the task of being a
history teacher, a chemist, an athletic director, a mathematician? It is
not always easy to answer this question, but the vocational demands of
discipleship require that we give it our best shot.

Whatever we do, however, it is important that we restore to our culture an image of Jesus Christ as an intelligent, competent person who
spoke authoritatively on whatever subject he addressed. The disciples of
Jesus agreed with Paul when he said that all the wisdom of the Greeks
and Jews was ultimately wrapped up in Jesus himself (Col 2:2-3). For
them, Jesus was not merely a Savior from sin; he was the wisest, most
intelligent, most attractive person they had ever seen.

In the early centuries of Christianity the church presented Jesus to
unbelievers precisely because he was wiser, more virtuous, more intelligent and more attractive in his character than Aristotle, Plato, Moses or
anyone else. It has been a part of the church's self-understanding to locate the spiritual life in a broader quest for the good life, that is, a life of
wisdom, knowledge, beauty and goodness. So understood, the spiritual
life and discipleship to Jesus were seen as the very best way to achieve a
life of truth, beauty and goodness. Moreover, the life of discipleship was
depicted as the wisest, most reasonable form of life available so that a life
of unbelief was taken to be foolish and absurd. *Our schools need to recap-*

---

[4]Harry Blamires, *A God Who Acts* (Ann Arbor, Mich.: Servant Books, 1957), p. 67.

ture and propagate this broader understanding of following Christ if they are to be thoroughly Christian in their approach to education.

3. *Biblical teaching about the role of the mind in the Christian life and the value of extrabiblical knowledge requires integration.* The Scriptures are clear that God wants us to be like him in every facet of our lives, and he desires commitment from our total being, including our intellectual life. We are told that we change spiritually by having the categories of our minds renewed (Rom 12:1-2), that we are to include an intellectual love for God in our devotion (Mt 22:37-38), and that we are to be prepared to give others a reasonable answer to questions others ask us about why we believe what we believe (1 Pet 3:15). As the great eighteenth-century Christian thinker and spiritual master William Law put it, "Unreasonable and absurd ways of life . . . are truly an offense to God."[5] Learning and developing convictions about the teachings of Scripture are absolutely central to these mandates. However, many of Jesus' followers have failed to see that an aggressive pursuit of knowledge in areas outside the Bible is also relevant to these directives.

God has revealed himself and various truths on a number of topics outside the Bible. As Christians have known throughout our history, common sense, logic and mathematics, along with the arts, humanities, sciences and other areas of study, contain important truths relevant to life in general and to the development of a careful, life-related Christian worldview.

In 1756 John Wesley delivered an address to a gathering of clergy on how to carry out the pastoral ministry with joy and skill. In it Wesley catalogued a number of things familiar to most contemporary believers—the cultivation of a disposition to glorify God and save souls, a knowledge of Scripture, and similar notions. However, at the front of his list Wesley focused on something seldom expressly valued by most pastoral search committees: "Ought not a Minister to have, First, a good understanding, a clear apprehension, a sound judgment, and a capacity of reasoning with some closeness?"[6]

---

[5]William Law, *A Serious Call to a Devout and Holy Life* (1728; reprint, Grand Rapids: Eerdmans, 1966), p. 2.
[6]John Wesley, "An Address to the Clergy," in *The Works of John Wesley*, 3rd ed. (Grand Rapids:

Time and again throughout the address Wesley unpacked this remark by admonishing ministers to know what would sound truly odd and almost pagan to the average congregant of today: logic, metaphysics, natural theology, geometry and the ideas of important figures in the history of philosophy. For Wesley study in these areas (especially philosophy and geometry) helped train the mind to think precisely, a habit of incredible value, he asserted, when it comes to thinking as a Christian about theological themes or scriptural texts. According to Wesley the study of extrabiblical information and the writings of unbelievers was of critical value for growth and maturity. As he put it elsewhere, "To imagine none can teach you but those who are themselves saved from sin is a very great and dangerous mistake. Give not place to it for a moment."[7]

Wesley's remarks were not unusual in his time. A century earlier the great Reformed pastor Richard Baxter was faced with lukewarmness in the church and unbelief outside the church. In 1667 he wrote a book to meet this need, and in it he used philosophy, logic and general items of knowledge outside Scripture to argue for the existence of the soul and the life to come. The fact that Baxter turned to philosophy and extrabiblical knowledge instead of small groups or praise hymns is worth pondering. In fact, it is safe to say that throughout much of church history, Scripture and right reason directed at extrabiblical truth were used by disciples of Jesus and prized as twin allies.

In valuing extrabiblical knowledge our brothers and sisters in church history were merely following common sense and Scripture itself. Repeatedly, Scripture acknowledges the wisdom of cultures outside Israel; for example, Egypt (Acts 7:22; cf. Ex 7:11), the Edomites (Jer 49:7), the Phoenicians (Zech 9:2) and many others. The remarkable achievements produced by human wisdom are acknowledged in Job 28:1-11. The wisdom of Solomon is compared to the wisdom of the "people of the east" and Egypt in order to show that Solomon's wisdom surpassed that of people with a longstanding, well-deserved reputation for wisdom (1 Kings 4:29-34). Paul approvingly quotes pagan philosophers (Acts 17:28), and Jude does the same thing with the noncanonical book *The*

Baker, 1979), p. 481.
[7]John Wesley, *A Plain Account of Christian Perfection* (London: Epworth Press, 1952), p. 87.

Assumption of Moses (Jude 9). The book of Proverbs is filled with examples in which knowledge, even moral and spiritual knowledge, can be gained from studying things (ants, for example) in the natural world. Jesus taught that we should know we are to love our enemies, not on the basis of an Old Testament text but from careful reflection on how the sun and rain behave (Mt 5:44-45).

In valuing extrabiblical knowledge our brothers and sisters in church history were also living out scriptural teaching about the value of general revelation. We must never forget that God is the God of creation and general revelation just as he is the God of Scripture and special revelation.

Christians should do everything they can to gain and teach important and relevant knowledge in their areas of expertise. *At the level appropriate to our station in life, Christians are called to be Christian intellectuals, at home in the world of ideas.*

4. *Neglect of integration results in a costly division between secular and sacred.* While few would actually put it in these terms, faith is now understood as a blind act of will, a sort of decision to believe something that is either independent of reason or makes up for the paltry lack of evidence for what one is trying to believe. By contrast, the Bible presents faith as a power or skill to act in accordance with the nature of the kingdom of God, a trust in what we have reason to believe is true. Understood in this way, we see that faith is built on reason and knowledge. We should have good reasons for thinking that Christianity is true before we completely dedicate ourselves to it. We should have solid evidence that our understanding of a biblical passage is correct before we go on to apply it. We bring knowledge claims from Scripture and theology to the task of integration; we do not employ mere beliefs or faith postulates.

Unfortunately, our contemporary understanding of faith and reason treats them as polar opposites. A few years ago I (J. P.) went to New York to conduct a series of evangelistic messages for a church. The series was in a high school gym and several believers and unbelievers came each night. The first evening I gave arguments for the existence of God from science and philosophy. Before closing in prayer, I entertained several questions from the audience. One woman (who was a Christian) complained about my talk, charging that if I "proved" the existence of God, I would leave no room for faith. I responded by saying that if she were right, then we should pray that currently available evidence for God would evaporate and be refuted so there would be even more room for faith! Obviously, her view of faith utterly detached it from reason.

If faith and reason are deeply connected, then students and teachers need to explore their entire intellectual life in light of the Word of God. But if faith and reason are polar opposites, then the subject matter of our study or teaching is largely irrelevant to growth in discipleship. Because of this view of faith and reason, there has emerged a secular-sacred separation in our understanding of the Christian life with the result that Christian teaching and practice are privatized. The withdrawal of the corporate body of Christ from the public sphere of ideas is mirrored by our understanding of what is required to produce an individual disciple. Religion is viewed as personal, private and a matter of how we feel about things. Often, Bible classes and paracurricular Christian activities are not taken as academically serious aspects of the Christian school, nor are they integrated into the content of "secular" areas of teaching.

There is no time like the present to recapture the integrative task. Given the abandonment of monotheism, the ground is weakened for believing in the unity of truth. This is one reason why our *uni*versities are turning in to *multi*versities.[8] The fragmentation of secular education at all levels and its inability to define its purpose or gather together a coherent curriculum are symptoms of what happens when monotheism, especially Christian monotheism, is set aside. At this critical hour the Christian educator has something increasingly rare and distinctive to offer, and integration is at the heart of who we are as Christian educators.

5. *The nature of spiritual warfare necessitates integration.* Today, spiritual warfare is widely misunderstood. Briefly, spiritual warfare is a

---

[8]See Julie Reuben, *The Making of the Modern University* (Chicago: University of Chicago Press, 1996).

conflict among persons—disembodied malevolent persons (demons and the devil), human beings, angels and God himself. So far, so good. But what is often overlooked is that this conflict among persons in two camps crucially involves a clash of ideas. Why? The conflict is about control, and persons control others by getting them to accept certain beliefs and emotions as correct, good and proper. This is precisely how the devil primarily works to destroy human beings and thwart God's work in history; namely, by influencing the idea structures in culture. That is why Paul makes the war of ideas central to spiritual conflict:

> For though we live in the world, we do not wage war as the world does. The weapons we fight with are not the weapons of the world. On the contrary, they have divine power to demolish strongholds. We demolish arguments and every pretension that sets itself up against the knowledge of God, and we take captive every thought to make it obedient to Christ. (2 Cor 10:3-5 NIV)

Spiritual warfare is largely, though not entirely, a war of ideas, and we fight bad, false ideas with better ones. That means that truth, reason, argumentation and so forth, from both Scripture and general revelation, are central weapons in the fight. Since the centers of education are the centers for dealing with ideas, they become the main location for spiritual warfare. Solid, intelligent integration, then, is part of our mandate to engage in spiritual conflict.

6. *Spiritual formation calls for integration.* It is crucial that we reflect a bit on the relationship between integration and spiritual/devotional life. To begin with, there is a widespread hunger throughout our culture for genuine, life-transforming spirituality. This is as it should be. People are weary of those who claim to believe certain things when they do not see those beliefs having an impact on the lives of the heralds. Among other things, integration is a spiritual activity—we may even call it a spiritual discipline—but not merely in the sense that often comes to mind in this context. Often, Christian teachers express the spiritual aspect of integration in terms of doxology: Christian integrators hold to and teach the same beliefs about their subject matter that non-Christians accept but go on to add praise to God for the subject

matter. Thus, Christian biologists simply assert the views widely accepted in the discipline but make sure that class closes with a word of praise to God for the beauty and complexity of the living world.

The doxological approach is good as far as it goes; unfortunately, it doesn't go far enough in capturing the spiritual dimension of integration. We draw closer to the core of this dimension when we think about the role of beliefs in the process of spiritual transformation. Beliefs are the rails on which our lives run. We almost always act according to what we really believe. It doesn't matter much what we say we believe or what we want others to think we believe. When the rubber meets the road, we act out our actual beliefs most of the time. That is why behavior is such a good indicator of our beliefs. The centrality of beliefs for spiritual progress is a clear implication of Old Testament teaching on wisdom and New Testament teaching about the role of a renewed mind in transformation. Thus, *integration has as its spiritual aim the intellectual goal of structuring the mind so we can see things as they really are and strengthening the belief structure that ought to inform the individual and corporate life of discipleship to Jesus.*

Integration can also help unbelievers accept certain beliefs crucial to the Christian journey and aid believers in maintaining and developing convictions about those beliefs. This aspect of integration becomes clear when we reflect on the notion of a plausibility structure. Individuals will never be able to change their lives if they cannot even entertain the beliefs needed to bring about that change. By "entertain a belief" we mean to consider the *possibility* that the belief *might* be true. If someone is hateful and mean to a fellow employee, that person will have to change what he or she believes about that coworker before treating the coworker differently. But if a person cannot even entertain the thought that the coworker is a good person worthy of kindness, the hateful person will not change.

A person's plausibility structure is the set of ideas the person either is or is not willing to entertain as possibly true. For example, few people would come to a lecture defending a flat earth, because this idea is just not part of our common plausibility structure. Most people today simply cannot even entertain the idea. Moreover, a person's plausibility structure is largely (though not exclusively) a function of beliefs already held. Applied to accepting or maintaining Christian belief, J. Gresham Machen got it right when he said:

> God usually exerts that power in connection with certain prior conditions of the human mind, and it should be ours to create, so far as we can, with the help of God, those favorable conditions for the reception of the gospel. False ideas are the greatest obstacles to the reception of the gospel. We may preach with all the fervor of a reformer and yet succeed only in winning a straggler here and there, if we permit the whole collective thought of the nation or of the world to be controlled by ideas which, by the resistless force of logic, prevent Christianity from being regarded as anything more than a harmless delusion.[9]

If a culture reaches the point where Christian claims are not even part of its plausibility structure, fewer and fewer people will be able to entertain the possibility that they might be true. Whatever stragglers do come to faith in such a context would do so on the basis of felt needs alone, and the genuineness of such conversions would be questionable, to say the least. And believers will not make much progress in the spiritual life because they will not have the depth of conviction or the integrated noetic structure necessary for such progress. This is why integration is so crucial to spirituality. It can create a plausibility structure in a person's mind, "favorable conditions," as Machen put it, so Christian ideas can be entertained by that person. As Christians, our goal is *to make Christian ideas relevant to our subject matter appear to be true, beautiful, good and reasonable to increase the ranking of Christian ideas in the culture's plausibility structure.*

　　7. *Integration is crucial to the current worldview struggle and the contemporary crisis of knowledge.* Luther once said that if we defend Christ at all points except those at which he is currently being attacked, then we have not really defended Christ. The Christian must keep in mind the tensions between Christian claims and competing worldviews currently dominating the culture. Such vigilance yields an integrative mandate for contemporary Christians that the Christian Worldview Integration

---

[9]J. Gresham Machen, address delivered on September 20, 1912, at the opening of the 101st session of Princeton Theological Seminary, reprinted in *What Is Christianity?* (Grand Rapids: Eerdmans, 1951), p. 162.

Series (CWIS) will keep in mind. There is a very important cultural fact that each volume in the series must face: *There simply is no established, widely recognized body of ethical or religious knowledge now operative in the institutions of knowledge in our culture.* Indeed, ethical and religious claims are frequently placed into what Francis Schaeffer called the "upper story," and they are judged to have little or no epistemic authority, especially compared to the authority given to science to define the limits of knowledge and reality in those same institutions. This raises pressing questions: *Is Christianity a knowledge tradition or merely a faith tradition, a perspective which, while true, cannot be known to be true and must be embraced on the basis of some epistemic state weaker than knowledge? Is there nonempirical knowledge in my field? Is there evidence of nonphysical, immaterial reality (e.g., linguistic meanings are arguable, nonphysical, spiritual entities) in my field? Do the ideas of Christianity do any serious intellectual work in my field such that those who fail to take them into consideration simply will not be able to understand adequately the realities involved in my field?*

There are at least two reasons why these may well be the crucial questions for Christians to keep in mind as they do their work in their disciplines. For one thing, Christianity claims to be a knowledge tradition, and it places knowledge at the center of proclamation and discipleship. The Old and New Testaments, including the teachings of Jesus, claim not merely that Christianity is true but that a variety of its moral and religious assertions can be known to be true.

Second, knowledge is the basis of responsible action in society. Dentists, not lawyers, have the authority to place their hands in our mouths because they have the relevant knowledge—not merely true beliefs—on the basis of which they may act responsibly. If Christians do little to deflect the view that theological and ethical assertions are merely parts of a tradition, ways of seeing, a source for adding a "theological perspective" to an otherwise unperturbed secular topic and so forth that fall short of conveying knowledge, then they inadvertently contribute to the marginalization of Christianity precisely because they fail to rebut the contemporary tendency to rob it of the very thing that gives it the authority necessary to prevent that marginalization, namely, its legitimate claim to give us moral and religious knowledge. Both in and out of the church Jesus has been lost as an intellectual authority, and Christian intellectuals should carry out their academic vocation in light of this fact.

We agree with those who see a three-way worldview struggle in academic and popular culture among ethical monotheism (especially Christian theism), postmodernism and scientific naturalism. As Christian intellectuals seek to promote Christianity as a knowledge tradition in their academic disciplines, they should keep in mind the impact of their work on this triumvirate. Space considerations forbid us to say much about postmodernism here. We recognize it is a variegated tunic with many nuances. But to the degree that postmodernism denies the objectivity of reality, truth, value and reason (in its epistemic if not psychological sense), to the degree that it rejects dichotomous thinking about real-unreal, true-false, rational-irrational and right-wrong, to the degree that it believes intentionality creates the objects of consciousness, to that degree it should be resisted by Christian intellectuals, and the CWIS will take this stance toward postmodernism.

Scientific naturalism also comes in many varieties, but very roughly a major form of it is the view that the spatiotemporal cosmos containing physical objects studied by the hard sciences is all there is and that the hard sciences are either the only source of knowledge or else vastly superior in proffering epistemically justified beliefs compared to nonscientific fields. In connection with scientific naturalism some have argued that the rise of modern science has contributed to the loss of intellectual authority in those fields like ethics and religion that supposedly are not subject to the types of testing and experimentation employed in science.

Extreme forms of postmodernism and scientific naturalism agree that there is no nonempirical knowledge, especially no knowledge of immaterial reality, no theological or ethical knowledge. *The authors of the CWIS seek to undermine this claim and the concomitant privatization and noncognitive treatment of religious/ethical faith and belief.* Thus, there will be three integrative tasks of central importance for each volume in the series.

HOW DO WE ENGAGE IN INTEGRATION? THREE INTEGRATIVE TASKS

As noted earlier, the word *integration* means "to form or blend into a whole," "to unite." One of the goals of integration is to maintain or increase both the conceptual relevance of and epistemological justification for Christian theism. To repeat Augustine's advice, "We must show our Scriptures not to be in conflict with whatever [our critics] can demonstrate about the nature of things from reliable sources."[10] We may distinguish three different aspects of the justificatory side of integration: direct defense, polemics and Christian explanation.

1. *Direct defense.* In direct defense we engage in integration with the primary intent of enhancing or maintaining directly the rational justification of Christian theism or some proposition taken to be explicit within or entailed by it, especially those aspects of a Christian worldview relevant to our own discipline. Specific attention should be given to topics that are intrinsically important to mere Christianity or currently under fire in our field. Hereafter, we will simply refer to these issues as "Christian theism." We do so for brevity's sake. Christian theism should be taken to include specific views about a particular area of study that we believe to be relevant to the integrative task, for example, that cognitive behavioral therapy is an important tool for applying the biblical mandate to be "transformed by the renewing of your minds" (Rom 12:2).

There are two basic forms of direct defense, one negative and one positive.[11] The less controversial of the two is a negative direct defense where we attempt to remove defeaters to Christian theism. If we have a justified belief regarding some proposition P, a defeater is something that weakens or removes that justification. Defeaters come in two types.[12] A rebutting defeater gives justification for believing not-P, in this case, that Christian theism is false. For example, attempts to show that the biblical concept of the family is dysfunctional and false, or that homosexuality is causally necessitated by genes or brain states and that therefore it is not a proper object for moral appraisal are cases of rebut-

---

[10]Augustine *De genesi ad litteram* 1.21.
[11]See Ronald Nash, *Faith and Reason* (Grand Rapids: Zondervan, 1988), pp. 14-18.
[12]For a useful discussion of various types of defeaters, see John Pollock, *Contemporary Theories of Knowledge* (Totowa, N.J.: Rowman & Littlefield, 1986), pp. 36-39; Ralph Baergen, *Contemporary Epistemology* (Fort Worth, Tex.: Harcourt Brace, 1995), pp. 119-24.

ting defeaters. An undercutting defeater does not give justification for believing not-P but rather seeks to remove or weaken justification for believing P in the first place. Critiques of the arguments for God's existence are examples of undercutting defeaters. When defeaters are raised against Christian theism, a negative defense seeks either to rebut or undercut those defeaters.

By contrast, a positive direct defense is an attempt to build a positive case for Christian theism. Arguments for the existence of God, objective morality, the existence of the soul, the value and nature of virtue ethics, and the possibility and knowability of miracles are examples. This task for integration is not accepted by all Christian intellectuals. For example, various species of what may be loosely called Reformed epistemology run the gamut from seeing a modest role for a positive direct defense to an outright rejection of this type of activity in certain areas; for example, justifying belief in God and the authority of Holy Scripture. *The CWIS will seek to engage in both negative and positive direct defense.*

2. *Polemics.* In polemics we seek to criticize views that rival Christian theism in one way or another. Critiques of scientific naturalism, physicalism, pantheism, behaviorist models of educational goals, authorless approaches to texts and Marxist theories of economics are all examples of polemics.

3. *Theistic explanation.* Suppose we have a set of items that stand in need of explanation and we offer some overall explanation as an adequate or even best explanation of those items. In such a case our overall explanation explains each of the items in question, and this fact itself provides some degree of confirmation for our overall explanation. For example, if a certain intrinsic genre statement explains the various data of a biblical text, then this fact offers some confirmation for the belief that the statement is the correct interpretation of that text. Christian theists ought to be about the business of exploring the world in light of their worldview and, more specifically, of using their theistic beliefs as explanations of various desiderata in their disciplines. Put differently, we should seek to solve intellectual problems and shed light on areas of puzzlement by using the explanatory power of our worldview.

For example, for those who accept the existence of natural moral law, the irreducibly mental nature of consciousness, natural human rights or the fact that human flourishing follows from certain biblically mandated ethical and religious practices, the truth of Christian theism provides a good explanation of these phenomena. And this fact can provide some degree of confirmation for Christian theism. *The CWIS seeks to show the explanatory power of Christian ideas in various disciplines.*

WHAT MODELS ARE AVAILABLE FOR CLASSIFYING INTEGRATIVE PROBLEMS?

When problem areas surface, there is a need for Christians to think hard about the issue in light of the need for strengthening the rational authority of Christian theism and placing it squarely within the plausibility structure of contemporary culture. We will use the term *theology* to stand for any Christian idea that seems to be a part of a Christian worldview derived primarily from special revelation. When we address problems like these, there will emerge a number of different ways that theology can interact with an issue in a discipline outside theology. Here are some of the different ways that such interaction can take place. These represent different strategies for handling a particular difficulty in integration. These strategies will be employed where appropriate on a case-by-case basis by the authors in the series.

1. *The two-realms view.* Propositions, theories or methodologies in theology and another discipline may involve two distinct, nonoverlapping areas of investigation. For example, debates about angels or the extent of the atonement have little to do with organic chemistry. Similarly, it is of little interest to theology whether a methane molecule has three or four hydrogen atoms in it.

2. *The complementarity view.* Propositions, theories or methodologies in theology and another discipline may involve two different, complementary, noninteracting approaches to the same reality. Sociological aspects of church growth and certain psychological aspects of conversion may be sociological or psychological descriptions of certain phenomena that are complementary to a theological description of church growth or conversion.

3. *The direct-interaction view.* Propositions, theories or methodolo-

gies in theology and another discipline may directly interact in such a way that either one area of study offers rational support for the other or one area of study raises rational difficulties for the other. For example, certain theological teachings about the existence of the soul raise rational problems for philosophical or scientific claims that deny the existence of the soul. The general theory of evolution raises various difficulties for certain ways of understanding the book of Genesis. Some have argued that the big bang theory tends to support the theological proposition that the universe had a beginning.

4. *The presuppositions view.* Theology may support the presuppositions of another discipline and vice versa. Some have argued that many of the presuppositions of science (for example, the existence of truth; the rational, orderly nature of reality; the adequacy of our sensory and cognitive faculties as tools suited for knowing the external world) make sense and are easy to justify given Christian theism, but are odd and without ultimate justification in a naturalistic worldview. Similarly, some have argued that philosophical critiques of epistemological skepticism and defenses of the existence of a real, theory-independent world and a correspondence theory of truth offer justification for some of the presuppositions of theology.

5. *The practical application view.* Theology may fill out and add details to general principles in another discipline and vice versa, and theology may help us practically apply principles in another discipline and vice versa. For example, theology teaches that fathers should not provoke their children to anger, and psychology can add important details about what this means by offering information about family systems, the nature and causes of anger, and so forth. Psychology can devise various tests for assessing whether a person is or is not mature, and theology can offer a normative definition to psychology as to what a mature person is.

A WORD ABOUT THIS BOOK

We are very pleased to present to you *Education for Human Flourishing* by Paul Spears and Steven Loomis. It is a first-rate guide into the sometimes confusing territory of integrating Christianity and education. The central purpose of the book is to revive and ground a perennial philosophy of education that integrates essential tenets of Christianity. The authors are thoroughly acquainted with the main issues and options in current educational theory, and they present them in the pages to follow with skill and clarity. But the book's real strength lies in the way they weave foundational philosophical insights about human persons, truth, knowledge and related themes into that educational theory in such a way as to present the reader with a deep worldview approach to education from a penetrating Christian perspective.

We hope you can see why we are excited about this book. Even though you're busy and the many demands on your time tug at you from different directions, we don't think you can afford not to read this book. So wrestle, ponder, pray, compare ideas with Scripture, talk about the pages to follow with others and enjoy.

A FINAL CHALLENGE

In 2001 atheist philosopher Quentin Smith published a remarkably insightful article of crucial relevance to the task of integration. For over fifty years, Smith notes, the academic community has become increasingly secularized and atheistic even though there have been a fair number of Christian teachers involved in that community. How could this be? Smith's answer amounts to the claim that Christians compartmentalized their faith, kept it tucked away in a private compartment of their lives and did not integrate their Christian ideas with their work. Said Smith:

> This is not to say that none of the scholars in their various academic fields were realist theists [theists who took their religious beliefs to be true] in their "private lives"; but realist theists, for the most part excluded their theism from their publications and teaching, in large part because theism . . . was mainly considered to have such a low epistemic status that it did not meet the standards of an "academically respectable" position to hold.[13]

Smith goes on to claim that while Christians have recaptured considerable ground in the field of philosophy, "theists in other fields tend to

---

[13]Quentin Smith, "The Metaphysics of Naturalism," *Philo* 4, no. 2 (2001): 1.

compartmentalize their theistic beliefs from their scholarly work; they rarely assume and never argue for theism in their scholarly work."[14]

This has got to stop. We offer this book to you with the prayer that it will help you rise to the occasion and recapture lost territory in your field of study for the cause of Christ.

Francis J. Beckwith
J. P. Moreland
Series Editors

---

[14]Ibid., p. 3. The same observation about advances in philosophy has been noted by Mark A. Noll in *The Scandal of the Evangelical Mind* (Grand Rapids: Eerdmans, 1994), pp. 235-38.

Authors' Preface

Education is a task we have all been involved in from a young age. At around the age of five or so, we begin the long journey of climbing to the top of the academic mountain. According to Robert Fulghum, a Grammy nominee for the Spoken Word Award, we learn some of the most important things in life during this time. In his book *All I Really Need to Know I Learned in Kindergarten*, Fulghum points out the importance of learning to share, play fair, say sorry when you hurt someone, and make sure that you wash your hands and flush (not in that order).[1] Clearly, this list is important, but as we progress in our intellectual training, we are told that there is much more that we need to come to understand. So leaving the basics of "Flushing 101" behind us, we move on to subjects like reading, writing and mathematics.

We quickly become enmeshed in the life of academic expectation. We develop the ability to navigate academic standards without putting forth too much effort ("Is this going to be on the test?") and learn the value of pleasing our teacher and parents with good grades. What is not clear to most of us is why we are going to school in the first place. We realize that every day our parents take us to this institution which regiments our day and promises us that our diligent work will be rewarded with a prosperous vocation years down the road. Mostly, we enjoy recess, try to avoid bullies, look forward to vacation times and do our best to comport ourselves with the expectations of the social institution in which we are immersed. A few of us find that we can excel at this form of instruction and find our identity in success.

---

[1]For the complete list see Robert Fulghum, *All I Really Need to Know I Learned in Kindergarten* (New York: Random House, 1989).

As we progress through the educational system, you would think it would become increasingly clearer to us what exactly education is for, but this is not often the case. Instead, we become increasingly adept at navigating the system without learning the fundamental knowledge and skills that enable us to flourish. This becomes apparent when as adults we find we are not well equipped to wrestle with some of the more difficult questions of parenting, life, death and our own fragile existence. A driving belief of this book is that the formal activity of education can better equip us to deal with such questions when grounded in a theological and philosophical foundation that is integrated with the Christian faith. Only then can we better understand (for ourselves and to teach others) who we are within God's created universe.

Within education (and most fields and disciplines, in fact), it is easy to separate ourselves into what are nearly two separate existences: one that works within the boundaries of the educational guild, and the other that pursues a life of following the teaching of Jesus Christ. During the day we work hard within our vocational pursuits, but seldom take into account our theological commitments—except perhaps when we encounter a dilemma that is strictly ethical in character. It is not uncommon to see people separate or compartmentalize their lives into these secular-sacred categories. As Christians we need to be able to understand our work first and foremost within the context of God's created universe, and to do so unapologetically.

Integration is often seen as a sort of veneer that we put over our academic work to make it acceptable to those within the Christian subculture. It is hard to come to grips with our larger culture, as a narrower view of reality, which no longer understands Christianity to be a viable source of understanding. Too often, our academic colleagues who have no religious inclinations look down on Christianity as (at best) some sort of antiquated way to think about the field of education. At times Christianity is even painted in an adversarial light, where it is defined as a tool of power and repression within the larger social institution. Both are products of an incomplete understanding of the role that Christianity plays in explaining humanity holistically.

Reflecting on the efficacy of institutionalized educational standards in light of a foundational commitment to the Christian faith may not seem overtly counterintuitive, but it can be like attempting to paddle upstream in class five rapids. For example, when a school of education credentials a teacher, it is because they judge that the student exhibits what has been deemed by the school as "best practice"—their ability to comport themselves with "well-tested standards"—and that the student's teaching reflects an understanding of "scientifically verified assessment criteria." This is not a question about whether or not the newly credentialed teacher is actually practicing the craft in a way that most properly educates students, but that their understanding of education aligns itself with dominant modern educational theory—which leaves no room for publicly held Christian commitments. The tendency within today's modern academic arena (which includes schooling and higher education) is to privilege knowledge as existing solely under the narrow purview of the discipline's accepted methodologies. What this does is to narrow, not widen, the information base available to knowledge and its creation and dissemination.

We believe that this view undercuts a proper investigation of education, because it does not have as its central aim the pursuit of truth: it is a commitment to whatever the guild (or the institution) deems to be true. Because education as a field engages with some of the most basic aspects of the human condition, a Christian foundation (which reveals to us the most fundamental aspects of humanity) gives us the best opportunity to successfully develop schooling and higher education in a manner which promotes human flourishing. Our desire is to encourage you to think more deeply about how you will ground your educational theory and practice, and how you can properly revivify your understanding of education's first principles.

This book will push you. It will cause you to reflect on preconceived notions about what education is about. It will push you to think hard about subjects you perhaps haven't considered as core to the educational project. We believe that the field of education deserves a rigorous, unflinching commitment to intellectual investigation: a high view of the teacher as a public intellectual and scholar. This project is broad in scope, but modest in expectation. We want to introduce you to some of the basic disciplines that we think most influence the field of education. We will discuss foundational theological, philosophical, historical, sociological, economic and leadership theory concepts that we believe lay the groundwork for quality educational theory. We don't expect that you will master all of these disciplines, but rather that you will begin to step outside of a traditional (technical) educational model that is driven by an arc of descent into technical procedures rather than an arc of ascent into the liberal arts skills and knowledge of the teacher as scholar. We want to encourage you to be committed to an investigation of education that is unwavering in its critique, but hopeful for the future of the field.

This book is the result of God's guiding hand in our lives. It was providential that the two of us were introduced to each other when we were doctoral students doing rigorous work in the philosophy of education. When we first met we rather quickly ascertained that we saw education in very similar ways. Our desire to think deeply and integratively about education was a significant aspect of both of our academic projects, and this became evident in our discussions over dinner with a small group of likeminded doctoral students and one amazing professor (our thanks to professor Joseph Weeres). We don't think we can estimate just how formative those conversations were in developing our educational theory. During the time of writing this book we have experienced loved ones struggling with cancer and the loss of family members, but these experiences only cemented our belief that a proper education with Christ at the core is necessary for humans to flourish during difficult times.

When J. P. Moreland and Frank Beckwith approached me (Paul) about writing a book on education and integration, I instantly thought of Steve Loomis as a coauthor. I have been privileged to work with an individual who carries himself in a godly manner and sees his academic work in terms of kingdom purposes. His work is academically rigorous—and that is not only a result of his intellectual acumen, but of his commitment to doing quality work for the Lord.

And when Paul approached me (Steve) about the possibility of this book, I knew instantly that a collaboration of this kind, with Paul, would generate a synergy of important old and new ideas, as well as make for an interesting read for thousands of new and veteran teachers. Both of us take a high view of teachers in society. We see them as scholars, public intellectuals whose institutional roles play out on the micro and macro levels of human reality. It is through this work, and others like it, as well as our teaching, that we serve our Lord.

I (Paul) would like especially to thank my friends and colleagues at Biola's Torrey Honors Institute for all of their support over the years, and, specifically, John Mark Reynolds, Fred Sanders and Melissa Schubert. Thank you for all your encouragement, discussions and thoughtful insights that have much improved this book. Finally, I thank Jennifer Hardy, my patient, insightful and wise-beyond-her-years research assistant. I cannot give enough thanks for all you have done for this book and how you have kept my life sane.

My (Steve's) gratitude to the immensely talented students of Wheaton College and the Claremont Graduate School with whom I've had the pleasure to work. They sense something is not right with the present system of education. I pray that they will develop the courage and insight to right the ship before that ship wrecks on the perilous reef of what we describe as the technical model. It is C. S. Lewis's abolition of man that we seek to avoid, and the only way to avoid it is to develop brilliant ideas that work. Wheaton students are certainly fit for that assignment.

We jointly are grateful to Jim Hoover, senior editor at InterVarsity Press, for the kind patience that he showed to us throughout the writing of this book, and to our general editors, J. P. Moreland and Frank Beckwith, who showed the way. We extend warm appreciation to our students who are first-rank scholars dedicated to the proposition that Christians can effectively serve Jesus and humanity with their minds. We also thank the G. W. Aldeen Memorial Fund of Wheaton College that helped to finance part of this project.

Précis of Book and Chapters
Thesis

The purpose of this book is to revive and ground a perennial philosophy of education that integrates essential tenets of the Christian faith. The text simultaneously reflects on the old and new, offering a new, critical, and integratively Christian educational agenda for a twenty-first-century global community, and secures this analysis within an appropriate framework of thought. This book makes a case that the complex educational good is not sustainable in the present technical environment of schooling and higher education. This technical environment within the educational field limits information and knowledge that makes us most human. For learning to contribute to human development and flourishing, including important dimensions of freedom, education as an institution requires conditions of knowledge and practice that are grounded in the Christian liberal arts tradition. As a text, the book is written specifically for emerging practitioners and scholars in the field, upperclassmen and graduate level college students in education degree programs in higher education across the world.

Main Skills

In chapters one through three readers will be encouraged to think about what it means to be human, and how their conception of humanity both theologically and philosophically affects how they go about educating others. They will learn to better consider how education developed throughout history, and how today's modern educational field is a result of those historical decisions. They will discover a proper sense of

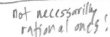
not necessarily rational ones!

what it means to pursue truth and knowledge in a way that enables them to have confidence in their educational endeavor.

Chapters four through six emphasize the intellectual virtues and the skill domains of the liberal arts: *logos* (reason), *mētis* (cunning, practical know-how), *aretē* (upholding virtue, including justice), *sophia* (the development of wisdom), *phronēsis* (habituated good action), and *praxis* (helping to realize individual and community excellences).

CHAPTER PRÉCIS

Chapter 1: In this first chapter, students will wrestle with theological and philosophical anthropology and how it impacts the field of education. To have an understanding of what it means to be human is necessarily at the core of the educational project. We believe that the project of education is fundamentally an investigation of Christian theological principles and philosophical understanding. As students develop these skills they will be able to assess the successes and failures of both broad and specific educational theories. It will also enable students to think carefully about what the primary role of education is. Fundamentally, this chapter will enable students to think about the field of education in terms of what role education plays in the pursuit of human flourishing for followers of Christ.

Chapter 2: The second chapter surveys the philosophical and historical development of educational theories as well as introducing students to the basic philosophical categories that they should know as educators. To have a clear understanding of modern educational theories we must be conversant with the philosophical commitments that have developed over the years within education broadly. We also need to be able employ basic philosophical tools so that we can grapple with various beliefs within the educational field. An increased ability to employ historical and philosophical tools will enable students to comprehend how educational theories develop from deeply held (often tacit) philosophical commitments. This skill is foundational for comprehending diverse educational theories.

Chapter 3: In chapter three students will wrestle with the nature of knowledge. It is important for students to know what counts as knowl-

"To Know and To Learn" — Yes!

edge because this is the cornerstone of both curriculum development and assessment. Having a strong working understanding of how we are to think of knowledge grants us confidence in our abilities to pursue what is truly real. Within the field of education knowledge should be understood as something more than convention. Education should be about revealing to students what is real or true about the world. Thus, normative skeptical philosophies are antithetical to an educator's epistemological commitments and educational project. This is to say that there are right and wrong ideas, and this chapter will enable students to make judgments about the rightness and wrongness of ideas as they become more conversant with the principles that undergird knowledge.

Chapter 4: In chapter four students will come to understand more fully the larger institutional and informational forces at work across education. Knowing the information economy of education will offer teachers an important strategic advantage in negotiating for better (more liberal) conditions for student learning. Unfortunately, many of these information forces work against the very integration that Christian educators are concerned with, nudging both teacher preparation and the schools in a narrow and technical direction. This trend presses education into conformity with conceptual systems and models which deny too much its primary nature. As a result, an improper model of education stunts institutional performance and human development. No other book on the market has made this argument available to Christian educators.

Chapter 5: This chapter contrasts social ethics and moral education seen as a mere technical procedure with social ethics and moral education seen as a result of the intellectual and moral virtues. In the technical procedure, virtue becomes less necessary: the focus is away from the achievement of human excellences and toward managing utility functions. Such people as John Dewey believed that the good of education (and human nature itself) could be molded by technical means. We show why this is an insufficient conception of social ethics. Teachers will be shown how to intelligently integrate Christocentric morality and character education into their practice.

technicians verses scholars (margin note)

Chapter 6: In general terms, there are two arcs of practice in the development of teachers: (a) practice that is a further descent into a technical model, where teachers are technicians, and (b) practice that moves away from the technical model and ascends toward the education good, where teachers are scholars. There are tremendous social costs when teachers are trained as technicians and not as scholars. Perhaps the most important cost is the loss of agency in the development and flourishing of individual human beings. Christian schools of education can awake to these costs and restructure the manner in which new teachers are educated. We take for granted that Christian educators will become school leaders. What are the necessary policy and leadership questions for the twenty-first-century education? How can teachers and leaders integrate their worldview by recasting these questions in the light of the truths of Jesus Christ? Hence, this chapter briefly examines where educational policy and leadership stands today and what future opportunities Christian integrationists might have to help reform the institution of education.

1

HUMANITY REVISITED

notice: Augustine is using reason as well as prayer – revelation

I at least, Lord, have difficulty at this point,
and I find my own self hard to grasp. . . . Great is the power
of memory, an awe-inspiring mystery, my God a power of profound
and infinite multiplicity. And this mind, this is I myself.
What then am I God? What is my nature?

AUGUSTINE *CONFESSIONS* 10.16.25-17.26

one of the central & enduring questions – one essential for education!

Education is a field of amazing possibilities. The opportunities and obstacles that present themselves in today's modern classroom are challenging. As educators ourselves we see great opportunity, and we know of many educators like ourselves who are deeply dedicated to enriching the intellectual lives of their students. We want to see education contributing to the long-term success of our students, but while we learn all about student assessment we find it hard to assess ourselves within our own discipline. When we try to understand the value of or reasons for a certain educational standard or assessment method, we often find ourselves unsatisfied with the explanations and unsure how to continue to question what seems to be in our eyes a problematic method. This is symptomatic of the fact that in education classes we are not often taught how to think in theological and philosophical categories, and how both theology and philosophy should be foundational to our educational theories.

College students who are studying to be teachers learn a great deal about things like classroom management, curriculum development and other practical standards, but they are missing underlying theory. We (the authors) were once college students caught in the academic whirlwind, and we understand being terrified at the thought of a class of twenty-four fourth graders that we would someday teach from 8:30 a.m. to 2:30 p.m. (What if they decide to jump me all at once?) To even begin to think about theology, philosophy and educational theory seems to pale in comparison to those fourth graders and our desperate need for practical answers. But once we start teaching, we learn classroom management skills, and the fourth graders are not quite so daunting.

When we start to get the technical basics of the classroom under control, we begin to realize that some of the curriculum and assessment methods we clung to during our early teaching experiences may not be very effective. We start to see that certain standards and methods are actually academically unhelpful or even limit some of our pedagogical goals. Without classes that ground them in educational theory, new teachers are often at a loss as to how to assess the supposed tried-and-true educational standards.

Even teachers who have been in the classroom for years find themselves in a similar predicament. Many veteran teachers who have attempted to question the standards end up unable to overcome the monolithic system, so they learn strategies that circumvent it. While we understand why this happens, it does nothing to address the ongoing inadequacies and inequities of the standards.

In order for education to train and develop its teachers and students effectively, it must focus on fundamental theological and philosophical principles that help educators articulate reality. Once we have laid a theological and philosophical foundation for inquiry, we can begin to craft the foundation for a coherent educational discipline that enables students to develop the intellectual virtues which allow them to become responsible participants within their family, church and community. Additionally, the theology and philosophy grounding a strong educational theory will give our teachers the tools to effectively assess current standards and teaching methods, and help them to not avoid methods and ideas that may be antithetical to human flourishing.

Education has always been a topic of intellectual inquiry. Every culture inculcates beliefs, knowledge and traditions. Education is the means by which communities equip their members with a holistic understanding of humanity. Throughout history important intellectuals have reflected on the nature of humanity and how, given a certain conception of human nature, we should go about educating the populace. As they become more familiar with education's lineage, educators develop better insights into their discipline.

The writings of the ancient Greek thinkers Plato and Aristotle convey early thoughts about the nature of education. Both Plato and Aristotle ground their educational theory on the study of philosophy, a word whose original meaning is "the love of wisdom." This love is actualized through a life of study, which is not chiefly concerned with the pursuit of new knowledge but with a more detailed explanation of the interconnectedness of beliefs. Plato and Aristotle attempted to craft clear descriptions of what it is to be human, and through these classical understandings educational ideologies were developed. Plato and Aristotle's belief in human rationality necessitated the development of educational principles. If humans are fundamentally rational, the question is how do we best actualize rational abilities? We will begin our discussion of educational practice with Aristotle.

An educated person is grounded in the essential concepts of reality so that he or she can act ethically. To act ethically we must have the proper desires and feelings or responses to reality. In his *Nicomachean Ethics* Aristotle states that humans are political animals, which means they are social beings by nature.[1] Proper existence within society requires proper treatment of others—we must act upon our knowledge of what is good. A developed understanding of human nature allows us to understand what true human flourishing looks like. Education, then, is the means by which humans are trained to be able to properly

---

[1]Aristotle *Nicomachean Ethics*, trans. Terence Irwin (Indianapolis: Hackett, 1999), 1097b.

evaluate diverse situations and act in such a way as to benefit themselves and their society. This can be understood as being educated for virtuous action.

Like Plato and Aristotle, great Christian thinkers such as Augustine and Calvin hold to the importance of being properly educated. They too believe that education enables humans to develop proper understandings about human nature and other aspects of reality. One important difference between Christians and thinkers like Plato and Aristotle is related to revelation. Rationality plays an important role in the Christian thinker's educational theories, but rationality itself does not give a complete understanding of reality. Humans need divine revelation. Plato and Aristotle would disagree. This disagreement plays a seminal role in how humans believe we access reality. If we believe that reality is only found in the physical senses (and we are wrong), this limits our access to information that may exist outside the empirical realm. Our beliefs about human access to reality structures the means we use to gain knowledge about the world, and how we teach others to pursue that knowledge.

Augustine, who was a man of amazing natural intellect, realized that he was unable to truly understand the nature of the reality around him without insight given to him by God.[2] In Augustine's autobiographical work *Confessions*, he describes his inability to truly understand God until God intervened through Scripture and the Holy Spirit.[3] For Augustine, we humans must understand ourself in relationship to God to fully actualize our human potential. Famously, he pens, "Our hearts are restless until they find their rest in you."[4] For us to be complete we need to understand existence in light of God's redemptive work and his kingdom purposes for all of humanity.

Calvin begins his monumental *Institutes of the Christian Religion*: "Nearly all of the wisdom we possess, that is to say, true and sound wisdom, consists of two parts: the knowledge of God and of ourselves."[5]

---

[2]See, for example, Augustine *Confessions*, trans. Henry Chadwick (Oxford: Oxford University Press, 1991), 4.16.30.
[3]Ibid., 8.
[4]Ibid., 1.1.1.
[5]John Calvin, *Institutes of the Christian Religion* 1.1.1. ed. John T. McNeill, trans. Ford Lewis

I wonder how the imagination fits into the picture? (see Frye, Educated Imagination)

Calvin realizes that our rational capacities are a foundational part of how we know the world around us, but to truly understand who we are we must be illuminated by God's revelation, which comes through his Word and the work of the Holy Spirit.[6] Human inability to completely discern the nature of reality is to be expected because of sin, but God, through his mercy, intervenes by his revelatory gift.[7] The combination of our rational capacities and the grace given to us through the revelation of God enables us to be educated. It has been tempting, historically, to abandon either rationality for revelation or revelation for rationality, but either extreme ends in an inability to access reality. The symbiotic relationship between rationality and revelation enables us to craft the most complete view of reality.

This chapter introduces some fundamental principles in the realm of theological and philosophical anthropology. We believe that the complexity of human beings necessitates a rigorous investigation of the essential makeup of persons, and because we believe humans are created in the image of God, to do anything less would craft a view of humanity that is incomplete and ultimately incoherent. C. S. Lewis points out that we need to see our neighbors in light of the glory of being created by God.[8] In this light, with humility and reverence, we seek to construct an understanding of humanity so we can educate our students for his kingdom service.

ANTHROPOLOGY INVESTIGATED

Understanding basic metaphysical concepts is essential to developing a proper anthropology.[9] Metaphysics is concerned with vital philosophical questions such as the nature and essence of things, cause and effect, and the nature of humanity. It is called "first philosophy" because it deals with basic principles of philosophy. Metaphysics analyzes the na-

---

Battles, Library of Christian Classics 20 (Louisville: Westminster John Knox, 1993).

[6]Ibid., 1.5.2.

[7]It is not the purpose of this book to argue for the place of Scripture as a centerpiece of educational theory within the Christian view of the discipline of education. It is granted as a fundamental avenue by which educators gain insight on human nature.

[8]C. S. Lewis, *The Weight of Glory* (San Francisco: HarperCollins, 2001), p. 45.

[9]Much more will be said about metaphysics in chap. 2.

ture of things that are not exhaustively comprehended by the physical senses. Things such as consciousness, the immortality of souls, freedom of the will and God are real entities that cannot be investigated empirically. Dualism is an important metaphysical concept that undergirds our anthropological investigations.

We believe that dualism, and specifically substance dualism, is the most effective way by which we can best explain fundamental issues in human ontology (the fundamental or essential properties of humans).[10] In *Body and Soul*, philosopher J. P. Moreland points out that throughout the majority of human history most people believed that human nature consisted of two parts: a physical body and a nonphysical soul. Formerly, professionals and laypeople believed that when a human person died his or her soul departed the body, which decayed, to exist in some sort of afterlife. This view of the dual nature of humans is commonsensical and develops out of self-reflection and our experience of others. Moreland writes, "Many philosophers who deny dualism admit that it is the commonsense view."[11] In the last two hundred years, however, the concept of dualism has increasingly come under attack, being undercut primarily by the scientific notion that humans are solely empirical (physical) constructs. What stems the tide of the scientific onslaught is Christianity's commitment to a supernatural reality, which stands outside of the physical realm. Christianity and a understanding of dualism, which is rooted in both theological and philosophical principles, will enable us to develop a holistic understanding of human persons.

SUBSTANCE DUALISM AND THE SOUL

Substance dualism is the view that human beings are made up of a body and a soul. Even further, substance dualists believe there is a great difference between the brain and mind, that the brain pertains to a per-

---

[10]This discussion of dualism does not preclude other views of human ontology. Clearly, it is the case that there are other people who are followers of Christ who would not call themselves dualists. It is not our goal to give an exhaustive overview or survey of all the philosophical options, but to begin to establish a point by which we can consider the implications of ontology and how it impacts educational commitments.

[11]J. P. Moreland and Scott B. Rae, *Body and Soul: Human Nature & the Crisis in Ethics* (Downers Grove, Ill.: InterVarsity Press, 2000), p. 18.

son's body and the mind to a person's soul. For example, the other day I (Paul) was reaching into the microwave to take out a plate of food, not knowing that the plate itself was hot. (I had assumed that the microwave would only heat the food.) When I touched the plate, signals were sent up my neural pathways to my brain causing physiological responses including jerking my hand away from the plate. All of this was brain activity. But the thought or experience of pain was not the physical event. Instead, it was the mental event that took place in the immaterial substance of my soul. Even now, as I reflect on the event, my memory of the event occurs in the substance of my soul, and not in my brain. Still, the substance dualist must account for the connection between body and soul. Philosopher Dallas Willard explains it in this manner:

> The soul is one non-physical dimension of the person. A human person is a non-physical (spiritual) entity that has an essential involvement with a particular physical body. The brain, then—a piece of meat that is of more than usual interest—is one part of the embodied dimension of the human person. It too is integrated by the soul into one life, along with all of the dimensions of the person (at least when all is well).[12]

Dr. Willard's point is that to think properly about our essential human nature is to think of it as an integrated whole between our material body and our immaterial soul. As we interact with the world around us, our body works in concert with our soul to enable us to consider, react and think about the world we live in.

This view of substance dualism is at odds with popularized notions of contemporary science. Broadly, views about human ontology comes in two major forms: physicalism and dualism. Basically, physicalism holds that humans are nothing more than material substances that can be examined through the senses. Physicalism, therefore, puts knowledge about human persons solely within the purview of the sciences. Since physicalism holds a place of authority inside modern academics, it is important that we understand the basic principles of this view.

---

[12]Dallas Willard, "Good Question: Gray Matter and the Soul," *Christianity Today*, November 18, 2000, p. 74.

PHYSICALISM BRIEFLY CONSIDERED

For a physicalist human ontology is understood in terms of what we can know through our senses, and these descriptions are best mediated through the disciplines that make up the hard sciences. The disciplines of physics and chemistry explain humanness as a grouping of particles that are configured in certain orderly ways. The sentence "Bob is human" only suggests that Bob is a set of complex structures that form in a multiplicity of properly ordered configurations that conform to a certain pattern, which is denoted as human.

Human beings turn out to be nothing more than a specific type of structure within the physical universe—which is made up of millions of other complex structures. A human can be described specifically as a system that has a body made up of tissue that has a brain and a nervous system. Humans are also categorized in terms of their brains' ability to perform complex computations as compared to other sentient life forms' ability. According to the physicalist, human beings are just one of many complex systems within the universe, and to think of humanness as special is the height of narcissism. Princeton ethicist Peter Singer states:

> The traditional view of the sanctity of human life will collapse under pressure from scientific, technological, and demographic developments. By 2040, it may be that only a rump of hard-core, know-nothing religious fundamentalists will defend the view that every human life, from conception to death, is sacrosanct.[13]

Singer's commitment to physicalism results in an ethic that devalues human life, rendering it no more important than any other life form.

The physicalist also has difficulty explaining first-person perspectives. Moments of self-awareness, such as when we are hungry or in pain, are expressed by using the pronoun *I*. The ability to self-identify and reflect on our internal conscious states are proper to and necessary for successful human existence. But the physicalist describes all phenomena from a third-person perspective, an objective external source that describes the object through the means of empirical methodolo-

---

[13]Peter Singer, "The Sanctity of Life," *Foreign Policy*, September-October 2005, p. 40.

gies. Subjective first-person experiences have no place in the physicalist world. So when a physicalist talks about "Bob," he or she will talk about things like Bob's weight, his height or his shoe size, but will be unable to talk about anything that has to do with Bob's subjective internal conscious states.[14] All the physicalist can do is describe internal states as material phenomena, which is insufficient.

When we think of ourselves, it is never through a third-person experience but through our own first-person acquaintance with ourselves—that is, our souls. Physicalism is unable to capture in any meaningful way our commonsense belief about our ability to know our internal conscious states; yet all of us believe with justification that the majority of times we consider our own condition we also apprehend it.

Additionally, physicalism cannot explain why personal identity endures through physical change. If our identity is solely contingent on us having the same grouping of properties, what happens when we change through the gain or loss of properties? To illustrate, imagine that someone you know (let's call him John) is in a tragic automobile accident, is badly burned and loses a limb. When we go to the hospital to visit our John, how are we able to identify him? The bundle of properties that we have always known as "John" has changed. Both his burns and the loss of his limb have changed the way that we perceive him, and yet when we visit with him we will still call him "John." Not only that, the person we are visiting in the hospital still self identifies himself as John, and he gives historical accounts of himself that are consistent with what we know about our friend John. Physicalism can give no adequate account of why we know our friend who has been disfigured is still John. Our ability to know John even though his external state has changed seems commonsensical to us because we interact daily with human beings on a soulish level. It is this interaction with one another's transcendent soul that is the foundation of interpersonal relationships. So we can see how physicalism fails to holistically articulate the fundamental properties that make up our anthropology. In this light we will consider a dualistic explanation of humanness.

---

[14]For a discussion of this problem see Thomas Nagel, "What Is It Like to Be a Bat?" in *Mortal Questions* (Cambridge: Cambridge University Press, 1979).

DUALISM CONTINUED

Dualism maintains that some reality (human persons) comprises two different types of things that are not identical to each other. Most versions of dualism fall into two camps: property and substance dualism. Property dualism holds that, like the physicalist, reality is made up only of physical substances, but that there are two types of properties of matter when it reaches a certain state of complexity. These are physical properties and mental properties. Mental properties are not the same as and cannot be reduced to physical properties. So when someone has an experience of pain two things happen. Within the brain certain physiological events happen (that of nerve fibers firing) along with a mental event (that of feeling a pain). A property dualist holds that both events happen in the brain, and that human beings are not essentially mental beings that have experiences and thoughts, rather mental events emerge from certain physical properties, and these mental events cannot exist outside of these physical properties of the brain. Property dualism falls under many of the same criticisms as physicalism and therefore will not be discussed at length in this section.

Substance dualism maintains that the body and the soul are two distinct substances. The soul (as opposed to the body) is the locus of personal identity. It is an immaterial substance that is not the same as the body but is related to the body. All thinking, feeling, wanting and acting resides in the soul. Augustine says this about the soul: "The soul is present as a whole not only in the entire mass of a body, but also in the least part of the body at the same time."[15] For Augustine a human person is a body and a soul. You cannot separate the two and have a fully functioning human being.

According to the substance dualist the soul is more than just the mind. The soul is understood as the basis for physical life.[16] It is the controlling force for both our biological functions and our mental functions. The soul is also immortal. It is not susceptible to degradation or atrophy. It is the place where our self resides. It is the substance that

---

[15]Augustine *On the Immortality of the Soul* 26.25, trans. Ludwig Schopp (New York: Fathers of the Church, 1947).
[16]Aquinas *Summa Theologica* 75.1.

endures after death. And while this might tempt us to think of the separation of soul and body as the apex of human experience, Augustine teaches otherwise. "Man is neither the body alone, nor the soul alone, but both together. And therefore the highest good, in which lies the happiness of man is composed of goods of both kinds, bodily and spiritual."[17] So, it is important to understand that fully functioning humans are neither just body nor just soul, but are complexly interwoven beings made of both body *and* soul.

What is truly interesting is that for most of intellectual history nearly all individuals have believed in the soul. Most people think of themselves as more than their bodies. They see themselves as both physical and mental beings. This seems to be the commonsense response of most individuals when they reflect on what they know about themselves and their interactions with others. Even philosophers who deny dualism recognize that it is the commonsense view.[18] The same can be said of the history of the church. Christians have believed that humans have souls. And Christian doctrine teaches that the soul will depart the body after death, apparently remaining disembodied until it receives a resurrection body.

Educators need to understand this holistic nature of humans. Since one of the basic ways humans gain information about reality is from the outside world, it is important to understand the interconnectedness of the body and the mind. External stimuli play an important role in how information is obtained. Experiences like physical touch inform our existence; but describing touch as merely sensory contact plus data transfer from neurons to the brain underreports the complexity of essential human properties, which include mental properties.

Philosophical anthropological constructs are important tools for a proper understanding of humanness. Still, the investigation would be incomplete without an investigation of biblical constructs of humanness. But there is a notable difference between the intentions of philosophers and those of the biblical authors. The writers of both the Old and New Testaments were not writing specifically to develop an an-

---

[17]Augustine *City of God* 19.3, trans. Marcus Dods (New York: Random House, 1950).
[18]See J. R. Searle, *The Rediscovery of the Mind* (Cambridge, Mass.: MIT Press, 1992).

thropology that answered questions about human body and soul, whereas philosophers are intentionally addressing questions about the ontological status of humans. Biblical constructions of anthropology should be understood in light of the Bible's larger project—the explication of God's justice, love, mercy and salvation through the redemptive work of his Son Jesus Christ and the establishment of his everlasting kingdom.

This does not mean that Scripture has nothing to say about the human body and soul. But arguments for dualism are not explicit within the text of Scripture. Clearly, human nature has a physical aspect, to which the Scriptures attest. Genesis 2:7 states, "The LORD God formed the man of dust from the ground and breathed into his nostrils the breath of life, and the man became a living creature." From this passage we can see God making humans a material thing, literally from the soil of the earth. Conversely, understanding the spiritual nature of humans takes some investigation of the Old and New Testament.

In theological circles it has recently become vogue to attack the notion of dualism. Some reject the notion of dualism because they believe it is not a biblical notion but a Greek idea smuggled into Christian theology. Nancey Murphy, a philosopher from Fuller Theological Seminary, writes that humans are "at our best complex physical organisms; . . . we are *Spirited bodies.*"[19] Given recent attacks inside of Christian philosophy and theology, it is even more important to turn to the Scriptures to gain an understanding of our anthropology. In the following sections we will develop briefly the basic scriptural principles that support a concept of biblical dualism.[20]

THE OLD TESTAMENT AND THE BODY AND SOUL QUESTION

The most significant terms in the Old Testament that deal with the spiritual aspect of humanness are *nephesh* and *ruach*. The word

---

[19]Nancey Murphy, *Bodies and Souls, or Spirited Bodies?* (New York: Cambridge University Press, 2006), p. ix, emphasis original.

[20]For a comprehensive account of dualism from the Scriptures see John W. Cooper, *Body, Soul, and Life Everlasting: Biblical Anthropology and the Monism-Dualism Debate* (Grand Rapids: Eerdmans, 1989). We are indebted to Cooper for much of the work on dualism and the Scriptures that follows in this chapter.

nephesh is used over seven hundred times in the Old Testament, and it has numerous meanings. *Nephesh* refers to the body's neck or throat and the physiological functions that go with them; breathing, drinking and eating are all a part of the conceptual construction of this word. It also is the stem of some Hebrew words that mean to breathe deeply or recover one's breath. Conceptually, it is also used to distinguish living things from dead—that is, *nephesh* makes a person a living human being. A translation of *nephesh* only as soul would be incomplete. *Nephesh* is necessary for life, but its loss seems more notable than its possession (i.e., a person is dead because his or her *nephesh* is gone).[21]

The Hebrew term *ruach* is often used to denote "the vital energy dwelling within [someone]."[22] It is also used to signify emotional or mental exhaustion. It describes internal mental states that cause physiological responses. In 1 Kings 21, King Ahab of Israel is upset when Naboth refuses to sell his land to him, and his internal state of frustration causes him to lose his appetite. His frustration is a troubled *ruach*.[23] It is also the term for substance that gives life to creatures. In Ezekiel 37 the prophet gives an account of his vision of the dry bones, where God gives theses piles of bones and sinews his *ruach* (breath) which causes them to live. Ezekiel 11:19 also uses the term to describe the new spirit God will give the people of Israel.

The Old Testament does not describe the body in mechanistic terms. The body, while a physiological construct, is not animated without the breath of life. This breath is not an additional physical substance added to the person but a noncorporeal power that comes from God which gives something necessary for life. *Ruach* is a nonbiological power given by God that enables humans to think and act. It is necessary for human existence, gives humans breath and causes physiological responses in humans.

Both *nephesh* and *ruach* inform the Old Testament view of the body

---

[21]Walter Eichrodt, *Theology of the Old Testament*, 5th ed. (Philadelphia: Westminster Press, 1967), 2:134-42.

[22]Ibid., pp. 131-33.

[23]"But Jezebel his wife came to him and said to him, "Why is your spirit *[ruach]* so vexed that you eat no food?" (1 Kings 21:5).

and soul. *Nephesh* is more internal while *ruach* seems to exist outside of individuals.[24] *Nephesh* also seems to denote the combination of a physical body and the breath of God, which holistically forms a human. Neither *nephesh* nor *ruach* are meant to construct an anthropology that is close to the philosophical concept of substance dualism. The terms do, however, describe an immaterial aspect of humanness, which is significantly different from the physicalist's construct. Though the Old Testament does not develop a robust notion of the distinction between body and soul, this is enough to begin to construct a broadly dualistic theological anthropology.

THE NEW TESTAMENT AND THE BODY AND SOUL QUESTION

While the writers of the New Testament do not explicitly make an argument for dualism, they provide enough information for a careful reader to defeat the incorrect anthropologies of materialism and monism. Further, the New Testament expresses thoughts that substantiate some philosophical views, such as dualism. As revelation the Scriptures provide a more complete understanding of humanity than is available through philosophic inquiry alone. Working with the New Testament concepts of body and soul without conflating or confusing them with preconceptions requires careful exegesis.

Non-Pauline writings. In the Greek New Testament the words *pneuma* and *psychē*, usually translated "spirit" and "soul," are the primary terms used to express the immaterial aspect of humans. We will examine the key passages that explicate body and soul distinctions as a part of the theological taxonomy of the New Testament.

The author of Hebrews 12:23 refers to the deceased who are in heavenly Jerusalem as "the spirits of the righteous made perfect." *Spirit* here refers to humans who are without their physical bodies but maintain their personal identity and humanity. In Hebrews 12:1 the author offers encouragement to "run with endurance the race that is set before us" because there is a crowd of witnesses (those who have died and are already in heaven) watching believers as they

---

[24]Eichrodt, *Theology of the Old Testament*, 2:136.

follow Christ. The sense of this passage is that humans dwell both on earth and in heaven. Those in heaven are in a disembodied state but still are existent, and they are even aware of some of the events transpiring on the earth.

The death of Jesus as presented in the Gospels can clarify various conceptual uses of the word spirit *(pneuma)*. Matthew 27:50 states that when Jesus died he gave up his spirit (NIV, ESV). In Luke 23:46 Jesus says, "Father, into your hands I commit my spirit." It could be said that this use of *spirit* was similar to the Old Testament use of the term *ruach*. But in investigations of intertestamental literature both *ruach* and *pneuma* have varied usages, one of them being describing the disembodied dead.[25] Later, Luke 24:37 again uses the word *spirit* to describe the appearance of Jesus in the upper room to the disciples on the day of his resurrection. It is clear by Luke's account that the disciples have a concept of a spirit without a physical body having some type of transcendent existence. Luke quotes Jesus a few verses later when he states, "Touch me, and see. For a spirit does not have flesh and bones as you see that I have" (Lk 24:39). When Jesus reassures his disciples of who he is, he uses the word *spirit* to distinguish his present bodily resurrected state from a purely spiritual presence.

Matthew 10:28 helps us distinguish the meaning of soul in the New Testament. Jesus is instructing the Twelve before he sends them out to do ministry and he states, "Do not fear those who kill the body *[sōma]* but cannot kill the soul *[psychē]*." Here we see Jesus making a distinction between the physical destruction of the body and the destruction of the soul. Clearly, Jesus sees humanness as a construct of both body and soul.

The passages we have examined indicate that the Scriptures distinguish body and soul. This seems to allow for a construction of a theological anthropology that is dualistic in nature. However, it is important to examine Pauline literature to see if Paul too has a dualistic conception of humans.

---

[25]Cooper, *Body, Soul, and Life Everlasting*, pp. 81-103.

Pauline anthropology.[26] Gamaliel, who was either the son or grandson of Hillel, trained Paul as a Pharisee. Hillel was a renowned Pharisee who developed eight rules *(middoth)* for biblical interpretation, which he used to interpret Scripture and apply the laws of the Pentateuch to first-century Jewish society. Many scholars believe that the tools Paul uses when he interprets the Old Testament come from this tradition. As we investigate Pauline anthropology we can assume that Paul's pharisaical training influences his interpretive grid. Because Pharisees believed in the doctrine of bodily resurrection and the afterlife, when Paul encounters Jesus on the road to Damascus, he interprets this event in light of his Jewish understanding of the resurrection. Paul's theological commitments prior to his conversion, while obviously not the same as a Christian's, did not have to undergo a radical paradigm shift for him to grasp his encounter with Jesus. He did not abandon his status as a Pharisee as he chooses to follow Jesus (see Acts 22; Phil 3). Apparently Paul's ideas of bodily resurrection and afterlife remained basically unchanged after his conversion to Christianity.

First Thessalonians 4:13-18 states:

> We do not want you to be uninformed, brothers, about those who are asleep, that you may not grieve as others do who have no hope. For since we believe that Jesus died and rose again, even so, through Jesus, God will bring with him those who have fallen asleep. For this we declare to you by a word from the Lord, that we who are alive, who are left until the coming of the Lord, will not precede those who have fallen asleep. For the Lord himself will descend from heaven with a cry of command, with the voice of an archangel, and with the sound of the trumpet of God. And the dead in Christ will rise first. Then we who are alive, who are left, will be caught up together with them in the clouds to meet the Lord in the air, and so we will always be with the Lord. Therefore encourage one another with these words.

---

[26]A concise survey of Paul's view may be found in W. R. Stegner, "Paul the Jew," in *Dictionary of Paul and His Letters*, ed. Gerald F. Hawthorne, Ralph P. Martin and Daniel G. Reid (Downers Grove, Ill.: InterVarsity Press, 1993), pp. 503-11. Detailed questions about Paul's specific beliefs about the nature of the afterlife will not be examined in this section.

Paul is addressing the concerns of some of the Christians who falsely thought that they would not die before Christ's return. (He uses the word *asleep* metaphorically to describe those who have already died.) Paul clarifies to the Thessalonians that Christians, when they die, do not undergo immediate resurrection. Persons who die do not wink out of existence but await Christ's return so they can be reembodied. In 1 Thessalonians 5:10 Paul clarifies the earlier passage writing that Jesus "died for us so that whether we are awake or asleep we may live with him." These concepts track with Paul's rabbinic training, and they expound on his view that a human can be disembodied and retain his or her identity. It also seems to point out that embodiment is the eschatological ideal for humanity.

Another Pauline passage on the resurrection is 1 Corinthians 15. Here, Paul argues both for Christ's resurrection and the resurrection of humanity. Again, he uses the sleep metaphor, which allows for human identity to continue while existing in a disembodied state. He also uses the analogy of the sowing of seeds which "does not come to life unless it dies" (1 Cor 15:36). This has its roots in the Pharisees' teaching that God could create a resurrected human from the smallest bit of one's flesh.[27] Paul uses this teaching to point out that the corrupted body is the seed by which God will reconstitute an imperishable body. Humanity in its present state is doomed to death. At the time of the resurrection God will create a new body from the seed of one's decaying body, and the reembodied individual will remain the same person. While this does not give an explanation of how personal identity endures it is a tacit assumption of Paul's.

In 2 Corinthians 5:1-10 Paul describes his earthly body as a tent over his self which will ultimately be destroyed. He is expectantly looking forward to his resurrection body, which will no longer be susceptible to the sufferings he experiences due to his current embodied state. Prior to the reception of our resurrection bodies we will live "naked" or disembodied in the intermediate state in the presence of God. It seems clear that Paul holds that being present and disembodied with God is better than his present circumstances. It is just as

---

[27]Anthony Thiselton, *The First Epistle to the Corinthians: A Commentary on the Greek Text* (Grand Rapids: Eerdmans, 2000), p. 1262.

clear that Paul sees embodiment as a more complete view of his essential humanity.

Paul, in Philippians 1:21-24, writes:

> For to me to live is Christ, and to die is gain. If I am to live in the flesh, that means fruitful labor for me. Yet which I shall choose I cannot tell. I am hard pressed between the two. My desire is to depart and be with Christ, for that is far better. But to remain in the flesh is more necessary on your account.

This passage is similar to the 2 Corinthians passage—Paul is describing the importance of his earthly ministry juxtaposed with his desire to be with Christ. Clearly, Paul understands that his kingdom work on the earth is necessary, but he wishes to be in a better place with Christ. Again, we can see how Paul differentiates himself from his body— seeing his flesh as the thing which ties him to the earth. Departing through death to be with Christ means leaving the flesh behind. Obviously, Paul conceives of his person in dualistic terms.

It is clear that some type of anthropological dualism is espoused in the Scriptures, and substance dualism most properly articulates this view. The concepts of body and soul enable us to develop a robust anthropology. Our anthropology is grounded in fundamental theological, philosophical and commonsense concepts of body and soul. The work of education must begin with these fundamental tools.

HUMANITY, PURPOSE AND SUCCESS

Intellectual history is pervaded by the question, How can I live up to my full potential as a human? The question's simplicity contrasts with the complexity of the answer. For millennia great thinkers, such as Plato and Augustine, have sought an answer and still do today.

Questions about living up to one's full potential are tacitly questions about happiness. The concept of happiness has always been associated with, in one way or another, the flourishing of humanity. Classical descriptions of human flourishing are often expressed in terms such as *ends*, *purpose* and *teleology*. Ultimately, this is a discussion of what it means to be truly successful as a human being.

True, whenever you hear educational types talk of various "programs" it is always with the "unsuccessful" children as the "program"'ed.

Today the word *success* has mixed connotations. It is often incorrectly associated with the acquisition of money and power, particularly in our individualistic and materialistic culture. Yet, when we reflect on the transitory nature of both money and power, it is unclear why anyone would count these as a measure of true success. History is rife with examples of individuals who were one day rich or powerful and the next day bankrupt or in prison. We need a more enduring concept of success that is not subject to such things as the law of entropy or the whimsical nature of the human political system.

For the concept of success to have any value to us it must be measured by some sort of transcendent standard. Classical views of success have been normative; that is, they have endured for generations. In today's culture, though, everything is transitory, and beliefs that do not "change with the times" are quickly seen as outmoded and unimportant. To be successful as educators we must understand our students as more than just their physical selves; their identities transcend the limitations of the empirical realm. (Hence the importance of an understanding of dualism and metaphysics.) We will begin our investigation of success with the teachings of Plato and Aristotle.

Plato's and Aristotle's writings have had a lasting impact on the world of scholarship, and it would be hard to overstate their importance or our debt to their work. So much of what they have written has laid the groundwork from which other intellectual greats (Augustine, Aquinas, Calvin, etc.) have investigated the human condition. Indeed, they set the stage for discussion that will go on for millennia, but their views of human purpose ultimately fall short of a holistic explanation of human existence. These shortcomings we will discuss later in this chapter.

Plato held that the universe was created in the image of essential realities or forms. The forms exist in the "world of being" where nothing changes. All things in the physical world are particular instances of their true form in the world of being, where the true form of the thing exists.[28] For example, the chair we sit on exemplifies what philosophers

---

[28]Plato *Phaedo* 74a–e.

call "chairness." A chair is an instantiation of the form "Chair," that is, the chair is made from the "blueprint" of the ideal chair. While objects in the physical world go in and out of existence, the forms always exist without change.[29] Both inanimate and animate objects that exist in the physical world are shadows of the true thing that exists in the ideal world of form. Particular things in the physical world will never be able to reach the ideal: as soon as they are created they begin to atrophy and become less and less like the ideal.

According to Plato human existence is to be understood in light of a transcendent ideal. That is, as we attempt to evaluate how we are living, there is actually some unchanging standard by which we can measure ourselves. Platonic notions of human flourishing or success are inextricably linked to these abstract objects of reality (forms) that ground our ability to evaluate our existence.

Unlike the physicalist described earlier in this chapter, Plato conceives of humanity as much more than a physical body. Some of the most essential aspects of humanity are not related to the physical realm. To describe humans Plato points to the soul, which is made up of appetites, passions and rationality.[30] For Plato our soul is a fundamental aspect of our humanity, which constitutes the immaterial part of our person. Platonic discussions of humanity do not include such things as height, weight, hair or skin color. These attributes are external and transitory, and are, as Plato says, "passing away." When humans mature and their bodies lose some of their physical abilities, they do not become less human. Ultimately, for Plato, the pursuit of human flourishing has little to do with bodies.

Platonism understands rationality as one of the most fundamental components of humanity. Rationality distinguishes humans from animals, and humans must use it properly if they are actually going to be successful. Success is actualized when we pursue "the good." Plato believed that all human beings were meant to pursue the good, which would lead to happiness.[31] The good is a normative, overarching con-

---

[29]Plato *Timaeus* 27d-28a.
[30]Plato *Republic* 441a-e.
[31]Ibid., 517c.

cept that subsumes all other forms. Plato taught that we are to pursue it by means of philosophy, which is the love of wisdom. The good is the pinnacle of our human pursuit; it is what is best or most excellent, and it is the direct object of the life of study. Understanding the forms, especially the good, enables us to think well and act accordingly.

Plato's dialogue *Gorgias* teaches that the good is actually knowable and therefore pursuable. In this work Plato describes a conversation between his mentor, Socrates, and the rhetorician Gorgias. While they begin to discuss the nature of oratory, the dialogue becomes an investigation of the foundations of knowledge.[32] Gorgias is a verbally dexterous person who uses his rhetorical skills to sway those who are less intellectually rigorous. Plato, through the person of Socrates, takes pains, through the use of the dialectic (the give and take of dialogue to examine the truth of an opinion), to point out the relativistic nature of Gorgias's "art." Gorgias and others that subscribed to his ideology of rhetoric are not concerned with truth but with how their use of language can help them gain personal power. His view is contrasted with Socrates's, who points out that life is not about persuasion but adhering to an understanding of the world that is at its foundation unchanging. Only this kind of understanding allows for humans to properly judge the rightness and wrongness of an action.[33]

How does Plato think we gain knowledge so we can make proper judgments? Humans, at the most basic level, possess the ability to access the empirical world around them. They are also able to reflect on their experience of the empirical world through their rationality. Through our rational abilities we are able to refine our understandings of things we contact in the empirical world. So, the more we experience and reflect on an object in this world, the more we can come to understand it.

Oftentimes in Plato's dialogues, Socrates, his mouthpiece, undertakes grandiose projects where he attempts to know what concepts like *virtue* or *justice* are "in themselves." He wants to know what these ab-

---

[32]Plato *Gorgias* 449d.
[33]A. E. Taylor, *Plato: The Man and His Work*, 4th ed. (Mineola, N.Y.: Courier Dover, 2001), pp. 104-6.

stract objects are in their essential nature. Many times his dialogue partners attempt to describe the concept according to its effects or instances or parts. However, long lists of virtuous acts do not satisfy Socrates when he seeks knowledge of virtue.[34] What he is looking for is an account of virtue that explains all the different virtuous acts, because he does not want to live according to principles that are derived from the physical world, which is changing. He wants to know unchanging principles so that he can pursue them in an unwavering manner. These transcendent principles can only be found in the forms, and only the forms transcend the limitations of the physical world. They are not restricted by the constraints of space and time.

Plato does not think that a detailed physical description of a thing counts as understanding. So when we initially consider human beings we will notice physical properties (e.g., humans are bipeds and binocular). Eventually, though, we will notice that human beings all seem to have qualities that transcend their physical states. (Plato suggests that something noticed early on is that all humans are beautiful.)[35] Then we will begin to notice that other things (e.g., roses) also are beautiful. Plato argues that this idea of beauty is a transcendent thing that is unchanging, and that more than one being can participate in the form of Beauty. When we keep a rose on our table for an extended period of time it begins to participate less and less with the form of Beauty as it decomposes. The form of Beauty isn't changing, but the rose's ability to instantiate beauty in the corporeal world is limited because of its physical makeup.

Plato's concept of human purpose is teleological. For instance, someone does not see because he or she has eyes, but has eyes in order to see. It is important to notice the distinction—we were given eyes to fulfill the intention of our Designer to be a creature who sees. Eyes are the tools that fulfill the design intention. This teleology stands in direct opposition to the naturalism, which holds that we see because we have eyes. Plato believes that mechanistic explanations do not fully account for the nature of things. Understanding how things work is

---

[34]Plato *Meno* 72d.
[35]Plato *Symposium* 209a-c.

valuable, but it does not explain the intention or purpose of things—only the way they are carried out. To be able to explain the purpose of humanity entails a commitment to a reality that stands outside a physical instantiation. For Plato human purpose or teleology comes from the realm of forms, which is unchanging and when understood enables us to flourish as humans.

Returning to the earlier discussion of success, a successful person turns out to be, for Plato, an individual who pursues accurate understanding of the world through the means of education. This pursuit allows a person to act with the courage necessary to live well. The life of study, contemplation and education develops a person who has "an absolutely assured personal conviction about the universal order and his place in it."[36] The life of inquiry enables a person to better achieve success because he or she will acquire a more robust understanding of how to live within the created order.[37]

These Platonic notions of human existence have deeply informed Christian theological views. The view that humans were created for a purpose that is larger than themselves comports well with basic Christian theological commitments. Christians believe that humans are created by God for his purpose, and our proper understanding of our purpose cannot be derived by empirical inquiry. Numerous Christian intellectuals have relied on aspects of Plato's philosophical framework as they crafted their theological anthropologies.

Before we say more about Plato's influence on Christian thought, let's briefly consider Aristotle, who also has contributed much to the Christian consideration of anthropology and, by extension, to the pursuit of education. As we consider the thoughts of Aristotle (and Plato) we will begin to see how our beliefs about humanity have historical roots in the ideas of these classic thinkers.

In his *Nicomachean Ethics* Aristotle develops a method to understand what it means to pursue the most excellent functioning of a human, which he calls happiness. For Aristotle human flourishing, what we have been calling success, is a combination of theory and

---

[36]Taylor, *Plato*, p. 284.
[37]Plato *Republic* bk. 4, esp. 4.443c-d.

action. Humans always pursue their own personal good.[38] While it may be the case that what they pursue ultimately is not good, that does not mean that they desire bad things for themselves. No one gets up in the morning and thinks, *I want what's bad for me.* Even those who perform horrendously evil deeds do so believing it will bring them happiness.

Some methods of pursuing happiness are more effective than others. Aristotle shows that there are many types of goods, which lead to various ends, but there is only one highest good, and that is happiness. All other goods that we pursue are "so that" goods. We learn to play guitar *so that* we can accompany ourselves when we sing. We practice singing *so that* we can improve and get a recording contract. We sign a recording contract *so that* we can be famous and make lots of money. All "so that" goods are subordinate to other goods. Aristotle suggests the only good not subordinated to other goods is happiness. Again, common sense tells us that our ultimate pursuit is happiness. No one seeks happiness *so that* something else happens; indeed, obtaining happiness eliminates all other needs.[39]

Happiness, though, requires the possession of virtue. For something to be virtuous it must properly fulfill the purpose for which it was made, according to Aristotle. For example, a knife is virtuous when forged from a quality metal that is easy to sharpen and holds its edge a long time. Similarly, to understand human virtue we must understand the purpose humans are made for, and for this we need to understand the nature of the soul.

Aristotle believes that the soul consists of both rational and nonrational parts.[40] The nonrational has two components: the autonomic part, which is not influenced by reason, and the appetites and desires, which may be influenced by the rational part of our soul, which is the seat of the intellect, and controls our appetites and desires. Human virtue requires the training of both the appetitive and rational parts of the soul.

---

[38]Aristotle *Nicomachean Ethics* 1095a.1-27.
[39]Ibid., 1097a-b.
[40]Ibid., 1144a.

Training the appetite consists of developing habits through repetitive practice of right activities. Training the intellect takes place through a life of study. This studious life is not merely theoretical but also active. Through study, the intellectual part of the soul enables the appetites to develop good habits. A person may practice the piano for long periods of time and not improve if he or she does not practice correctly. The development of proper habits must work in concert with a rational understanding of what makes that habit excellent.

Therefore, if we agree with Plato and Aristotle's basic commitment to teleology, we believe education and a life of study are necessary to a successful life. Education enables us to understand, through our rational capacities, the world around us. A properly educated human responds to quandaries in a manner that corresponds properly to the realities of this orderly universe.

The classical tradition of inquiry lays the foundation for anthropology. Investigating the work undertaken by Plato and Aristotle allows us to consider our own anthropological commitments and how they should inform our actions as educators. We find it helpful that Plato and Aristotle conceived humanity in terms of purpose, and established principles to evaluate human action. Historically, Christianity has embraced these Platonic and Aristotelian philosophical commitments, incorporating them into theological discourse. Such great theologians as Augustine, Aquinas, Calvin and Wesley learned from the work of Plato and Aristotle. While both philosophers brought their tremendous intellects to bear on the question of anthropology, their apprehension of humanity was incomplete without God's revelation to and about humanity.

THE LIMITS OF CLASSICAL TELEOLOGY

Classical teleology establishes a principle of being that is not constrained by a mechanistic view of existence. Teleological concepts of reality hold that all objects have an intended goal, and when an object obtains its intended goal it has reached its natural state. Something is in its natural state when it is operating within its constituted parameters. The teleology of inanimate objects is pretty easy to understand. When we examine a knife, we can rather quickly determine whether or not it is able to actualize its intended purpose. It becomes much more complex however when we consider humans.

The point of much of this chapter has been to establish what a biblical anthropology should comprise. We have argued that human beings are composed of a material body and an immaterial soul, and that the soul directs the body's actions ultimately through its rational capacities. The development of these rational capacities through a life of study most effectively allows humans to pursue excellence, by which we mean actions that best enable them to obtain their most proper state. Through education, we are able to understand who we are and how to seek our proper end, which ultimately leads to our happiness. When we think about the life of study and how it can increase our own and our students' happiness, this resonates with us as educators. Giving others the opportunity to become happy is a rewarding endeavor.

In a limited sense teleology can enable us to help ourselves and others be more satisfied with our current existence. However, classical teleologies are constrained by a limited viewpoint, that is, from a human perspective alone. Classical teleology is eminently superior to a physicalist view of human beings; however, compared to a robust Christian theological anthropology, it falls far short.

ATONED HUMANITY AND OUR VOCATION

As Christians, we understand that human beings are in an unnatural state. We have inherited sinful nature or what is often called "original sin." The apostle Paul points out in Ephesians 2 that before accepting Christ we were "dead in [our] trespasses and sins," following the "prince of the power of the air," and that we were "carrying out the desires of the body and the mind, and were by nature children of wrath, like the rest of mankind." Our sin affects every part of our being, making us unable to know or pursue what is truly best. The prophet Jeremiah points out that the level of corruption in our own hearts makes it impossible for us to understand ourselves (Jer 17:9). Our state of sin places us in epistemic crisis. Swiss theologian Karl Barth states that because of our sinful nature we are blind and deaf to the real source of truth, and that we live in a world of dreams where what we think we know only shows the depth of our ignorance.[41] To put it mildly, sin compromises our capacity to clearly understand what we as humans need for our success and happiness.

Only by the grace of God and the atoning work of his Son Jesus Christ on the cross are we able to come to an accurate understanding of what it means to flourish as a human being. This is not something we can learn from Plato and Aristotle. Salvation through the work of Jesus Christ not only changes our position before God but also enables us, through the Holy Spirit's labor, to be able to comprehend our humanity. Prior to our salvation our ignorance of reality is repeatedly illustrated in Scripture through the concept of darkness. First Peter 2:9 states that God "called you out of darkness into his marvelous light." In Acts 26:18 the apostle Paul says Jesus sent him to the Gentiles "to open their eyes, so that they may turn from darkness to light and from the power of Satan to God, that they may receive forgiveness of sins and a place among those who are sanctified by faith in me." God calls us out of our own intellectual and spiritual darkness into the illumined world of understanding.

To have a notion of what our true purpose is, God must illumine our minds. Karl Barth writes:

> Illumination, however, is the seeing of which man was previously incapable but of which he is now capable. It is thus his advancement to knowledge. That the revelation of God shines on him and in him, takes place in such a way that he hears, receives, understands, grasps and appropriates what is said to him in it, not with new and special organs, but with the same organs of apperception with which he knows other things, yet not in virtue of his own capacity to use them, but virtue of the missing capacity which he is now given by God's revelation.[42]

God's illumination enables us to gain knowledge that we could not have without his intervening revelation. Consequently, prior to God's illumination, even our best attempt to craft a coherent anthropology falls woefully short.

---

[41]Karl Barth, *Church Dogmatics* IV, part 3.2, trans. Geoffrey W. Bromiley (Edinburgh: T & T Clark, 1962) p. 512.
[42]Ibid., p. 509.

Most teleologies do not take into account the necessity of human redemption. Even if they do consider certain revelatory facts as they develop their anthropologies, they do not clearly explicate humanity's purpose. Natural teleology, because it is a construct of human rationality, is unable to holistically explain the essential nature of our existence—this can only be understood in light of God's eschatological purposes. While we do not want to completely abandon helpful teleological constructs, we believe a more complete view comes only when we think of humans in terms of God's eschatological purposes.

Eschatology is a study of the last things or "end times." From creation through the Fall and to the eventual second coming of Jesus Christ, God has been purposefully moving his creation toward restoration. When Adam and Eve sinned by eating of the fruit of the tree of the knowledge of good and evil, all creation abandoned its natural state. Not only were Adam and Eve out of fellowship with God and doomed to death, but also the entire natural world ceased to function properly. Paul writes in Romans 8:22, "For we know that the whole creation has been groaning together in the pains of childbirth until now." In Romans 8 we see Paul's expectant hope in God's future plans for his creation. Right now things are unnatural, but God is at work to make things right again.

When God gives us illumination, he is revealing eschatological truths, which are revealed facts about the already perfected future kingdom of God. When we think about the future, we consider it in light of contingencies. We realize that our plans and hopes for the future are volatile, subject to myriad situations that cause us to adjust our expectation. Human conceptions of the future are uncertain. Conversely, according to a biblical eschatology, the establishment of God's kingdom on the new earth is certain. For Christians it is not our past or even our present that creates our future, but God's plan for his kingdom to come. What God has revealed of his perfect future kingdom enables us to live as we should today.[43]

---

[43]Wolfhart Pannenberg, *Theology and the Kingdom of God* (Philadelphia: Westminster Press, 1969), pp. 53, 133.

Our knowledge of reality is to be shaped by God's illumination. This means that our understanding of present goods is predicated on God revealing his eschatological kingdom, which he brings about himself. Classical teleology fails to give a clear understanding of human purpose. Only through God's revelation do we have an idea of what we should become, what our vocation is.

Today, we commonly think about vocation in terms of occupations. Sadly, much of what we think about ourselves and our educational goals has more to do with our jobs rather than who we are. As Christians we should not think of ourselves in these limited terms. We are eternal beings who are destined to live forever with God. In 2 Corinthians 4:17 Paul writes, "This light momentary affliction is preparing for us an eternal weight of glory beyond all comparison." What we do and experience presently shapes our eternal being.

Our understanding of self and others should be mediated by eternal realities. When God saves us, we become an inextricable part of his kingdom purposes. Christians are called to be ministers of the gospel of Jesus Christ. First Peter 2:9 expresses our Christian vocation: "You are a chosen race, a royal priesthood, a holy nation, a people for his own possession, that you may proclaim the excellencies of him who called you out of darkness into his marvelous light." The first words Peter used are almost exactly the same as the charge that God gave the people of Israel at Sinai: "a kingdom of priests and a holy nation" (Ex 19:6). As followers of Jesus Christ we are now acting as his priests, and we are charged to proclaim God's kingdom—praising the one who set us free from sin. Our focus as Christian educators needs to take seriously the fact that we educate our students for work in God's kingdom, and not just to enable them to obtain gainful employment. In a world driven by performance it is too easy to find ourselves obsessing over test scores rather than loving our students as Christ loves us.

It is easy to think that the proclamation of the gospel is only the calling of the clergy or occasionally our responsibility when we are questioned about our foundational beliefs. This is a false understanding. We fully belong to God, and he, because of his love, gives us proper guidance.[44] This means that we are absolutely committed to the kingdom purposes God has constructed, and we plan on understanding and dedicating ourselves to that mission. This commitment should radically reconstruct how we think of our daily lives.

CONCLUSION

A strong anthropology will be grounded in both philosophical and theological principles.

Ultimately, understanding the foundational role theology plays in anthropology is needed to properly respond to and assess the various pedagogical and curricular paradigms within education. Most important, Christians need to realize that our work in the classroom transcends the normal expectations of "meeting state standards." As followers of Jesus Christ we are participants in God's kingdom purposes, blessed individuals who by God's grace have been given the opportunity to share with others what it means to truly have purpose.

Mastering the discipline of education can be a daunting task. To come to a clear understanding of what it means to properly educate our students, we have begun to consider the complex philosophical, historical, biblical and theological concepts that ultimately shape our educational views. We need to be able to show others through our rigorous intellectual pursuit of education that we are a serious voice for change in this discipline. This will happen through dedicating ourselves, not to our own external success, but to the larger project of God's kingdom. We have an opportunity to speak to others in a way that can make an eternal difference. It is our belief that the rest of this book lays out a project that will enable Christian educators to do that.

---

[44]Karl Barth, *The Doctrine of Reconciliation, Church Dogmatics* IV, part 3.2 (Edinburgh: T & T Clark, 1962), pp. 536-37.

2

Historical Perspectives
on Education
Looking Back to the Future

Educators are inundated with myriads of competing educational theories, and these theories dictate the methods and goals that are actualized in the classroom on a daily basis. These educational theories are a product of a commitment to a certain philosophical paradigm. Teachers are overwhelmed, understandably, with the amount of work it takes to properly manage the classroom: preparing the next day or week's classes, meeting with parents, grading papers and so forth. This doesn't leave a teacher much time (if any at all) to reflect on educational theory—let alone the theories' underlying philosophical commitments. If teachers are going to be properly equipped for their task of education, they must begin to grapple with the historical development of educational practice.

Broadly speaking, modern education lacks a unified purpose or goal to direct its curricular and pedagogical commitments. This lack of unity exists because education has many competing allegiances to different educational methodologies, which are driven by a variety of diverse philosophical commitments. Education is no longer understood in terms of training that enables us to pursue a true conception of reality. Formerly, education was conceived as a tool by which we came to properly understand our humanity, ourselves and our right role within society. Education was about pursuing and understanding objective value, as C. S. Lewis points out: "the belief that certain attitudes are really true, and that others really false, to the kind of thing the universe is and the kind of things we are."[1] Today, education is not so much about truth or morality as it is about tolerance and contributing to the nation's economic growth.

The following is an example of education's paradigmatic shift away from the pursuit of truth. Every year the University of Chicago offers a lecture for its incoming freshmen called "Aims of Education." This lecture is given, ostensibly, to describe what their next four years will be like at the university. In 1998, Professor John Mearsheimer was selected to give the "Aims of Education" speech, and he said that the pursuit of truth is not a goal for any faculty member at the University of Chicago. In his speech he states: "There is a powerful bias at the University of Chicago against providing you with the truth about the important issues we study. Instead, we aim to produce independent thinkers who can reach their own conclusions."[2] He points out that the University of Chicago is not alone in this bias:

> Not only is there a powerful imperative at Chicago to stay away from teaching the truth, but the University also makes little effort to provide you with moral guidance. Indeed, it is a remarkably amoral institution. I would say the same thing, by the way, about all other major colleges and universities in this country.[3]

The argument made by Professor Mearsheimer seems self-refuting. He and the University of Chicago hold that there *is* a truth to be taught—you should not teach truth. It is his desire not to teach objective values (truth), which is itself an objective value.

What is very troubling is that Professor Mearsheimer is not alone in his belief; his speech to the incoming freshmen at the University of Chicago is just one example of the difficulty that today's Christian educator faces. Christian academics should pursue truth and objectivity, and it is important for us to understand how philosophical ideologies have influenced the discipline of education. It is also the case that many academic institutions have started out with the desire to pursue truth, but through

---

[1]C. S. Lewis, *The Abolition of Man* (San Francisco: HarperOne, 2001), p. 18.
[2]John J. Mearsheimer, "The Aims of Education," *Philosophy and Literature* 22, no. 1 (1998): 147.
[3]Ibid., p. 149.

the influence of competing philosophies they have abandoned their commitment to a Christian theological and philosophical worldview. Additionally, much of our educational system no longer sees the value of philosophy and philosophy of education, which ground the methods that enable us to discern or even discuss truth and reality. For the most part, schools of education have relegated philosophy to an afterthought. For Christian educators to properly respond to current educational views, like those held by Mearsheimer, we need to understand what principles undergird our ability to assess the truth of a theory.

Educational assessment necessitates the ability to identify and evaluate foundational commitments that underlie pedagogical theories. Along with this evaluative aspect, we must be able to examine the philosophical commitments behind a theory's view of the educational task and its view of students. These theoretical principles, whether tacit or overt, undergird pedagogy. To flourish in the discipline of education, we should have a basic understanding of philosophical categories and the views of the most influential philosophical thinkers. It behooves educators to understand how these influence educational theory. A survey of these foundational categories and philosophical thinkers will help us understand some of the basic differences between various philosophical positions, and make us more aware of some of the pitfalls that have enveloped most of our prestigious institutions of higher education.

Thinking about philosophy may seem like a daunting task, but educators do not need a graduate degree in the discipline to be able to understand philosophy. This chapter is designed to enable educators to develop the basic framework needed to think philosophically. Ultimately, philosophy is an intellectual tool kit, and by becoming more competent with these tools we are enabled to recognize fundamental ideological commitments certain educational theories draw upon.[4]

Christians have often been nervous about the place of philosophy within academic discourse. Historically, medieval scholars held that

---

[4]J. P. Moreland has two books that will help develop philosophical acumen: *Love Your God with All Your Mind* (Colorado Springs: NavPress, 1997), and *Philosophy Made Slightly Less Difficult: A Beginner's Guide to Life's Big Questions* (Downers Grove, Ill.: InterVarsity Press, 2005), which he cowrote with Garrett J. DeWeese.

theology was the queen of the sciences (that is the most important domain of knowledge), and that philosophy was her handmaiden. In the late seventeenth century, Enlightenment philosophy usurped theology's throne. Since then, not only has philosophy been seen as more important than theology but much of Western philosophy has been bent on undermining theology as a knowledge tradition. Christian skepticism about philosophy's help in the pursuit of knowledge is therefore understandable. Our goal is to understand that philosophy is a means by which educators can better guide themselves and their students to truth.

Philosophy enables us to become more confident in the things that we believe, and it thereby can play a more fundamental role in the way we evaluate educational theory. This, of course, does not remove the importance of robust theological knowledge within our educational theory.[5] Philosophy enables us to develop our intellectual tools to the best of our abilities. C. S. Lewis points out that we, as Christians, are called by God to be intellectually rigorous: "He wants a child's heart, but a grown-up's head. . . . He also wants every bit of intelligence we have to be alert at its job, and in first-class fighting trim. . . . God is no fonder of intellectual slackers than of any other slackers."[6] Subsequently, both as believers in Christ and academically minded individuals, it is morally incumbent upon us to develop our intellect, and philosophic "tools" are an important part of this development.

First, we investigate some of the basic categories under which philosophy organizes itself: metaphysics, logic, aesthetics, ethics and epistemology.[7] What follows is an overview of each of these categories, and as we understand these organizing principles of philosophy we are able to use these philosophical categories as tools to assess philosophical and educational commitments.

METAPHYSICS

The term *metaphysics* was coined by Aristotle and means literally "after

---

[5]This will be discussed in chap. 3.
[6]C. S. Lewis, *Mere Christianity* (New York: Macmillan, 1960), p. 75.
[7]This list is not exhaustive.

physics"; it is the investigation we do after the study of the natural sciences or "physics." Metaphysics is concerned with the fundamental essence of things and the study of reality. It attempts to investigate things which are not completely accessible through the means of the five senses. Consciousness, the immortality of souls, freedom of the will and our ideas of God cannot be understood through the senses. Metaphysics enables us to develop a clearer understanding of things that stand outside of the empirical realm.

To understand the world around us, we need to have a well-developed metaphysics. Metaphysics enables us to develop categories by which we can understand fundamental aspects of our world of experience. Metaphysics analyzes and explains real things so we can deliberate on the various categories of existence. It seeks foundational principles that enable us to pursue other philosophic and academic enterprises.

What is a human being? Why do we exist? What is my purpose in life? To answer these questions successfully, we need to develop a list of properties that constitute humanity; that is, we need to develop an "ontology" of humanity. Ontology is a view of what exists and a description of the essential properties different things have. An ontology of human persons would hold, for example, that from the point of conception a person is fully human and cannot be anything else (i.e., cannot become a tree or a dog). The person is a physical body existing in space and time, and is not just a brain but is also made up of immaterial substance (a soul), which is not mechanistic or dependent on brain function for existence. A soul is not coextensive, that is, occupying the same space at the same time, with the body, but is a necessary component of the body. A body without a soul is no longer a body in the strict sense. Instead it is a corpse. Humans have a purpose for existence, have proper ways of functioning, are libertarian free agents and are made in God's image. These concepts provide starting points for a full account of human ontology.

On the other hand, the commitments of modern natural science prevent it from a complete description of what it means to be human. This is because the object of scientific understanding is solely the empirical world, which is the realm of the senses. If modern science is right, humans then become property things, a grouping of parts that function in a machinelike manner with no unifying essence. This commitment to empiricism radically undercuts the possibility that science can provide a holistic account of what it means to be human.

Another important aspect of metaphysics is the concept of universals. A universal is a thing that can be had by more than one object at a time or be had by an object at different times. The color blue, humanness, being round are examples of universals. Some universals are *essential* to the nature of a thing, and some are *accidental* properties. An essential property is necessary to the existence of an object, and if an object looses that essential property it ceases to exist. An essential property of Steve Loomis is his humanness, that is to say it is necessary for Steve to have the property of being human to continue to exist. But an accidental property can be lost without causing its host to lose its existence. So if Steve loses all of his height he does not cease being Steve, because his height is an accidental property.

Universals can also be subdivided into singular properties or relations. A singular property is possessed by an object without a relation to another object, for example, colors or geometrical shapes. A universal is relational when there is a relationship between at least two different objects. Features such as bigger, taller or heavier (a volleyball size compared to that of a baseball, a Sumo wrestler's weight compared to that of a jockey) are all relations. Universals are permanent foundational sources of order, which do not change regardless of our interaction with the external, sensory world. So while various instantiations of a circle may be different, the universal "circle" will not change. Universals, therefore, are absolutes: features (such as justice, being intelligent, being painful) that are the same throughout various times, places or cultures.

Universals do not exist on their own; rather, they are owned by a substance. A substance contains a group of properties, but it is more than just the sum of its properties or parts. For example, let's consider my friend Fred, who is six feet tall, has brown hair and weighs 185 pounds. Suppose Fred goes away for the summer and starts a rigorous workout routine. When I see him next fall, he has gained ten pounds of muscle mass, dyed his hair blond and tattooed a dove on his left bicep.

Is he now a new Fred? What if he lost two fingers in a weightlifting accident? Is he now a new Fred? No, "Fred qua Fred"—that is, the essential properties that make Fred who he is—exist regardless of the fact that he is sporting a new tattoo or that he lost two fingers. The changes that took place in Fred were not changes on an essential level but were changes of his accidental properties, such as the change of skin color, which are not essential to Fred being Fred or being human.

We know, since Fred is human, that he has basic metaphysical properties that make up his essence, and that he is able to exist as a unified whole throughout time. This is because Fred's metaphysical properties are not subject to entropy; that is, unlike his physical body, the fundamental properties that make Fred human will not decay. Metaphysics enables us to properly describe why every time we lose or gain a new property, our essential selves do not change.

Consider how an understanding of metaphysics will affect the way we teach our students. If we espouse a modern scientific ideology, human beings turn out to be just bundles of different physical properties, and a potential teaching model we could adopt is the behaviorist model (advocated by B. F. Skinner). From this perspective, students respond to the teacher's inputs, and the teacher evaluates his or her effectiveness by their students' output, much like programming a computer. Thus students are trained by reinforcing their behavior with a series of rewards and punishments; eventually they respond properly to certain stimuli. As long as students gave the right responses, the teacher would be successful. Teachers would no longer need to think longitudinally about their students, because once students are effectively trained they will respond properly to stimuli. Ethics turns out to be a study of the correct types of stimuli that enable students to function within the parameters of what society dictates as good interpersonal behavior. Behaviorists cannot appeal to transcendent realities (i.e., universals grounded in God) that exist independently of the physical world, because such realities don't exist. Within a modern scientific paradigm they are nonsensical. So an immortal soul with free will turns out to be an incoherent belief that plays no role in how we think about our actions.

Logic

Everyone uses logic every day, but it is important to understand logic in a slightly more technical way. Logic is the daunting side of philosophy; it even makes many academics nervous because so often we are afraid of looking ignorant. Chiefly, logic is skillful thought and argument. It is foundational to the proper use of rational capacities. Logic is the tool used to deduce the consequences of a set of premises. Logic allows us to construct ideas to clearly communicate concepts to one another. The better we are able to identify logical flaws in an argument, the more adept we will be at getting at the crux of a person's improperly held beliefs.

God is a God of truth, wisdom and logic. Jesus' use of logic shows us its value as a tool for teaching and learning. Jesus' debate in Matthew 12 with the Pharisees on the nature of sabbath rest is a perfect example of the importance of logic. It would be helpful for anyone to continue their study with a good introductory text on argumentation, such as *With Good Reason: An Introduction to Informal Fallacies* by Morris Engel.

A deductive argument presents a conclusion which necessarily follows from the premises. The premises in a deductive argument include all of the necessary information to reach a conclusion. An example of a deductive argument follows:

All men are mortal.
Socrates is a man.
(Therefore)
Socrates is mortal.

An inductive argument presents a conclusion as a probable truth. To know whether an inductive argument is true requires information outside of its premises.

The following is an example of an inductive argument:

The sun, since the beginning of time, has always risen in the morning.
Therefore, the sun will rise tomorrow morning.

Inductive arguments are relying on probability, but not on necessity. The probability that the sun will rise in the morning is very high, but it is still only probable. Just because it has happened many times before does not make it certain in the future.

It is important, as an educator, to be able to spot errors of reasoning. Here are a few examples of informal fallacies or informal logic. The first type of informal fallacy is called *begging the question,* where the truth of the conclusion is assumed by the premises. Here is an example of question begging: Abortion is wrong because murder is wrong, and killing an unborn child is murder. Now this may be true, but the speaker is equating abortion to murder without explaining why killing an unborn child is murder. The speaker needs to think of a better way to form the argument without that assumption.

Another informal fallacy is called *tu quoque,* which is Latin for "you also." Basically the speaker is saying, "Oh yeah, you should talk." Grandma would call this "the pot calling the kettle black." This fallacy holds that an opponent's argument is empty because his or her own advice has not been followed. "Bob told me to stop eating fatty foods because they are bad for me, but why should I listen to him? He eats a pound of French fries every day."

Equivocation occurs when a key term in an argument can have more than one meaning. For example: When I ask my son if he "picked up" the toys in his room, he can say yes because of equivocation. Of course, when you look at his room it is obvious he picked up the toys and put them right back on the floor where he found them, not into the toy box.

As educators we are always assessing the quality of students' argument to ascertain whether they understand the concepts they are using. Teachers should instill in their students an understanding of what constitutes good and fallacious arguments. As Christians we should be able to counter the daily bombardment of anti-Christian rhetoric with strong rational skills. Dallas Willard writes, "Paying careful attention to how Jesus made use of logical thinking can strengthen our confidence in Jesus as master of the centers of intellect and creativity, and can encourage us to accept him as master in all of the areas of intellectual life in which we may participate."[8]

---

[8]Dallas Willard, "Jesus the Logician," *Christian Scholar's Review* 28, no. 4 (1999): 614.

Epistemology

Humans are inquisitive. Aristotle states, "All human beings by nature desire to know."[9] When we spend time with elementary school children, we quickly observe that much of their life revolves around inquiry. Epistemology is the branch of philosophy that investigates what knowledge is, and how we understand whether our beliefs are justified. One of the goals of our work as educators is to train our students to consider the world around them in such a way that they understand and function properly within it as human beings. The pursuit of knowledge should be the cornerstone of the academic discipline of education.

There are three different ways we talk about knowledge. They are (1) *technical* knowledge or what is more commonly called know-how, (2) *propositional* knowledge, which is knowledge of facts, and (3) knowledge by *acquaintance*, which is knowledge about something by direct awareness.

Consider this sentence: I know how to play basketball. This is an example of technical knowledge, possession of the skill that enables me to properly perform a certain type of task. Other examples of know-how are juggling, cooking and parachuting. Such knowledge is gained through repeated practice and familiarity with the task. It is often the case that once we get a certain level of skill through practice, we are no longer consciously aware of all the necessary steps taken to complete the task well. As I type my thoughts into the computer I am not reflecting on the actions of my fingers. This is because I have mastered the technical knowledge necessary to type.

"Propositional knowledge is the type of knowing whose instances are labeled by means of a phrase expressing some proposition."[10] More simply, propositional knowledge is knowledge of a fact that is the case. For example, you may have a great deal of knowledge about Winston Churchill, which comes from extensive time reading his writings, studying his biographies and even visiting his home of Chartwell, England. The knowledge you have of Churchill is propositional because

[9]Aristotle *Metaphysics* 1.1.
[10]Robert K. Shope, "Propositional Knowledge," in *A Companion to Epistemology*, ed. Jonathan Dancy (Malden, Mass.: Blackwell, 1992), p. 396.

you have "knowledge that" X obtains or is true about Churchill, such as he was prime minister of Great Britain during World War II.

Knowledge by acquaintance involves experience of a thing. We may have theoretical knowledge of an object, say a baseball, but when we hold the baseball in our hand we have knowledge by acquaintance. We come to know the baseball through our senses. Through acquaintance we can also know our own internal mental states, such as feelings or thoughts. So when we reflect on our feelings we are aware of them by direct acquaintance, which is a source of knowledge.

The standard definition of propositional knowledge is "justified true belief." Knowledge as justified true belief offers a conceptual grid that allows us to determine whether or not someone actually knows something. Often we equate truth with knowledge. Truth is certainly a fundamental aspect of knowledge, but in and of itself it is an incomplete account of knowledge. When we assess students in a classroom situation, we understand that it is not enough for their answer on the test to be true. A guess on a test (and who hasn't done that before) may turn out to be true, but it says more about a student's luck than his or her knowledge. Consider how this understanding of knowledge can change the way we determine the best models of assessment. Correct answers on a standardized test do not necessarily evidence student knowledge. Teachers want more than good test scores for their students. They want their students to actually have knowledge about a subject. This is just one way philosophy, and in this case specifically epistemology, allows us to reflect on how we go about the educational project.

If a person believes something, he or she is willing to act in accordance with that belief. It would be incoherent for me to say that I believe alligators are dangerous and then wade into an alligator-infested swamp. If I believe that alligators are dangerous, I must reasonably avoid being close to such a dangerous place. Belief in itself is not sufficient for knowledge; many people believe in things they don't know are true.

If we want to have knowledge, true belief is not enough. We must be justified as to why we have that belief. Our reasons for holding something to be true must meet a certain set of standards depending on the concept in question. So justification uses criteria by which we can judge whether or not the belief we have is warranted. Much more will be said about this in chapter three.

ETHICS

Ethics, which is the philosophical study of proper moral attitudes, character traits and behavior, is a synthesis and outworking of metaphysics and epistemology. Ethics uses the knowledge we have about our universe and ourselves in an attempt to put together a coherent ideology that enables us to properly live. Historically, ethics is grounded in the belief that there is a certain orderliness to our human existence. Because of the normative nature of our human existence, we are able to recognize (knowledge of how humans *should* or *should not* function) and then create principles individuals should live by in society.

Our actions have consequences. Sometimes we know instantaneously when we have done something right or wrong. At other times, bad decisions will not manifest themselves until a much later date. We need to be able to judge what decisions are improper and which are correct. If we have to make decisions at the spur of the moment without a well-constructed ethical system, we'll often lean in the direction of expediency or personal satisfaction. This is because what seems to be a right decision at a certain time does not always take into account larger foundational beliefs that transcend the moment of decision.

An example of this can be seen, tragically, when a woman decides to end the life of her unborn child through an abortion. When a woman finds herself pregnant out of marriage, she often faces multiple pressures to end the pregnancy. She wants to avoid bringing shame to her family and herself. Perhaps she is too young to be able to afford to care for the baby. She could be under pressure from her boyfriend, who doesn't want to pay child support, to end the pregnancy. All of the pressures and emotions she feels are very real. If she succumbs to the pressure at that time and aborts the baby, there will be long-term effects that she could not have foreseen. Depression, guilt, pain (both emotional and physical) will affect her for a long time.

When life decisions are complicated, ethics provides categories through which we can consider the implications of our decision. A good ethic would have us think about the rights of both the woman and the unborn baby. It would help us understand the value of this unborn child. The father of the child would be apprised of his responsibility to both the woman and his unborn child. Ethics would also help a community develop a support system for a woman who has a child out of wedlock. Ethics help mitigate the pressures of the moment in light of a transcendent understanding of reality.

Ethics is a profoundly important subject. If we want to be able to live the most successful type of life, we must think ethically. As Christians we realize that we should govern our lives by moral laws, that they enable us to do what is most proper for ourselves and those around us. A study of ethics will give us the tools to better understand the fundamental principles that undergird moral and ethical actions, and to be able to choose well amidst difficulty.

IMPORTANT HISTORICAL AND PHILOSOPHICAL MOMENTS THAT INFLUENCE EDUCATION

As educators not only do we need to understand the basic philosophical categories that enable us to think critically about our discipline, but we also need to develop a clear understanding of how different philosophical paradigms have affected the development of the discipline of education. Modern educational commitments are inextricably linked to the philosophical upheaval brought about by the thirteenth-century recovery of Aristotelianism, which led to the birth of modern science and the Enlightenment in the sixteenth and seventeenth centuries.[11] Investigating these developments will allow us to lay a foundation for more examination of pedagogical and theological commitments that are mainstays of modern educational theories.

The growth of formalized education in the West can reasonably be thought to begin in the late eleventh century with the conquest of two important centers of learning that had previously been under Muslim control: the city of Toledo in Spain and the island of Sicily. The capture of these two centers of learning begins the dissemination of these long-

---

[11]For more on this discussion see Rik Van Nieuwenhove and Joseph Wawrykow, eds., *The Theology of Thomas Aquinas* (Notre Dame, Ind.: University of Notre Dame Press, 2005).

lost methods of thinking about the world of ideas. Most of this new intellectual insight comes from the recovery of disciplines of science and natural philosophy. Some of the most important written works found in Toledo and Sicily were Euclid's mathematical writings, the scientific works of Archimedes, the *Almagest* of Ptolemy, which is a treatise on math and astronomy, and volumes by the Greek philosopher Aristotle.[12]

It is hard to believe that the major works of Aristotle were lost to the West until the late twelfth century, and yet the re-introduction of Aristotle's writings fundamentally changed the way academics do their intellectual investigations. Aristotle introduced a new intellectual rigor that did not exist in the West. He held that the most fundamental aspect of humanity is rationality—it is the substance that distinguishes us from common animals.[13] By making the intellectual life the focal point of the human endeavor, a person comes to know true fulfillment and happiness.[14]

Aristotle focused his intellectual pursuits not on restating things that are already known but by wrestling with difficult intellectual conundrums and forcing them to submit to his intellectual rigor. In *Nicomachean Ethics* Aristotle shows his fidelity to a life of intellectual investigation:

> As in the other cases we must set out the appearances, and first of all go through the puzzles. In this way we must prove the common beliefs about these ways of being affected—ideally, all the common beliefs, but if not all, then most of them, and the most important. For if the objections are solved, and the common beliefs are left, it will be an adequate proof.[15]

For Aristotle the intellectual puzzle is not threatening but is an invitation or opportunity for inquiry.

The pursuit of scholarly puzzles and the intellectual rational tools that Aristotle brought to bear on them changed the academic paradigm

---

[12]Much of this section is indebted to the work of Edward Grant: *God and Reason in the Middle Ages* (Cambridge: Cambridge University Press, 2001).
[13]Aristotle *Politics* 1253a.10.
[14]Aristotle *Nicomachean Ethics* 1178a.15-22.
[15]Ibid., 1145b.1-7.

of the time. The academy began to move away from handbooks and encyclopedic works, which was the staple of an education in the West, and forged a new direction in which logic, natural philosophy and methods of inquiry are driven by Aristotelian analytic methodology. Aristotle dominated the thinking of the Middle Ages because no other scholar at the time was even marginally close to his caliber and breadth. In *God and Reason in the Middle Ages* Edward Grant states, "Aristotle's importance lies in the way he elevated reason and thought to the highest level of activity in the universe, and, even more than that, he actually used reason to understand and resolve problems and to organize his thoughts."[16] Aristotle's dedication to rationality and his confidence in his ability to gain knowledge through his experiences of the universe—a universe which at its core is orderly and logical—brought long-lasting changes to the Western approach to academic inquiry.

As educators became part of corporations, organized bodies of individuals dedicated to pursuing academic work and community, important institutions of higher learning were established. One of the most influential academic corporations established in the Middle Ages was the University of Paris, where theology and secular academic disciplines came together in a structured manner. It's not that theologians hadn't pursued or even written about the secular disciplines, but these new universities put theologians and secular academics in close proximity to one another outside of the direct control of the church.

The University of Paris was one of the institutions where theology was seen as a professional discipline. The establishment of theology as an academic pursuit outside of the direct control of the church in a so-called secular setting brought many challenges to the church and to the discipline of theology. The church had to confront the influence of natural and analytic philosophy within theological discourse.

Prior to the thirteenth century, theology always saw itself as the preeminent discipline far superior to any other science. All other learning was to help theological understanding. As Aristotelian methodologies of inquiry thrived at the universities, the question of

---

[16]Grant, *God and Reason in the Middle Ages*, p. 90.

the role of theology within the developing academic environment became a crucial question.

From the thirteenth century forward academics wrestled with the place of theology as a knowledge tradition. Could theology be understood by using the same methods of scientific investigation that were flourishing during the Middle Ages? Science in the late medieval period largely used Aristotelian methodology which pursued knowledge as "an organized body of systematically arranged information" that accurately and immediately explained the phenomenon at hand.[17]

In his groundbreaking work *Summa Theologica*, thirteenth-century theologian Thomas Aquinas establishes within the first few pages that the discipline of theology is a science. But an important distinction between theology and the other sciences is where theology focuses its investigations. For Aquinas the source of these investigations is Scripture, which is the fundamental way that fallen humans come to properly understand God. Humanity is limited in its investigations of reality because of the Fall. All of the other academic disciplines or sciences are unable to craft a clear conception of God. The only way humans can attain full knowledge of God is if God, out of his graciousness, chooses to reveal himself to them.[18] This revelation allows us to understand the "deep things of God" that lead to our salvation.

While theology and the other sciences systematically investigate what constitutes their "sources of knowledge," their discipline-specific goals are very different. Most disciplines use science to develop an understanding of some observed phenomena (e.g., why water becomes a solid). The examination of the phenomenon is exhausted when we arrive at basic truths of that particular discipline (e.g., water exists in solid, liquid and gaseous forms). Theology is distinct because it focuses on the nature of God, which is given by God through the Scriptures. Theology examines these revelations not to gain new information about God, but to gain wisdom, which is "rational clarity"

[17]R. J. Hankinson, "Philosophy of Science," in *Cambridge Companion to Aristotle*, ed. Jonathan Barnes (New York: Cambridge University Press, 1995), p. 109.
[18]Thomas Aquinas, "What Is Faith?" in *The Sermon-Conferences of St. Thomas Aquinas on the Apostles' Creed*, ed. Nicholas Ayo (Notre Dame, Ind.: University of Notre Dame Press, 1988).

about the interconnectedness of God's divine nature.[19] Wisdom pursues understanding how knowledge, within a discipline, is coherent, and recognizes how the seemingly discrete pieces of knowledge within a discipline fit together as a unified whole. The study of theology is a unique pursuit of "wisdom" because it is the study of God—the one who created and makes coherent all of the universe. Ultimately, Aquinas believed that the reason we should pursue the discipline of theology is because we love God and want to better understand what he has revealed about himself.[20]

Another distinctive of theology, for Aquinas, is its place within the hierarchy of other academic disciplines. Theology holds a place of epistemic primacy because it focuses on the revelation of God, who as the cause and architect of the cosmos set the foundation for all order in the universe. No scientific concept is true when it conflicts with fundamental theological principles. However, the epistemic high ground that Scripture holds over the other disciplines is limited to the discipline of theology itself. This is because different academic disciplines focused on areas of exploration that are not within the purview of theology. All disciplines establish what constitutes proper science within their field of inquiry. There are times when academics within a scientific discipline hold competing views about the nature of a thing. Theology should not be seen as the final arbiter that determines the truthfulness of those competing claims. To do so would involve theology in fields outside of its discipline.

Aquinas's view gave academic investigations more leeway, as long as they are not in conflict with fundamental theological principles. Academic investigation had a new paradigm, and the investigative methods of the new sciences was now grounded in empiricism. As these new scientific methods developed, it became increasingly important to establish evidence in measurable and quantifiable ways. By the middle of the thirteenth century famous Oxford professors Robert Grosseteste and Roger Bacon both held that the more that scientists are able to quantify empirical data and analyze it through

---

[19]Nieuwenhove and Wawrykow, eds., *Theology of Thomas Aquinas*, p. 15.
[20]Aquinas *De Trinitate* 2.2.7.

mathematics, the more certain they can be about the outcomes of their investigation.[21]

By the end of the thirteenth century theology still held a place of preeminence over the other fields of knowledge. However, professors within these new institutions were determined to ensure the place of faculty autonomy.[22] The establishment of this autonomy enabled faculty members to pursue lines of investigation that might be seen by the church as questionable. While the faculty members did hold to the fidelity of the theological discipline, as most of the faculty were members of the church, their commitment to the pursuit of the other sciences in an empirical and systematic manner was a paradigm shift in research and academic discourse.

The new sciences were successful means by which academics investigated the world around them. The sciences enabled the logical/rational aspect of human inquiry to move forward aggressively. Scientific investigation was driven by a methodology committed to empirical investigation, rigorous quantification and rational/logical analysis of the phenomenon being examined. This new scientific approach led investigators to standardize their methods and retest their observations to see if their hypothesis was true. This also allowed other individuals to investigate a scientific claim by using the same agreed-upon empirical procedure.

As the new method of empirical scientific investigation became a more prevalent part of academic discourse, research grew exponentially. Not only was academic research enabling disciplines to understand their fields better—it also allowed researchers to develop a more rigorous manner of investigation within their own fields. Tried-and-true investigation techniques were refined through the fire of Aristotelian logic. The success of the new method combined with its adoption by many diverse academic disciplines supercharged academic growth.[23]

[21]Marcia L. Colish, *Medieval Foundations of the Western Intellectual Tradition*, Yale Intellectual History of the West (New Haven, Conn.: Yale University Press, 1999), pp. 321-22.

[22]Ibid., pp. 268-69.

[23]Nancy R. Pearcey and Charles B. Thaxton, *The Soul of Science: Christian Faith and Natural Philosophy* (Wheaton, Ill.: Crossway, 1994), chap. 1.

As the academic disciplines outside of theology continued to grow in their acquisition of knowledge, the belief in the coherence of all the disciplines became strained. By the sixteenth century Galileo, the great mathematician, astronomer and physicist, explained planetary phenomenon by using mathematical and mechanistic models. For Galileo, mathematics not only explains how God created the universe but it explains the way the universe must *necessarily* be constituted. It is certainly the case that God created the universe, but, Galileo believed, given our mathematical understanding of it, God could not have created it any other way. Galileo believed that the universe is unchanging and acts by "immutable laws which she never transgresses."[24] By holding to the necessity of mathematics, Galileo placed his empirical investigations of nature on par with revelation. Galileo is but one example of how the laws of nature began to be understood as an independent source of knowledge on par with Scripture and theology.

It was not long before empirical science as a knowledge tradition was seen as superior to Christian revelation. Isaac Newton continued this view of the superiority of empirical science through his groundbreaking work on universal gravitation titled the *Philosophiæ Naturalis Principia Mathematica*. He believed that God was in control of the universe causing it to be orderly, and he hoped that through his work he could explain how God fit in the world. For Newton, nature was a universal system of mathematical reason, a machine, in which all subjects are reducible to their component parts, all the way down to the level of particles. These particles react to external forces, which Newton held to be mass, length and time.[25] Newton's process of understanding the physical universe—as a mechanistic construct to be grasped by empirical methods—is foundational to Enlightenment ideology.

Newton's work on universal gravitation explained much about how the planets orbit the sun, and was also foundational to the Enlightenment view of the preeminence of humanity's rational capacities. If Newton could unlock one of the laws of God's universe, what would

---

[24]E. A. Burtt, *The Metaphysical Foundations of Modern Science*, rev. ed. (New York: Anchor Books, 1954), p. 75, quoted in ibid., p. 131.
[25]Isaac Newton, *Principia* (Amherst, N.Y.: Prometheus, 1995), p. 8.

keep humans from discovering all of God's laws, given enough time and effort? The intellectual aristocracy, in response to the success of Newton's work, began to conceive of a world in which human rational capabilities would be able to answer the problems of the ages. The new scientific methodology would find the truth through investigation of the natural world alone. And once science displaced theology as the superior knowledge tradition, humanity would be free of what some came to believe was the church's attempt to limit scientific inquiry.

The Enlightenment laid the groundwork for today's modern scientific worldview. Prior to the new empirical shift, the senses were seen as a starting point for the quest of knowledge. The essential nature of a thing was never limited to external sensible properties. Academic investigations of knowledge were understood in terms of teleology. To ponder the nature of X was an attempt to understand the purpose of X within the holistic scheme of the universe. It was far more than just a question of function; it sought the teleological and ontological status of X. What makes a dog a dog? What makes a human a human? These questions transcend the realm of empirical investigation and necessarily lean heavily on metaphysics. But such questions were abandoned as Enlightenment ideology permeated the academic milieu.

JOHN LOCKE

Bolstered by the success of the new scientific method of Newton, philosophers began to adopt a more empirically driven construct of knowledge. In *An Essay Concerning Human Understanding*, John Locke accommodated the new scientific method in his account of knowledge. Essentially, he wrote a textbook on how to think well. All of Locke's work was instrumental in redirecting philosophical thoughts on knowledge in the eighteenth century.

In the *Essay* Locke attempts to define the limits of human understanding. To explain the treatise's purpose, Locke writes, "it was necessary to examine our own Abilities, and see, what Objects our Understandings were, or were not fitted to deal with."[26] He tried to

---

[26]John Locke, *An Essay Concerning Human Understanding* (Indianapolis: Hackett, 1996), p. 2.

determine what we can and cannot know, and what is the best way to formulate our inquiry. Locke continues that his goal is "to enquire into the Original, Certainty, and Extent of human Knowledge; together with the Grounds and Degrees of Belief, Opinion and Assent."[27] To have true knowledge of a thing, Locke believes that we must understand what justifies knowledge. Beliefs based on testimony, for example, are not knowledge. For Locke, most knowledge is at best probable and never obtains adequate justification.

Locke is the first in a line of famous British empiricists. Many British empiricists adopted Locke's epistemology as a starting point. According to all empiricist philosophers, knowledge starts with and is based in sense experience. Locke believed that the mind comes unfurnished, and the only way we come to know anything is through sensory experiences of the external world. When we have these experiences, we are able to reflect on them and come to an understanding about what they are.[28]

Locke's understanding of human thought was strictly empirical. Locke believed a person to be "a thinking intelligent being that has reason and reflection, and can consider itself as itself, the same thinking thing at different times and places."[29] Locke held that thoughts are derived from the brain and not from a type of consciousness that is supervened[30] on the brain. Locke believed the brain is thinking matter.

In terms of human self-identity, Locke believed that there are two important features: First, if we question whether or not we have self-existence, then we do.[31] Second, as long as we have psychological continuity, that is, we are continually aware of ourself, then we have endurance over time. The endurance of the self over time is an important part of Locke's argument (whether it obtains or not is another question) because it lays the foundation for the acquisition of knowledge. Human agents must be able to endure over time because

---

[27]Ibid., p. 4.

[28]Ibid., p. 33.

[29]Ibid., p. 138.

[30]*Supervenience* is the idea that mental properties are separate from brain functions and yet act in concert with brain functions.

[31]This view was also held by Augustine and Descartes, who said to doubt one's own existence presupposes that one exists.

they need to be able to hold discrete ideas together to form complex ideas. Endurance allows for an agent through experience to acquire ideas and then form the different ideas into coherent and useful pieces of knowledge.

Locke believed that humans have two types of knowledge: demonstrative and intuitive. Demonstrative knowledge is obtained by a chain of mediating ideas. These are all ideas that are derived from sense impressions. Since these mediating ideas are sense impressions, Locke believes that logical connections between the chains of ideas in demonstrative knowledge are almost perceptible. Intuitive knowledge, on the other hand, is seeing the sameness or difference between two ideas "without the intervention of any other. . . . Thus the mind perceives that white is not black, that a circle is not a triangle, that three are more than two, and equal to one and two."[32] Locke believed that intuitive knowledge (such as less and more) are relations between other ideas or objects and is the foundation of all other knowledge.[33]

Locke believed that the mind is a *tabula rasa* (blank slate), the only way to gain knowledge is by experiencing the perceptible world. He was one of the first empiricists to gain a hearing with his contemporaries. Locke's disdain for metaphysics, encapsulated by his belief that experience alone is sufficient to construct ideas and knowledge, constructed a bulwark of epistemic theory that enabled scholars to pursue the Enlightenment project.

It is important to note that John Locke did not believe the scientific method gave humans the ability to understand the essence of things down to their most fundamental level. At best, science generalizes about the relationships between various phenomena. Locke believed that the scientific method, while limited, is the best means of investigation, and that all claims produced through these investigations should be held modestly. While science provides the best explanation of the world around us, it is unable to explain all the levels of a substance, down to its most fundamental properties.[34]

---

[32]Locke, *Essay Concerning Human Understanding*, p. 228.
[33]Ibid., p. 229.
[34]John Losee, *Historical Introduction to the Philosophy of Science* (Oxford: Oxford University Press,

DAVID HUME

Locke's modest claims about the nature of knowledge leads us to David Hume. Hume was influenced by the work of both Isaac Newton and John Locke, and while he was a thoroughgoing empiricist he was skeptical about the success of the scientific project. Hume believed knowledge claims could be grounded only in experiences, and even knowledge grounded in experience is limited in what it can explain about the world in which we live.[35]

For Hume knowledge comes through our sense perceptions, and these make up our ideas and impressions. When we see something, say an apple, we're having an impression of the apple, and this impression enables us to have an idea called "apple." Hume held that impressions are the more "lively" of the two types of perceptions; that is, they are actually present to us through our senses. On the other hand, ideas are "faint images" of impressions, and we must have a prior impression to have an idea. To have a belief about an apple we must have a sense impression attached to the apple; otherwise, our idea of the apple is not a belief but merely epistemically probable, because what we know of the apple may change when we no longer directly have a perception of it in the form of an impression.[36]

Hume believed all of our attempts to understand the core of reality is an investigation of causation, which is only accessed through our senses. Hume states, "All reasonings concerning matter of fact seem to be founded on the relation of *Cause and Effect*."[37] To know a fact about something is to understand its relationship to causes and effects. Additionally, Hume believed developing an understanding of a matter of fact comes from experience and not from reason. "Cause and effects are discoverable, not by reason, but by experience."[38] Hume held that reason is an ability that comes about when inferences are made based on

1972), pp. 101-3.

[35]David Hume and Eric Steinberg, *An Enquiry Concerning Human Understanding; A Letter from a Gentleman to His Friend in Edinburgh; An Abstract of a Treatise of Human Nature*, 2nd ed. (Indianapolis: Hackett, 1993), p. 6.

[36]David Hume, *A Treatise of Human Nature* (Oxford: Oxford University Press, 1965), p. 191.

[37]Hume and Steinberg, *Enquiry Concerning Human Understanding*, p. 16.

[38]Ibid., p. 17.

experiences. For example, if every year we travel to a lake and swing on the same tree swing, we might infer that the tree swing is always hanging from the same tree at all times of the year. Hume suggests that this is a patently unjustified belief. The amount of justification that we have for the tree swing being attached to the tree is limited to the few hours a year (at best) of observation we have of the tree swing. It could be the case that every fall someone comes and removes the swing and stores it for the winter, but we would not know it and our belief is therefore a presumption and unfounded.[39] Since we do not have any object continuously under our perceptive gaze, we cannot have confidence in our understanding of an object continuing to exist in the manner in which we first perceived it. Any belief that we know something about a object we have experienced in the past is fictitious. Hume's skepticism is driven by his belief that knowledge cannot be independent of sense experience. Can knowledge about an object endure if we are not continuously monitoring it with our senses?

Hume claimed that our belief in cause and effect, and first causes, is driven by a faulty understanding of the information we derive from our senses as well as our socialized belief or custom about how the world functions. He believed our interaction with the world and our community builds within us certain inferences about what constitutes knowledge. Hume acknowledged that it is understandable for us to think certain types of events are necessarily connected to each other—but it usually is the case that they do not constitute knowledge for Hume.[40] Custom causes us to believe that the sun will rise in the east tomorrow—not knowledge. We have observed the sun rising in the east so many times before that we begin to expect it to happen every day, but there is no external reason to believe that it will. Again, according to Hume, this inevitably drives us to skepticism.

Hume's project is to get us to understand that whatever we believe to be true we should hold onto very lightly. Most of our beliefs, and the methods of basic reasoning we use to obtain these beliefs, are either false or are not held for rational reasons. Hume states that knowledge

---

[39]Ibid., p. 79.
[40]Ibid., pp. 31-37.

can be found only in mathematics or ideas that are grounded in facts (sense impressions of cause and effect) or we should "commit it then to the flames: For it can contain nothing but sophistry and illusion."[41] Humean skepticism shakes philosophical ideas to the core because Hume does not allow for principles that have historically been grounded in the realm of metaphysics. This threatens the very concepts that have undergirded the fields of scientific investigation, which caused Immanuel Kant to state, "'I openly confess my recollection of David Hume was the very thing which many years ago first interrupted my dogmatic slumber and gave my investigations in the field of speculative philosophy a quite new direction."[42] We will investigate more fully this awakening of Kant and his attempt to counter Hume's skepticism.

IMMANUEL KANT

David Hume's skepticism was the driving force in Kant's writing his groundbreaking philosophical book *The Critique of Pure Reason*.[43] Kant realized he must defend empirical science (and the laws governing science) against Hume's skepticism, while at the same time not allowing classical views of metaphysics to play a role in the determination of what is knowledge.[44] Hume and Kant agree that knowledge comes by observation of the external world, and both believe that knowledge is gained through our initial contact with objects in the empirical world. The important distinction to make here is that Hume believed that knowledge comes directly through sense perception, and any belief that is not grounded in our sensory experience does not constitute knowledge, but probability. Kant likewise believed that knowledge arises out of sense perception, but that it is not limited to the actual sense perception. Unlike Hume, Kant did not believe that sense impressions "de-

[41]Ibid., p. 21.

[42]Immanuel Kant and Gordon Treash, *Der einzig mögliche Beweisgrund* (The One Possible Basis for a Demonstration of the Existence of God) (New York: Abaris, 1979), p. 260.

[43]This is a simplified presentation of Kant's complex view of knowledge. For a thoroughgoing explanation please read Justus Hartnack's excellent book *Kant's Theory of Knowledge: An Introduction to the Critique of Pure Reason*.

[44]What follows is a distillation of Kant. His writing is dense and technical with very nuanced distinctions, but a total exposition of his philosophy is not possible nor needed for our purposes.

grade." For Kant sense perceptions are the fundamental building blocks of knowledge, and in combination with the faculties of human reason, which exist prior to experience, perceptions enable us to make judgments regarding our experiences. Reason is a prescriptive regulatory method by which we organize our scientific principles that brings knowledge.[45] We come to know things through our sense perceptions and the activities of our rational mind.

Kant held that there are two aspects of reality—phenomenal and noumenal. The phenomenal world is knowable through our five senses. The noumenal world is the arena where things exist in themselves. We cannot form any ideas of the noumenal world. We don't have access to anything noumenal. Kant believed that most traditional concepts of knowledge are falsely grounded in the "metaphysical world," which is not justified by evidence that comes from the senses, where, Kant believes, all concepts are derived.

Kant makes a fundamental distinction between two types of knowledge—knowledge a posteriori and a priori.[46] *A posteriori knowledge* is based on having previous experiences in the sensible world. But it can only give us knowledge of appearances since it is directly linked to experiences in the sensible external world. *A priori knowledge* is not based on experience. It is prior to our experience of sensory inputs. The project for Kant is to be able to explain how a priori knowledge is phenomenal, that is, grounded in the world of the senses.

Kant held a view called "transcendental unity of apperception." Apperception is the idea that when we have a sense perception of something it necessarily relates to "our thinking" (about the object). These acts of thinking happen within us and are distinct from the act of sensing. Kant argued that all minds are structured in such a way that we are able to synthesize the incoming pieces of empirical information along with our intuitions into coherent concepts of the world, and that we are aware of the unifying nature of our intuitions and perceptions within ourselves.

---

[45]Losee, *Historical Introduction to the Philosophy of Science*, pp. 112-14.
[46]Immanuel Kant and Norman Kemp Smith, *Immanuel Kant's Critique of Pure Reason* (New York: St. Martin's Press, 1963), p. 266.

For Kant both intuitions and concepts are basic parts of our human thought and knowledge. Our intuitions have their source in our direct sensing of an object, and concepts result because of the understanding. When we see something (this discussion could work for any of the five senses) the object is understood in terms of intuitions. The act of seeing brings an immediate condition about that is an intuition. These intuitions relate immediately to the sensible object (e.g., the act of seeing a tree). Concepts work in terms of synthesizing the things that objects have in common.[47] Both intuitions and concepts can be "pure." By pure Kant means a priori (not coming from experience). Kant holds that the concept of space is a "pure intuition." For example, consider our intuition of space. We observe things in particular places, and we know that all things must exist in space. Additionally, space is something we cannot imagine not existing. We can imagine nothing existing in a particular space, but not the non-existence of space itself. As a matter of fact, without space we would not be able to observe anything at all.

Examples of pure concepts are existence, necessity, cause and possibility. They are pure concepts of understanding, that is, they do not arise out of experience (again, they are a priori). These concepts do not exist as a result of our sensory experiences, but are "abstracted from the laws inherent in the mind (by attending to its actions on the occasion of an experience)."[48] So these laws only emerge through experience. They do not exist transcendently as classical metaphysics would hold.

Kant believed that when we see a tree we have a sense experience of the tree, which comes through intuition. When we consider the tree (its similarities and differences to other trees, the possibility that it could not be there, the shape of the tree), we put ideas together about the tree (synthesize). Sense experience coming through intuition combines with concepts to create understanding. Understanding emerges from our sensory experiences of the tree, and are not a product of any transcendent views of trees, leaves, colors or shapes. Our understanding

---

[47]Ibid.
[48]Immanuel Kant, "On the Form and Principles of the Sensible and the Intelligible World" (Inaugural Dissertation, 1770) in Immanuel Kant, *Theoretical Philosophy 1755-1770*, ed. David Walford and Ralf Meerbote (Cambridge: Cambridge University Press, 1992), pp. 387-88.

of the tree is grounded in our sensory experience of the tree, and we make a judgment of and understand the experience from "the laws inherent in the mind"—not from some transcendental universal or Platonic Form.

Kant believed that traditional metaphysics holds no value; belief in traditional metaphysics is a transcendental illusion. A transcendental illusion happens when we attempt to construct categories of knowledge and understanding that transcend the realm of sensory experience. According to Kant, these illusions are "grounded in the nature of human reason, and gives rise to an illusion which cannot be avoided, although it may, indeed, be rendered harmless."[49] Transcendental laws may exist, but only in the sense that they are particular to empirical events (e.g., the laws of chemistry). The legitimate use of the noumenal and the corresponding concept of metaphysics must instead be restricted to the physical world, to the ordering of our empirical senses.[50]

Kant's version of empiricism does away with Hume's sensationalism by showing that there must be a basic interpretive grid in place prior to a human agent's interaction with external phenomena. Kant keeps the belief (held in common with Locke and Hume) that knowledge is grounded in empirical experience, but he does away with Hume's skepticism by explaining the phenomenal roots of a priori laws of science.

Kant is the paradigmatic philosopher of the Enlightenment. He completely destroyed the last vestiges of medieval philosophy and synthesized rationalistic and empiricist epistemology. Kant laid the groundwork for the paradigm shift within the university. University of Chicago professor Alan Bloom says, "The unity of the university is now Kant."[51] Empiricist epistemology has now become the primary framework by which academics pursue knowledge within their fields. Kant saved knowledge and the project of science from Humean skepticism, but knowledge must be grounded in sense experience alone.

---

[49]Kant and Smith, *Immanuel Kant's Critique of Pure Reason*, p. 659.
[50]Ibid.
[51]Allan David Bloom, *The Closing of the American Mind: How Higher Education Has Failed Democracy and Impoverished the Souls of Today's Students* (New York: Simon & Schuster, 1987), p. 300.

WHAT THE "NEW SCIENCES" ABANDON

This paradigm shift in epistemology allowed the new sciences to flourish. With each of science's successes, society distanced itself from classical metaphysical principles that are foundational to belief in a transcendent reality. With every new discovery in science the empiricist project seems more and more justified. Because of the new scientific paradigm, humanity no longer needs a transcendent set of truths to determine ethical and moral norms. Given enough time and energy, humans believe they will eventually master the earth and all of its problems.

Even though the new sciences are radically successful, they lack the tools by which humanity has historically come to understand itself. The new scientific method should not be construed as evil; it is just incomplete. Science in the last two hundred years has fundamentally changed our world as we know it. Consider a medical doctor at the end of the Civil War. That doctor has more in common with a medical practitioner at the time of Christ than he does with today's modern physician. Because of technological advances, today's doctor knows more about the body and is able to diagnose illness in a much more accurate manner. The progress of science is a great testament to human ingenuity, and it has enabled us to eliminate a great deal of physical suffering in the world. Still, humans are more than just a complex grouping of cells that comprise an amazing "computer made of meat," and we should not limit our understanding of human persons to one avenue of access to reality.

Humans are very complex beings. We are not just aggregates of observable phenomena. Yet some of the most important aspects of our makeup are ignored because their investigation takes us beyond the realm of the empirical sciences. We are soulish beings who need to be understood through a combination of empirical and metaphysical investigation. To say something as simple as "I am sad" transcends the limits of science.

While it is true that a full-orbed understanding of humanity goes beyond the pale of scientific investigation, it is also true that an exhaustive understanding of humanity transcends our rational capacities. The complexity of the human condition is known fully by God alone. David points this out in Psalm 139:23-24, and he asks God to reveal his own heart to him:

> Search me, O God, and know my heart!
>   Try me and know my thoughts!
> And see if there be any grievous way in me,
>   and lead me in the way everlasting!

This is one of the many places where Scripture reveals that God understands us better than we understand ourselves. Prior to the adoption of the scientific method, Scripture was understood to be the primary method through which God revealed himself to humanity. Without God graciously revealing himself, we would be unable to understand with any clarity the current difficulties we find ourselves in. Nor would we know how to extricate ourselves from our problems without the grace of God.

Today's science, in all its permutations, is a driving force behind education and a major force behind secularism. As Christian educators we must understand the underlying philosophical principles that are deconstructing all vestiges of understanding that articulate what it means to be human. The pressure behind secularism is not only intellectual but also comes in the form of social pressure. Richard Dawkins, professor of zoology at Oxford University and a preeminent atheist, says:

> What has theology ever said that is of the smallest use to anybody? What has theology ever said that is demonstrably true and is not obvious? I have listened to theologians, read them, debated against them. I have never heard any of them ever say anything of the smallest use, anything that was not either platitudinously obvious or downright false.[52]

As we write this, Richard Dawkins is on the lecture circuit touting his book *The God Delusion*. It seems that we cannot look at the Internet or watch TV without seeing Dawkins or hearing someone talk about this work. He continues to rail against the idiocy of religion—especially Christianity—and he is not alone. Though it is socially acceptable to be

---

[52]Richard Dawkins, "The Emptiness of Theology," *Free Enquiry* 18, no. 2 (1998): 94.

a Christian when our belief is only personal, when we believe that Christianity has something to say about the way we should live, people become much more negative toward us. They go as far as questioning our rational capacities, wondering how we can be a Christian when science has shown the incoherence of faith. Obviously, in education, Christianity has to fight against the cultural pressures that have deemed Christians to be at best naive and perhaps dangers to society.

Christian educators must be trained intellectually to constructively dialogue with their intellectual adversaries. The pressures of the secular world will entice us to conform to its ideology, but in doing so we abandon what we know as fundamentally true. Dallas Willard observes we are under

> the crushing weight of a secular outlook that permeates or pressures every thought we have today. Sometimes it even forces those who self identify as Christian teachers to set aside Jesus' plain statements about the reality and total relevance of the Kingdom of God and replace them with philosophical speculations whose only recommendations is their constancy with a modern mind-set.[53]

When we understand the origin of this worldview, we can begin to alleviate the ongoing pressures that are placed on us by our culture.

As we understand fundamental theological and philosophical principles that undergird our discipline, we will be able to more effectively grapple with the different curricular and pedagogical methodologies that limit our students from achieving their full potential. It is morally incumbent upon educators to develop a holistic view of our students so that they can properly come to terms with what is truly real and knowable in the universe.

---

[53]Dallas Willard, *The Divine Conspiracy* (San Francisco: HarperCollins, 1998), p. 92.

WHO KNOWS?

EDUCATION AND EPISTEMOLOGY

Educational standards are the foundation of the modern educational endeavor. Statements about educational success imply standards. Measuring whether or not students are being properly educated involves testing them in a particular subject with its prescribed set of grade-appropriate standards that they must meet or exceed. In the United States most students are put through a battery of tests on a yearly basis to ascertain how students, teacher and schools are performing in comparison to the state standards. From these multiple-choice standardized tests both teachers and schools determine whether their work is successful, as deemed by their state's department of education. The question is, what do such tests actually tell us about the student's intelligence, ability, creativity, insightfulness or grasp of reality? Do the current standards provide an accurate way to assess a genuine education?

What does it mean to be educated? How do educators determine the success or failure of our educational project? These questions are about knowledge itself. Standards are necessary to determine whether someone is educated. On the other hand, all too often in today's academic institutions much "education" turns out to be mindless submission to a set of educational expectations. When these criteria are inflexibly put into practice, students suffer. Imagine, for example, a fifth-grade girl in California who has been attending a classical elementary school since kindergarten. Her family moves to another part of the state where there is no classical school for her to attend, so her parents decide to have her attend a traditional elementary school. When her academic ability is tested, her teacher informs her parents that she is behind the other students academically. The reason is not that the student lacks some fundamental academic skill such as reading, writing or mathematics, but that there is a gap in her knowledge of the daily lives of people who occupied the Catholic missions in the state of California. How do we assess the importance of her having knowledge of the early Catholic missions in California? What role does it play in her fundamental academic development? Are people in other states not flourishing because they have not learned about mission life? While an understanding of state history is good, it is not as fundamental as reading, writing and mathematics, nor does the lack of it indicate some sort of academic deficiency.

Often, the expectations embedded in the standards are peripheral to the core of education. Additionally, many standards are grounded in a fundamental philosophical commitment that may be antithetical to a robust Christian worldview. For example, a California third grade history/social-sciences standard reads, "Discuss the relationship of students' 'work' in school and their personal human capital."[1] The concept of "human capital" is that humans may be understood in light of the skills they bring to the marketplace. Persons change their value in the marketplace by investing or not investing in educational opportunities. So third graders are being trained to think of their schooling not as a good in and of itself but in light of their future wage-earning potential. At an early age children are not taught to think of themselves as whole souls but as tangible assets. A student's personal assessment becomes grounded in transitory economic measurements rather than transcendent understandings of human flourishing.

EDUCATION'S PURPOSE

In a talk given to the English Society at Oxford called "Our English Syllabus," C. S. Lewis discussed what it truly means to educate some-

---

[1]"History-Social Science Content Standards for California Public Schools," California State Board of Education (April 25, 2007), p. 11 <www.cde.ca.gov/be/st/ss/documents/histsocs cistnd.pdf>.

one. To educate individuals is to enable them to become the type of persons who contribute both to their own happiness (i.e., human flourishing) and to the happiness of the society they live in. Ultimately, education leads a person to a life of leisure (exemplified as a life of thoughtful contemplation), not a career. It is not the belief of Lewis that we should have no vocational training, but that life's true purpose cannot be actualized within a vocation. Lewis points out that only animals are exclusively focused on their vocation. They are the perfect working professionals. They would, if they could speak, "only talk shop" to one another. Lewis states, "Lions cannot stop hunting, nor the beaver building dams, nor the bee making honey."[2] In *Nicomachean Ethics* Aristotle points out that what makes us uniquely human is our rational capacities, not our vocation: "We have found, then, that the human function is activity of the soul in accord with reason or requiring reason."[3] Intellectual instruction is the means by which humans properly actualize their human capacities. Educators should understand that a love of learning is a fundamental aspect of human flourishing, and not see it as a means of proper investment in human capital. Conversely, vocation should only be seen as a means to free us to pursue a life of reflection that enables us to come to knowledge of what is true.

For education to be successful, educators must understand what constitutes truth. C. S. Lewis wrote, "Truth is always about something, but reality is that about which truth is."[4] That truth is important might seem obvious, but in today's society truth is seen as malleable and relative. If we are going to be able to navigate the quagmires of standards and assessment, we need to clearly understand what it means to say something is true, and how this enables us to arbitrate between a student's correct and incorrect beliefs.

Truth is the engine that drives inquiry. The pursuit of the truth involves a desire to understand what is real and avoid what is false. Education enables students to come into contact with what is real. Things

---

[2] C. S. Lewis, *Rehabilitations, and Other Essays* (St. Clair Shores, Mich.: Scholarly Press, 1979), p. 83.
[3] Aristotle *Nicomachean Ethics*, trans. Terence Irwin (Indianapolis: Hackett, 1999), 1098a.8.
[4] C. S. Lewis, "Myth Became Fact," in *God in the Dock* (Grand Rapids: Eerdmans, 1970), p. 66.

we believe are either true or false—that is, the things we believe either correspond to reality or do not. There are consequences to discovering the truth. If our beliefs match what is real, then we, logically, must act in accordance to what we know about reality or face the consequences.

KNOWLEDGE, REALITY AND EDUCATION

To say we grasp reality implies something about knowledge. Epistemology (the study of knowledge) is a fundamental tool of proper education. How we define knowledge, how we assess others' knowledge and how we pursue knowledge is at the core of our project. Therefore, it is important to separate what we merely think knowledge is from what truly constitutes knowledge.

Let's review the types of knowledge discussed in chapter two. There are three types of knowledge: (1) *technical* knowledge or what is more commonly called know-how, (2) *propositional* knowledge, which is knowledge of facts, and (3) knowledge by *acquaintance*, which is knowledge about something by direct awareness.[5]

Most of the abilities that we associate with knowledge in the educational field turn out to be mostly a capacity to recite. The original meaning of *recitation*, which was derived from the Latin, is vocal repetition of a perfectly memorized text. This, of course, is not necessarily knowledge. The only thing done in recitation is a rehearsal of the piece memorized. Today's tests are the same. When students take a test, they do not have to believe that their answers are true, let alone knowledge. They merely have to make sure their answers correspond to the teacher's expectations.

As humans we are constantly engaged in mental activities. We constantly assess and categorize everything around us. We experience the world around us and we have beliefs about the world, some of which are true and some of which are false. We justify our ideas through our rational capacities, by which we set up a system of understanding that arbitrates what can be constituted as knowledge, what is and is not an accurate depiction of reality.

---

[5]See pp. 78-80.

To claim we know something implies we have sufficiently good reasons to say the things we believe are as we say they are. Knowledge is *justified true belief*. Each of these categories—justification, truth and belief—plays a necessary but not sufficient role in determining knowledge, and each should be explained in order to see how belief, justification and truth form an integrated concept of knowledge.

BELIEF

Belief is fundamental to knowledge. There may be sufficient reason to justify that something is true, but without believing it we cannot have knowledge. There are basically two types of beliefs: *dispositional* and *state-object*. which holds that belief is a certain kind of mental state. *Dispositional* beliefs, which dispose us to behave in a certain way, can be understood through an example from the movie *Monty Python and the Holy Grail*. The Knights of the Round Table are seeking the Holy Grail when they come upon a rabbit guarding a cave they must enter. The knights are disposed to believe that the rabbit is not dangerous (who has ever heard of a dangerous rabbit?), but unbeknownst to them the rabbit is the Killer Rabbit of Caerbannog. When King Arthur sends his knights to kill the rabbit, it kills three of King Arthur's knights before it is dispatched by the use of the Holy Hand Grenade of Antioch. This belief disposed the knights to behave in a certain way. Their belief about the docile nature of the rabbit was wrong, but it was nonetheless a belief. It led them to certain action (attempting to kill the rabbit) and for three of them a rather gruesome and untimely death.

But dispositional belief cannot account for beliefs that do not lead to actions or behaviors. A description of belief should not be limited to its manifestation to an external observer. When we are doing conceptual thinking, such as in the area of physics, the beliefs that we have about physics are not usually followed by a physical response. When we assent to the belief that $E=mc^2$, we show no *outward sign* of belief.

The *state-object* view says beliefs are held in a certain kind of mental state. That is, an affirming mental state is directed at an object associated with a proposition. For example, when I say I believe that

Joe Montana played quarterback for the Kansas City Chiefs, I am stating that I believe that the proposition represents a fact about the world we live in. The affirming mental state is directed toward an object (Joe Montana) associated with the proposition "that Joe Montana played quarterback for the Kansas City Chiefs," which I affirm.

Beliefs should be understood as either occurrent or standing. Occurrent beliefs are present to our consciousness and require our assent (e.g., the key that I hold in my hand will unlock my car door). Standing beliefs are beliefs that we hold but are not conscious of at the time we act on them (e.g., mathematical beliefs such as 2 + 2 = 4). We do not have to be consciously aware of all the beliefs in our mind while we are holding them. It would be rather impossible (and confusing) if all beliefs were occurrent. Our minds function in such a way that we do not always have to be attending to a true belief in order to act on it.

Neither verbal assent nor commitment to something is the same as believing. In today's society many people say they believe things. But for belief actually to obtain we need to do more than just say we believe it— we must conduct ourself accordingly. Verbal assent is often confused with actually believing. To say we are committed to something is to act *as if* we believe it. When we say we are committed to something, this does not necessitate that we believe it to be true. Occasionally, children will read or see something on television that frightens them. A dutiful parent will assure the children that they will be fine, and that mom and dad are right down the hall if need be. The children will say they believe that mom and dad will protect them, but the parent will not be out of the room for more than four seconds before being called back. Of course, the children said they believe, but did not, and are still frightened. The danger here is that people often conflate commitment or verbal assent to a proposition (e.g., Daddy, I know that monsters are not real) with belief, and they try to convince someone to stay committed rather than enabling him or her to come to a true understanding of reality (e.g., teaching the child that monsters are not really under the bed). [6]

Belief assents to a claim and acts according to that claim. To believe

---

[6]Dallas Willard, "How People Perish for Lack of Knowledge," *Knowledge of Christ in Today's World: A Series of Eight Talks by Dallas Willard*, Eidos Christian Center, 2003, Audio CD.

something does not necessarily make it true, but to have knowledge it is necessary that it is true.

TRUTH

Truth is about reality. We do not have knowledge if what we believe is false. Truth is the correspondence of an idea of a thing to its reality. It represents things as they are. We cannot fight against truth and expect to win. While belief can be a verb (I believe *x*), truth cannot. It's impossible to say, I truth *x*. In discussing truth in *Mere Christianity*, C. S. Lewis writes,

> We are now getting to the point at which different beliefs about the universe lead to different behavior. Religion involves a series of statements about facts, which must be either true or false. If they are true, one set of conclusions will follow about the right sailing of the human fleet: if they are false, quite a different set.[7]

Christianity makes claims about the nature of reality. If these claims are true, then certain events should or should not happen because of that reality. We need to determine which beliefs are true and what follows logically from those beliefs. This is what makes understanding truth so important; having the truth gives us the opportunity to comport ourselves to reality.

Today, truth has become relativized. Most individuals do not want to be weighed down by the obligations of truth. Winston Churchill was profoundly aware of people not wanting to deal with the realities that were staring them in the face.[8] Prior to World War II, Churchill had been warning the British nation that the German war machine was gearing up, which threatened the nation's security. He counseled that the British needed to prepare to stand up to this growing military menace. No matter how much some individuals denied that the Germans were building up their military, the truth was they were building tanks and practicing simulated bombing runs on London while hosting the

---

[7]C. S. Lewis, *Mere Christianity* (New York: Macmillan, 1960), p. 58.
[8]To read more on Churchill's role in British politics in the 1930s see Roy Jenkins, *Churchill: A Biography* (New York: Penguin, 2002), chap. 25, esp. pp. 464-80.

1936 Olympics in Munich. At what point would those "appeasers," as Churchill called them, have thought it true that Germany's intention was to control Western Europe? Maybe not until Hitler's army drove its tanks through the streets of Paris. Of course, their denial of the truth that Germany was rearming did not make it less true; it merely put them out of contact with reality.

Technically, truth for us is *objective truth*. Objective truth exists regardless of our recognizing it. It is not created but is discovered by us. Truths are independent of our personal disposition. They are only true in relation to reality itself, a reality that is not created by our recognition of it. Understanding this leads us to some very useful tools of logic that enable us to determine how we understand truth: the laws of noncontradiction, identity and excluded middle.

The laws of noncontradiction, identity and excluded middle are related to propositions (e.g., 5 + 5 = 10) about reality. The law of noncontradiction states that a proposition (5 + 5 = 10) cannot be true and false at the same time; that is, 5 + 5 cannot equal both 10 and 11. Either the answer 11 is wrong or the answer 10 is wrong. The law of identity states that the proposition is equal to itself and different from everything else (nothing else can be 5 + 5 = 10). The law of the excluded middle states that the proposition is either true or it is false; there cannot be some intermediate state between the truth and falseness of a proposition.

Of course, we know that some people believe that truth is relative. We all hear individuals say, "It may be true for you, but it's not true for me." They may say "truth" is a human construct built upon societal norms. Things become true when a society agrees to accept some proposition as true. Some truths (really a societal norm) are relative to cultures, such as in India a person should not use his or her left hand when eating or interacting with others because it is the hand used for personal hygiene, but in the United States that is not a concern. On the other hand (pun intended), a relativist would say though it is true that sexual relations between a man and a woman was immoral outside of marriage in early twentieth-century America, it is not true in America today.

When discussing the difference between relativism and objective views of truth, how do we know which is right? If relativism is objectively true, then it is self-refuting. A view that states it is objectively true that there are no objective truths is contradictory. If relativism is true via relativism, then truth is mere custom and is not necessarily viable for all individuals or cultures.

What constitutes the conditions in which a relativist can say something is true? It is easy to see that people could justify what they believe to be true and not realize they lack all of the evidence necessary to properly judge the correctness of their belief. Justification for holding a belief to be true is not the same thing as having a criterion for truth. Until the nineteenth century, bloodletting was a common practice in the medical community. Bloodletting was thought to balance the human system by draining out disease with the blood. Bloodletting continued as a common practice even as medical understanding of the body increased, because it calmed patients (from loss of blood pressure) and offered a placebo effect. As physicians began to better understand the body and the nature of disease, they realized that bloodletting was doing more harm than good. It is true that the information the doctors possessed at one time justified bloodletting, but by the early twentieth century most doctors no longer believed that bloodletting was helpful. Just because doctors were justified in their beliefs does not make a criteria for truth relative. Bloodletting as a cure for disease is always false, regardless of what our evidence leads us to believe. Justification for the truth of a belief can come and go as the evidence changes. But the truthfulness of the belief (and the criterion for truth, namely, correspondence to reality) does not change.

Relativism is pervasive in our culture. Former University of Chicago professor Allan Bloom wrote *The Closing of the American Mind*, a critique of American higher education. In the introduction to the book he describes the intellectual condition of an incoming college freshman:

> The one thing a professor can be absolutely certain of: almost every student entering the university believes, or says he believes, that truth is relative.
> . . . That anyone should regard the proposition as not self-evident astonishes them, as though he were calling into question 2 + 2 = 4.

. . . The danger they have been taught to fear from absolutism is not error but intolerance.[9]

Bloom's book was a bestseller more than twenty years ago, and things only seem to be getting worse. Students see relativism as openness, and hold it to be a moral injunction. In that same introduction Bloom states, "The point is not to correct mistakes and really be right; rather it is not to think you are right at all."[10] This indoctrination against reality must be vigorously opposed if students are going to see education as a necessary aspect of human flourishing. Otherwise, they will only see education as a means to make themselves more attractive in the job market.

We hold to the correspondence theory of truth, which has roots as far back as Plato and Aristotle. Aristotle famously asserted, "to say that [either] that which is is not or that which is not is, is a falsehood; and to say that that which is is and that which is not is not, is true"[11] Aristotle holds that truth corresponds with what reality is. We believe that our academic investigations, when they are true, properly describe reality "in virtue of that correspondence."[12] This view changes the way teachers face their tasks. The pursuit of knowledge is the most real activity we can practice. When students are properly educated about truth, they should feel the weight of responsibility to act accordingly or risk the consequences—not from their teachers but from reality itself.

We can have contact with truth. Truth is a necessary condition for us to say we have knowledge. We must also believe in the truth for it to have an affect on our lives, but believing in the truth is not enough to call it knowledge. If we are going to say we *know* something we also must be justified.

JUSTIFICATION

We all have reasons for believing something. Justification sets a standard by which to measure whether or not we have enough evidence to

---

[9]Allan Bloom, *Closing of the American Mind* (New York: Simon & Schuster, 1987), p. 25.
[10]Ibid., p. 26.
[11]Aristotle "Metaphysics," in *Aristotle: Selections* (Indianapolis: Hackett, 1995), 4.7.1011b27-29.
[12]Robert Audi, *Belief, Justification, and Knowledge*, 2nd ed. (Belmont, Calif.: Wadsworth, 2007), p. 116.

say we should believe something. It is important to note that we could be justified in believing something and it still could be false, and therefore not knowledge. We also could have an unjustified true belief, but only by fortuitous circumstances.[13]

To call a proposition knowledge requires adequate reasons to hold that the proposition is true. In order to say we know something, humans have a basic intuition of the need to have adequate reasons for true beliefs. For example, imagine a student taking a test. If a student does not know the answer to a question but guesses correctly, does he or she know the answer? Of course not. The student was just lucky. Let's look at what constitutes evidence that justifies our beliefs.

Our view of justification is called modest foundationalism. Modest foundationalism maintains that knowledge is grounded on chains of beliefs, and these chains of beliefs actually terminate in beliefs that are not merely justified by other beliefs. Beliefs come in two forms: properly basic and nonbasic. All human beings have a noetic structure (all the things a person believes, and how they are related to each other) that is composed of properly basic and nonbasic beliefs.

A *nonbasic* belief is justified by its relationships with other beliefs, and is, ultimately, grounded in properly basic beliefs. A *properly basic* belief does not need external evidence (other propositions) to be true.[14] There are three important types of properly basic beliefs: self-evident, incorrigible and evident to our senses.[15] Self-evident beliefs are those which, when examined, cannot be seen to be false (e.g., mathematical propositions like $2 + 2 = 4$ or laws of logic). When you understand a self-evident proposition, you know that it could not be false. Self-evident propositions include basic truths of logic, math and ethics. In general, they are not known on the basis of experience. Incorrigible beliefs are those that cannot be mistaken. Examples of these include a person's belief about his or her own existence or that he or she is hungry or full. We cannot

---

[13]Ibid., p. 35.

[14]Alvin Plantinga, "Reason and Belief in God," in *Faith and Rationality: Reason and Belief in God*, ed. Alvin Plantinga and Nicholas Wolterstorff (Notre Dame, Ind.: University of Notre Dame Press, 1983), pp. 47-59.

[15]J. P. Moreland and William Lane Craig, *Philosophical Foundations for a Christian Worldview* (Downers Grove, Ill.: InterVarsity Press, 2003), p. 113.

say we are full and have someone successfully disagree with us about our belief (unless that person is our doting grandmother), because an individual is aware of his or her internal state of affairs. Beliefs about our perceptual experiences are a little trickier. When we have a sense experience, our belief that we are seeing or hearing something is properly basic, but the interpretation of the sensory experience can be wrong. If we see a man walking toward us, we can misidentify him as a friend, but the fact that we saw someone is true.

We need to say a little more about perception.[16] Fundamental to the notion of justification (and therefore of knowledge) is how we come to understand that our perceptions enable us to have access to the real world and therefore are tools by which we can gain knowledge. Some hold that our understandings are mediated through different interpretive grids; that is, we cannot actually come to know the world, but there are mediating factors between us and the object of our study. We hold to a different view, namely, that we have direct access to reality and can broadly have confidence in our human ability to understand reality. Our project of pursuing knowledge that corresponds to reality must be supported by the belief that we can access reality directly, without mediating interference.

Imagine we are walking through a forest and come upon a deer. What justifies our saying that we have seen a deer? When we perceive the deer, we have a basic sensory experience of shapes and colors, and out of that experience develops concepts that we have about the object. There are three aspects to seeing: simple seeing, seeing that and seeing as. *Simple seeing* happens when we see an object. All we are doing is having a sense experience—nothing interpretive is happening. *Seeing that* is a mental event in which we assess the validity of a proposition about that sense experience ("The object is a deer"). *Seeing as* involves applying a concept to the perceptual object (you see the object as a deer, as food or as vulnerable), which includes an element of interpretation.

The problem is that when we see something we can be wrong about what we are seeing. Does this mean that our sight is unreliable? Hardly.

---

[16]This discussion we are having about visual perception could easily be about any of the five senses.

While it is true that our perceptions can err, most of the time we can trust them. At this moment Steve perceives that he is looking at the computer keyboard and is editing this book chapter. He could be wrong, but almost certainly he is not. Saying Steve is justified in knowing something does not necessitate a system in which there is no error or certainty.[17] But it necessitates confidence in his ability to eventually correct an error in his experiencing or thinking. Humans do this all of the time. We may have originally misidentified the deer we saw in the forest as a bear, but as we continued to see the object, we were able to self-correct and properly describe the object as a deer.

In summary, knowledge as justified true belief needs all three components for us to have knowledge. We must assent to or affirm a proposition (believe), we must have reasons or criteria to hold to the proposition (justification), and it must correspond to reality (be true). When we say we actually know reality, we do not mean that we will know all things with absolute certainty. There are very few things that we know for certain (e.g., our own existence and basic principles of mathematics). When we conflate certainty with knowledge, this causes us to think that we cannot know.

CONCEPTS OF KNOWLEDGE AND EDUCATIONAL PRAXIS

Think about how a conflation of knowledge and certainty can affect students. If a student Googles something he or she is trying to understand, the student may realize it's not so straightforward; there are five views on the subject. But what's worse, each of the five views has three nuanced subviews. It is fine for a student to realize there is more to learn about a subject, and further investigation can cause the student to change his or her mind about the topic. Positively, this can lead a student to further investigation. But often, it leads to some sort of skepticism, where the student decides that nothing can be truly known (which itself is a circular statement).

Another problem is that some individuals hold we do not experience the external world directly through our senses. We only know

---

[17]Audi, *Belief, Justification, and Knowledge*, pp. 98-100.

the external world indirectly through our ideas or interpretations. Some type of barrier exists between the object and us, preventing direct access to the real object and all that exists in the external world. In this view, when we see a deer we are not looking at the deer but at an image of the deer in our mind. So when we say that we know something, we actually know a proposition. We do not know the deer but a proposition about the deer. Thus we do not know what is real because we never have any direct access to it. The pursuit of knowledge is merely pushing mental constructs around, not an interaction with reality.

Similarly, some individuals hold that knowledge is socially constructed. This view maintains that knowledge is not the active pursuit of external reality but a construct that is driven by those who control what is and is not called "knowledge." Sometimes the control is based on a ruling class, and sometimes it is based on societal norms, but it is always based on the construct of a combination of ethnic, political, societal pressures and linguistic practices. In this view truth is neither normative nor transcendent, but is a malleable thing based on practices of social groups who share a common narrative. There is no neutral viewpoint by which we are able to view the world. To be justified in a belief means that the assessment of conditions for truth is conditioned by nonobjective societally constructed views of reality.[18]

Neither the indirect view nor the socially constructed view advocates the objectivity of knowledge. Allowing either to control the development of curriculum or pedagogy undercuts students' access to what is truly real and knowable.

Chapter two discussed the nature of science and how scientific naturalism undercuts a holistic understanding of reality. Scientific methodology can achieve a certain type of knowledge, but that knowledge is limited by empirical methods. How are we educators to understand the role science plays in our educational system? The state of California's book on science standards explains the difference between the sciences, which brings knowledge, and faith: "Philosophical and religious beliefs

---

[18]For more on this topic see Douglas Groothuis, *Truth Decay* (Downers Grove, Ill.: InterVarsity Press, 2000).

are based, at least in part, on faith and are not subject to scientific test and refutation. . . . Ultimately, students should be made aware of the difference between understanding, which is the goal of education, and subscribing to ideas."[19] The state of California describes the goal of education as understanding, which is obtained and justified by the empiricist method of modern science. Conversely, philosophical and religious beliefs do not lead to knowledge but mere assent to ideology.

Obviously, there is a type of intellectual bullying going on in education. If we want to have knowledge, we use the scientific method. If we want to hold unsubstantiated beliefs, we can be uneducated and follow philosophy and religion. It is interesting to note how the competing worldviews were described by those who crafted the state standard. Notice the words used to describe science: *understanding*, *test* and *refutation*. These are words used for intellectual inquiry. On the other hand, note the words used to describe religion: *faith*, which is not subject to testing, and *subscription to ideas*, which do not evoke strong concepts of evidence gathering and knowledge getting. Students are immersed daily in this rhetorical tension between science and religion. Teachers have difficulty unpacking this rhetoric, but for a young student taking science classes it is nearly impossible.

SCIENTIFIC NATURALISM

Our society sees scientific naturalism as the salvation of the human race. Naturalism maintains that knowledge is exclusively limited to the realm of sense perceptions. E. O. Wilson, a Harvard sociobiologist (one who studies the biological basis of social behavior), is a staunch advocate of scientific naturalism. He says, "Science, its imperfections notwithstanding, is the sword in the stone that humanity finally pulled. The question it poses, of universal and orderly materialism, is the most important that can be asked in philosophy and religion."[20] Wilson believes that prior to the modern leaps in science, objective truth was an

---

[19]"California State Board of Education," National Center for Science Education (March 26, 2009) <http://ncseweb.org/media/voices/california-state-board-education>.
[20]Edward O. Wilson, *Consilience: The Unity of Knowledge* (New York: Alfred A. Knopf, 1998), p. 55.

elusive goal for any academic discipline.[21] Today, we know science is now the sole means to objective truth. Knowledge is attained through the scientific method.

Naturalists hold to a theory called scientism. Scientism comes in two forms: strong and weak. *Strong* scientism is the view that knowledge is only gained through the work of science. If a hypothesis, such as Christianity, is not knowable through empirical methods, then it is not an object of knowledge. *Weak* scientism holds that while science is the preeminent means of pursuing knowledge, other disciplines can have justified views about what is knowledge. A naturalist believes minimally that his view of knowledge is vastly superior to all other accounts, or maximally that it is the only means by which to know.

Daniel Dennett, professor of philosophy at Tufts University, is a staunch advocate of evolutionary biology and scientism (even though he hates the label). He recently wrote *Breaking the Spell: Religion as Natural Phenomenon*, in which he advocates an understanding of religion as a naturalized superstition. He argues that the only way to account for a religious inclination is through empirical investigation because that is how facts are known.[22] Dennett, quoted in an article in the *New Statesman*, argues that religion is "the nuclear weapon of rational discussion if, whenever it gets tough, you draw the blinds and play the faith card. It turns into a sham."[23] He points out that religion does have some positive aspects, "but then so does the Mafia. It keeps neighbourhoods quite secure; there's a very low petty crime rate if the Mafia's in control. That doesn't make it a good thing."[24] For Dennett, religion cannot withstand his epistemic criteria of being testable in the sense-perceptible world. But Dennett's own claim about the truth of scientism stands outside of examination in the empirical world. And since the assumptions of science (e.g., there is truth, the world is knowable) cannot be justified by science, Dennett's view undermines the philosophical support for science itself.

---

[21]Ibid., p. 60.
[22]Daniel Dennett, *Breaking the Spell: Religion as a Natural Phenomenon* (New York: Viking Adult, 2006), p. 4.
[23]Dennett in Sholto Byrnes, "When It Comes to Facts, and Explanations of Facts, Science Is the Only Game in Town," *New Statesman*, April 10, 2006, p. 30.
[24]Ibid., p. 29.

Ultimately, naturalism strips out all vestiges of transcendent reality. All that's left in the world is impersonal bits of matter bouncing off other bits of impersonal matter. Humans are simply stimulus-response organisms and are there no longer responsible for their actions. The following excerpt from a 1930s criminology textbook illustrates what rampant naturalism does to personal responsibility: "Man is no more 'responsible' for becoming willful and committing a crime than the flower for becoming red and fragrant. In both instances the end products are pre-determined by the nature of protoplasm and the chance of circumstances."[25] Concepts of justice, morality and honor no longer hold when humans are reduced to mere responders to external stimuli.

Because science continues to be the main arbiter of knowledge in our society, questions about faith are becoming completely privatized. Thus faith will play no role in educating students in the public arena. If education is about understanding, and understanding comes from science, then modern educational methods will eviscerate our discussion of theological anthropology and transcendent purpose.

RHETORIC VERSUS KNOWLEDGE

It is easy to feel defeated and confused given daily cultural pressure. No one is immune from doubt. Even someone like C. S. Lewis, who was a stalwart believer, had times of doubt.

It is July 1940 in England. Just months earlier, Winston Churchill was elevated to position of prime minster. The British Empire finds itself engulfed in a war with Germany, Italy and Japan. In June, Norway, Luxembourg, Belgium, the Netherlands and France fell to Germany, and Great Britain is in a desperate situation as the Battle of Britain begins.

On July 19, 1940, at 6 p.m., Hitler's Reichstag speech is translated by the BBC live. He makes a final appeal to the common sense of the British people, saying:

---

[25]Nathaniel Cantor, *Crime: Criminals and Criminal Justice* (New York: Henry Holt, 1932), p. 266.

It never had been my intention to wage war, but rather to build up a State with a new social order and the finest possible standard of culture. Every year that this war drags on is keeping me away from this work. . . . Mr. Churchill ought, perhaps, for once believe, when I say a great empire will be destroyed—an empire which it was never my intention to destroy or harm.[26]

Hitler is attempting to make his case that the people of Germany are only trying to save themselves from the oppressive Treaty of Versailles, which is controlled by a small group of capitalists and profiteers. Of course, this is all political rhetoric intended to justify the military actions of Germany.

The very next day, July 20, C. S. Lewis writes his brother, Warren, a letter in which he comments on Hitler's speech:

I don't know if I'm weaker than other people, but it is a positive revelation to me how while the speech lasts it is impossible not to waver just a little. I should be useless as a schoolmaster or a policeman. Statements which I know to be untrue all but convince me, at any rate for the moment, if only the man says them unflinchingly.[27]

Lewis does not finish the letter that day but on Sunday, after he has been to church. In his letter he reflects on an epiphany he has during service:

Before the service was over . . . I was struck by the idea for a book which I think might be both useful and entertaining. It would be called *As one Devil to Another* and would consist of letters from an elderly retired devil to a young devil who has just started to work on his first patient. The idea would be to give all the psychology of temptation from the other point of view.[28]

Lewis realizes that the rhetoric he had heard the night before is not unique to Hitler, but is a tool of the devil. From this insight Lewis goes on to write *The Screwtape Letters*, a series of letters of instruction be-

---

[26]Max Domarus, ed., *Hitler: Speeches and Proclamations, 1932-1945*, trans. Chris Wilcox (Wauconda, Ill.: Bolchazy-Carducci, 1997), p. 2062.

[27]C. S. Lewis, *The Collected Letters of C. S. Lewis* (San Francisco: HarperSanFrancisco, 2004), 2:425.

[28]Ibid., pp. 426-27.

tween the demon Uncle Screwtape and his nephew Wormwood. The letters teach Wormwood how best to tempt his patient away from God. Through these letters Lewis gives us insight into the devil's schemes.

The first chapter of *The Screwtape Letters* seems to respond directly to some of the confusion that Lewis is feeling when he writes to Warren. Uncle Screwtape, giving advice to his nephew Wormwood about his "charge," states:

> Your man has been accustomed, ever since he was a boy, to have a dozen incompatible philosophies dancing about together inside his head. He doesn't think of doctrines as primarily "true" or "false," but as "academic" or "practical," "outworn" or "contemporary," "conventional" or "ruthless." Jargon, not argument, is your best ally in keeping him from the Church. Don't waste time trying to make him think materialism is true! Make him think it is strong, stark, or courageous—that it is the philosophy of the future. That is the sort of thing he cares about.[29]

Uncle Screwtape suggests that language is not about truth claims but about "jargon." Rhetoric, not truth, must rule if evil is to be successful. Hitler was not interested in truth, but in rhetorically justifying his case.

The difficulty today is that knowledge is no longer understood holistically but as a competitive notion in which society determines its nature. Who gets to determine what is knowledge is at the forefront of our educational endeavor. The definition of *knowledge* has been changed. In today's society we have anointed our popular artists and our research universities as kings of knowledge.

Society and Knowledge

Our culture sees our actors and singers as spokespersons for many possible causes. People for the Ethical Treatment of Animals (PETA) understands how much our culture responds to celebrities who are outspoken for their cause. On their website GoVeg.com they list over fifty celebrities who are vegetarians. PETA has a darker side that rarely gets

---

[29]C. S. Lewis, *The Screwtape Letters* (New York: HarperCollins, 2001), pp. 1-2.

any play in public consciousness, which is that the organization often compares the slaughter of animals to the slaughter of humans. Ingrid Newkirk, founder of PETA has said, "There is no rational basis for asserting that a human being has special rights: A rat is a pig is a dog is a boy."[30] It is amazing that an organization with such outrageous views could get a hearing in our society, but the allure of the celebrity power around PETA seems to outweigh the large amount of negative press it has received. Few challenge PETA because societal consensus supports its public persona (that of protecting innocent animals) regardless of the fact that their founder claims a human boy's value is the same as that of a rat, pig or a dog.

Universities have their own clout as bearers of knowledge through the mechanism of research. By this "authority," research universities daily bombard the press with all their new discoveries. The news media daily details how science has found overwhelming evidence for X (such as global warming). Media coverage of a topic like global warming (a hypothesis that may or may not be true) fervently reports the preponderance of evidence about the untimely end of the earth. And yet, days later another group of researchers will claim that the earth's temperature is within acceptable parameters. Given the lack of unity on the side of research universities, it is difficult to see how their view of knowledge ultimately corresponds to reality. Not to say that science has no role to play in obtaining knowledge—it does. But science transgresses its true boundaries by attempting to be the all-encompassing standard for knowledge. When science attempts to undercut the reality of God's kingdom, it no longer contributes to understanding but lives in darkness without God.

To the Christian it should be obvious what is missing. Society does not avail itself of a fundamental source of truth—namely, the knowledge given to us by God about himself and his kingdom. The difficulty is that humans don't want to give up their freedom. We want to trust our own abilities to extricate us from the difficulties of this world. To a large portion of our society it is inconceivable to think of the Word of God as a source of knowledge of reality.

---

[30]Wesley J. Smith, "PETA to Cannibals: Don't Let Them Eat Steak," *San Francisco Chronicle*, December 21, 2003, p. D-1.

ANOTHER TRUE SOURCE OF KNOWLEDGE

The apostle Paul points out our confusion about true wisdom, how we falsely commit ourselves to knowledge that is woefully incomplete because it does not account for the reality of God's unseen kingdom.

> Yet among the mature we do impart wisdom, although it is not a wisdom of this age or of the rulers of this age, who are doomed to pass away. But we impart a secret and hidden wisdom of God, which God decreed before the ages for our glory. None of the rulers of this age understood this, for if they had, they would not have crucified the Lord of glory. (1 Cor 2:6-8)

Paul notes the transitory nature of "wisdom" that is strictly located in this age. The rulers of our age do not act out of a transcendent knowledge but out of a limited understanding of what is real. What God offers us is a world in which we can gain true wisdom that comes from him and is given to us for our glory. It is amazing to think that God is revealing himself to us for our own glory. Yet, so often we choose an incomplete knowledge because we don't understand holistically what is truly real.

AUGUSTINE'S REALITY CHECK

Augustine was the type of student who set the curve on a test. He described his academic pursuits in his work *Confessions*. At the age of eighteen he was reading Cicero's *Hortensius*, in which Cicero defends the importance of philosophic study within a society. By twenty Augustine read Aristotle's *Ten Categories*. While many of his peers understood Aristotle only after much tutoring, Augustine mastered the work on his own, stating, "The book seemed to me an extremely clear statement."[31] A voracious reader, Augustine recalled that he "read and undertood all the books [he] could get hold of on the arts which they call liberal."[32] He also said, "I was not aware that these arts are very difficult to understand even for studious and intelligent people, until I tried to explain them to such people and found the student of outstand-

---

[31]Augustine *Confessions* 4.16.28, trans. Henry Chadwick (Oxford: Oxford University Press, 1998).
[32]Ibid., 4.16.30.

ing quality was the one who did not lag behind me in my exposition."[33] Not many people could keep up with Augustine's amazing intellect.

It is difficult for the smartest person in the room to be humble, and Augustine was no exception. When he first read Scripture he found it to be "unworthy in comparison with the dignity of Cicero." He continues:

> My inflated conceit shunned the Bible's restraint, my gaze never pene-
> trated to its inwardness. Yet the Bible was composed in such a way that
> as beginners mature, its meaning grows with them. I disdained to be a
> little beginner. Puffed up with pride, I considered myself a mature adult.
> That is why I fell in with men proud of their slick talk, very earthly-
> minded and loquacious.[34]

The young Augustine was the intellectual superior of his peers. He grasped ideas that others could not follow. This caused him to trust in his own ability to overcome his personal foibles. Reflecting on his younger years, Augustine wondered what good it was to be able to "elucidate extremely complicated books, when [his] comprehension of religion was erroneous distorted, and shamefully sacrilegious?"[35] Unless we realize that the point of academic work is to understand God and his purposes, it is an erroneous pursuit.

In *Confessions* Augustine wrote that shortly before his conversion he had focused all of his mental energy on knowing God, but his life was still one of uncertainty.[36] But God began to show Augustine reality. He never before understood who he really was. He states, "You took me up from behind my own back where I had placed myself because I did not wish to observe myself, and you set me before my faces so that I could see how vile I was how twisted and filthy, covered in sores and ulcers."[37]

Although confronted with the starkness of his own sin, he was still trapped by his own lusts. In the midst of this struggle he turned to his good friend Alypius and cried out, "What is wrong with us? . . . Uneducated people are rising up and capturing heaven."[38] He could not

---

[33]Ibid.
[34]Ibid., 3.5.9-10.
[35]Ibid., 4.16.31.
[36]Ibid., 8.1.1.
[37]Ibid., 8.7.16.
[38]Ibid., 8.8.19.

understand why he couldn't find God. People much less intelligent than him were understanding the reality of God's kingdom—why couldn't he? Finally, while in a fit of tears, God graciously met Augustine through the prompting of an unknown voice that encouraged him to pick up the Scriptures, from which he read Romans 13:13-14. He recounts that moment, "It was as if a light of relief from all anxiety flooded my heart. All shadows of doubt were dispelled."[39] The Word of God illuminated Augustine's understandings. He was no longer limited to his human understanding; the Holy Spirit opened his mind to understand.

Christian educators need to understand the importance of the reality of the kingdom of God. Too often we neglect this source of knowledge as we attempt to meet agreed upon educational standards. We need to realize that God, through the work of the Holy Spirit, enables us to grasp a reality that is outside of our human limitations. One place we can observe this is in the gospel of Luke, where Jesus, the second person of the Trinity, models the work of the third person of the Trinity.

THE ULTIMATE TEACHING MOMENT

Let's look at Luke 24. Twice in this chapter Jesus teaches the disciples, giving them understanding that transcends the limitations of their intellect. The first encounter (Lk 24:13-35) takes place on the day of Christ's resurrection, when two disciples are walking on the road to Emmaus and Jesus starts to walk with them. These disciples are still unclear on who Jesus is and this manifests itself in their inability to recognize Jesus.[40] At this point they do not understand what has happened to Jesus. As he walks with these disciples, Jesus enables them to understand who and what Messiah is. Luke 24:27 states, "And beginning with Moses and all the Prophets, he [Jesus] interpreted to them in all the Scriptures the things concerning himself." Certainly, they had heard the messianic passages before, but they had not understood them.

---

[39]Ibid., 8.12.29.
[40]The disciples are unable to recognize him. This is more than likely due to spiritual blindness than Jesus' appearance. See I. Howard Marshall, *The Gospel of Luke: A Commentary on the Greek Text* (Grand Rapids: Eerdmans, 1978), p. 893.

When Jesus finally reveals himself to them and "their eyes [are] opened," they marvel at his teachings. The disciples say to one another, "Did not our hearts burn within us while he talked to us on the road, while he opened to us the Scriptures?" (Lk 24:32). New Testament scholar I. Howard Marshall points out that "The reality of the risen Jesus was already making itself known to the disciples as he spoke to them . . . only being recognized for what it was after the visual revelation of Jesus."[41] Only through the teaching ministry of Jesus are the disciples able to understand Jesus' whole ministry.

Luke records another meeting with the disciples on the same day (Lk 24:36-49). After the two disciples have walked with Jesus on the road to Emmaus they return to Jerusalem to inform the remaining eleven apostles of their encounter with Jesus. As they talked about this recent event, Jesus appears to them in the locked room.[42] After Jesus verifies that he is flesh and bones by having them touch him and by eating something, he teaches them: "These are my words that I spoke to you while I was still with you, that everything written about me in the Law of Moses and the Prophets and the Psalms must be fulfilled" (Lk 24:44). The Scriptures are a reliable source through which we can understand the reality of Jesus' messianic work and God's kingdom. Yet this does not seem to be enough. Jesus then "opens their minds to understand the Scriptures" (Lk 24:45). Hearing the Scriptures is not enough; to understand the depth of Scripture God must reveal the truth of Scripture to them. This illumination is necessary for all who wish to access the reality of God and kingdom.

In chapter one we discussed the importance of God's illumination. For us to begin to grasp the height and depth of his love and will for us, God must illumine our minds so we can understand his kingdom. Swiss theologian Karl Barth observes:

> In making Himself known, God acts on the whole man. Hence the knowledge of God given to man through his illumination is no mere apprehension and understanding of God's being and action, nor as such a

---

[41]Ibid., p. 899.
[42]Luke does not record that the room is locked. It is reported in John 20.

kind of intuitive contemplation. It is the claiming not only of his thinking but also of his willing and work, of the whole man, for God.[43]

When God reveals himself and his reality to us, he is not enabling us to have mere facts about himself, he is acting on all of our being. This encounter with ultimate reality causes change. When the apostle Paul confronted the reality of Jesus on the road to Damascus, he was not just "making a memory" but was encountering the God of the universe who was claiming Paul's whole life for his service.

THE TEACHER'S OBLIGATION

Truth is the expression of what reality is. As teachers who are followers of God, the King of the universe, we must not limit our teaching to what our senses reveal. Doing so makes our pursuit of knowledge godless. Teachers must be committed to a discipline that enables students to access *all* reality.

Christianity enables us to understand reality in a holistic manner. Through the revelation of God we are able to know and arbitrate what is truly good. The danger is that we are easily swayed by today's pop culture. Educators have a unique opportunity to influence the students we have daily contact with. We can enable our students to seek what is real and to live a life of true meaning rather than pursue a life of limited physical rewards. This stems out of our understanding and commitment to a transcendent reality. Through this commitment we can enable our students to fulfill their true purpose—to be ministers of God and his kingdom purposes.

---

[43]Karl Barth, *Church Dogmatics* IV, part 3.2, trans. Geoffrey W. Bromiley (Edinburgh: T & T Clark, 1962), p. 510.

4

The Information
Economy of Education

In the first three chapters we traced several important knowledge traditions vital to Christian thought and indispensable to a complete education. The next three chapters are an exercise in the ontology of education as a social institution. Ontology is the branch of philosophy investigating being and reality. No philosophy of education is complete without an accounting of the reality of education as a social institution. Social institutions like education are the environment in which the practical affairs of schooling and higher education occur. They are "hidden persuaders" that affect and influence the choices and decision making of all participants.[1] Christian educators exercise their craft in social reality as much as in physical reality. While we do not provide the "deep structure" of education in this particular book, the next chapters specifically show (1) how and why many of the background presuppositions discussed in chapters one through three have great difficulty in reaching institutional agendas, (2) how and why many Christian educationists compartmentalize knowledge and faith commitments, (3) how and why education has tended in the direction of least cost, and (4) what might be done about it.

Let us begin by noting that the least-cost direction has tended to mean an increased emphasis on technical practices that contribute to a descent in education practices, on training instead of education, an emphasis on mere rationality in place of the first principles of theoretical

---

[1]Geoffrey Hodgson, "The Hidden Persuaders: Institutions and Individuals in Economic Theory," *Cambridge Journal of Economics* 27 (2003): 159-75.

and practical reason. This has caused a dissipation of important sets of knowledge and skills necessary for sustaining liberal democracy. Democracy today is tied up with a retreat from classical economic liberalism (free markets) and a withdrawal from classical political liberalism (democratic government). Both these pillars of modernity are entering a disequilibrium between individual and collective goods: the collective is clobbering the individual in many spheres of social reality.[2] Further, within our field there has been great emphasis of late on mere educational attainment (acquiring more years of schooling) than on the complex development of commensurate levels of knowledge and skills (human, social and moral capital, higher reason, etc.). In a word, quantitative outputs such as testing and climbing the ladder of attainment have become more important to institutional agenda than qualitative inputs. Much of this trend results from the price factors of information, which we will get to in a moment.

A recent study showed that there has been something of a formal split or division between attainment and knowledge and skills.[3] The upshot is that educational attainment no longer reliably signals commensurate levels of knowledge, skills and reasoning ability. In economic terms the high school diploma (attainment) is a less reliable predictor of employment or higher education success today than in previous decades. This is so because the criterion on which success is based has less to do with the actual possession of knowledge, skills and reason than it does with a cheap proxy for human and social capital (a diploma). It is an interesting historical fact that the captains of industry had high levels of knowledge and skills without high levels of educational attainment. The typical high school graduate of 1910 could probably outthink many of today's college graduates. Yet today, unless the business professional has an M.B.A. degree, he or she is often locked out of the inner-ring of advancement; even the highly talented genius faces difficulty in a market geared for sustained consumption and credentialism.[4] This, incidentally,

---

[2]See the book by Steven Loomis and Jacob Rodriguez, *C. S. Lewis: A Philosophy of Education* (New York: Palgrave Macmillan, 2009).
[3]See the book by Jacob Rodriguez, Steven Loomis and Joseph Weeres, *The Cost of Institutions* (New York: Palgrave Macmillan, 2007).
[4]Randall Collins, "Credential Inflation and the Future of Universities," in *The Future of the*

is why the standards movement came to be. It was a concerted private-public effort to reconnect attainment and knowledge-skills at a time, in the early 1980s, when the U.S. business community began to notice the disparity. Businesses did not want to increase their own costs remediating the attainment—knowledge and skills—gap. The remedy was to bring schooling into a kind of production equivalency with McDonalds.[5] Standardization was thought to bring the two together. By 2007 the U.S. National Assessment Governing Board (NAGB) reported the following: "While, on average, high school graduates are taking more challenging courses and earning higher grades during their high school years, 12th-graders failed to produce gains on the 2005 National Assessment of Educational Progress (NAEP), according to The Nation's Report Card."[6] At their press conference on February 22, the NAGB could not answer how both could be true at the same time.[7] The asymmetry between educational attainment and the actual possession of knowledge and skills is a plausible answer as to why high-school students can be acquiring higher levels of attainment (passing challenging courses with higher grades) while at the same time failing to see those gains reflected in other demonstrations of knowledge and skills.

In colleges and universities the incongruency between attainment and knowledge manifests in lower-cost credentialing (e.g., diploma mills), often in order to capitalize on the vast demand for attainment and to grow the size of a university. The higher-cost pursuit of learning

---

City of Intellect: The Changing American University (Stanford, Calif.: Stanford University Press, 2002), pp. 23-46.

[5]See George Ritzer, *The McDonaldization of Society*, 2nd ed. (Thousand Oaks, Calif.: Pine Forge Press, 2004).

[6]"High School Students Show No Progress in Reading, According to the Nation's Report Card™: 12th-Grade Results at Odds with Data Showing That High School Graduates Are Taking More Advanced Courses and Earning Higher Grade Point Averages," National Assessment Governing Board press release., February 22, 2007, Washington, D.C. Copies of "The Nation's Report Card: 12-Grade Reading and Mathematics 2005" and "The Nation's Report Card: America's High School Graduates" and additional data from the 2005 12th-grade assessments are available at http://nationsreportcard.gov.

[7]See CSPAN under "video library: domestic/social": National Assessment of Educational Progress Report: 2/24/2007: Washington, D.C.: 1 hr. 27 min. <http://www.c-spanarchives.org/library/index.php?main_page=product_video_info&products_id=196765-1 or see http://nces.ed.gov/whatsnew/commissioner/remarks2007/9_25_2007.asp> (both URLs accessed 6/2/2009).

gives way to lower-priced, often standardized replica courses and degree programs. Franchising becomes a lucrative business model for many universities. Some education master's degree programs are like that. Because the teacher salary structure of school districts is tied directly to attainment, not knowledge and skills (a consequence of collective bargaining and the No Child Left Behind Act's qualified-teacher criterion), offering education master's degree programs is a profitable way to grow (and cross-subsidize) university budgets.

On one occasion one of us was guest lecturing in a philosophy of education course at such a program at a West Coast Christian university and the question was asked, "For what purpose are you taking this course?" After some awkward silence a hand slowly rose in the back of the room and the student replied: "To move up on the district's salary schedule." This is of course dispiriting for a scholar to hear, but it is an entirely understandable response. Today, the field incentivizes attainment (credentialism), which carries more motivational weight in the development of teachers than the acquisition of higher levels of knowledge and skill. It is a symptom of the descent into mere technical practice.

Still, the problem is broader and manifests itself in the inflationary problem of credentialism: a job that used to require a high school diploma now requires a bachelor of arts; what used to require a B.A. now requires an M.A., and so on. There is a built-in assumption that more attainment will achieve a higher functioning society. Ordinary citizens and others in the lower economic classes cannot keep pace with the inflationary pressures of credentialism. This problem is especially acute for Latinos and African Americans, who are more likely to be in the underclass and whose rates of high school graduation are roughly 60 to 65 percent (compared to the 75 to 80 percent graduation rate for all students). In order to recognize how serious these and other problems in education are, and how Christian educators (new or veteran) might respond to them, we need to understand a little bit about how the information economy of the institution works.

Our operating presupposition is that the redemption of reason requires a particular kind of faith, one that is familiar to reflective, mind-renewing followers of Jesus Christ. Here we join with philosopher Dallas Willard:

I think one of the greatest needs today is to help people to understand the changed situation between reason or understanding and revelation in our time—in particular, to understand that what is in trouble on our campuses today is reason itself. . . . My claim will be only the body of Christian knowledge—I will say this slowly—only the body of Christian knowledge and intellectual method can redeem reason.[8]

We put forth several philosophical, institutional and organizational issues and questions concerning important sectors of education that should occupy educators' attention for the next twenty to thirty years, if not much longer. This is by no means an exhaustive anticipation of institutional challenges and opportunities.[9] Like windows, challenges and opportunities open and close according to dynamic environmental conditions. Nevertheless, our logic and commentary generally signal to new and veteran educators a few of the areas that might yield community vision and action. New educators, like veteran educators, have a moral responsibility to steward the institution of education toward proper function and optimal performance.[10]

THE THREAT OF OPACITY TO THE LEARNING COMMUNITY

Survivor Maria Joffe shares a chilling account of the institutional effects of the Soviet Gulag system:

The only slender chance of salvation—is not to belong to any category. To be neither short, nor tall, nor of medium height. To be neither dark, nor white, nor grey. To be outside every gauge and measurement, out-

---

[8]Dallas Willard, "The Redemption of Reason" (keynote address at the academic symposium "The Christian University in the Next Millennium," Biola University, La Mirada, Calif., February 28, 1998).

[9]The study of institutions is a relatively new field of economic research. In this book we are studying the institutional environment of education that helps to form the framework from which human decision making and action take place; in the words of Douglass North, they are essentially the "rules of the game" that guide participant behavior. For key works, please see Douglass North, *Institutions, Institutional Change and Economic Performance* (Cambridge: Cambridge University Press, 1990); Samuel Bowles, *Microeconomics: Behavior, Institutions, and Evolution* (Princeton, N.J.: Princeton University Press, 2004); Richard Nelson, *Technology, Institutions, and Economic Growth* (Cambridge, Mass.: Harvard University Press, 2005); Jacob P. Rodriguez, Steven R. Loomis and Joseph G. Weeres, *The Cost of Institutions: Information and Freedom in Expanding Economies* (New York: Palgrave Macmillan, 2007).

[10]For further, see Alasdair MacIntyre, "Social Structures and Their Threats to Moral Agency," *Philosophy: The Journal of the Royal Institute of Philosophy* 74 (1999): 311-29.

side any shape or colouring. Dissolve completely in absolute obedience, submission to command and comprehend the meaning of every nod.[11]

To be opaque is to be impenetrable to sight, to be obscure, to live a dull and clouded existence, to be an undifferentiated unit, to give up individuality, to surrender divine uniqueness and to submit one's own identity to illegitimate power. When all is considered, being opaque is to be less than human. This loss of humanity is opposite to the Christian view of life, where an equilibrium is worked out on principles of human dignity and moral worth, where the individual maintains irreducible value in the face of any form of group, community or collective situation.

Yet technical models and systems that manifest in authoritarian, totalitarian or even democratic political regimes have more or less a similar capacity, though by much different means, to make human beings appear opaque through what Augustine, in *The City of God*, called *libido dominandi* (capricious rule). One of the many valuable contributions of C. S. Lewis to social thought is the recognition that democracy requires a certain form of education, one that optimizes human development and flourishing, otherwise it will slip into some form of tyranny. This can be true too of economic markets. Like cultural, political and social markets, where people relate to one another in a variety of contexts and for different purposes, economic markets can fall into disequilibrium when the individual human being becomes useful as though a mere cog in the social wheel, an abstract entity melded to the statistical curve. "In statistical affairs . . . the first care before all else is to lose sight of the man taken in isolation in order to consider him only a fraction of the species. It is necessary to strip him of his individuality to arrive at the elimination of all accidental effects that individuality can introduce into the question."[12] Estrangement from human purpose and flourishing may occur through either repressive coercion, as Joffe's account illustrates, or by voluntary assent to certain institutional incentives, such as when hu-

---

[11]Maria Joffe, *One Long Night: A Tale of Truth* (Chapham, U.K.: New Park, 1978), p. 166.
[12]From a 1835 report of four mathematicians on a statistical comparison of gallstone operations, cited Ian Hacking, *The Taming of Chance* (Cambridge: Cambridge University Press, 1990), p. 81.

man beings follow an illegitimate path-dependent pattern of belief or action (i.e., as when following a carrot as opposed to being threatened with a stick).[13] An example of the latter case is the corruption of the purpose of higher learning. This occurs when faculty and leadership choose new institutional incentives such as those brought about through processes of standardization,[14] as the costs against their resistance in personal prestige and professional reputation, or one's research agenda or practice become too high.

We sometimes forget that education systems are fragile institutions that require constant vigilance, including salting and lighting dynamics taught by Jesus Christ (Mt 5:13). Arguably most educators, including Christian educators, try to keep foremost in mind the perennial first principles of learning; the proper forms of means and ends, the fundamental reasons for providing an excellent education, the complex nexus between education and freedom. Even as Christian educators we sometimes forget or fail to realize that the realities of education in a secular age[15] make remote the direct apprehension in daily life of the belief that Jesus Christ should touch everything in our professional life and academic field (2 Cor 10:5). Yet we know

---

[13]We define *incentives* as rewards for actions by individuals who voluntarily align their behavior and even their "dispositions" or thought patterns to institutional priorities, prerogatives and direction. Incentives are also used to constrain activity and thought as much as they reward assent.

[14]For a leading thought on the subject of costs, see Ronald Coase's article, "The Problem of Social Costs," *Journal of Law and Economics* 3 (1960): 1-44. The work of historian George Marsden examines organizational assent to these incentives in higher education. See especially Marsden's, *The Soul of the American University: From Protestant Establishment to Established Nonbelief* (Oxford: Oxford University Press, 1994). Other examples could be drawn from sources like William Shirer's description of the Nazification of German higher learning, where he noted certain incentives that guided faculty capitulation. See his *The Rise and Fall of the Third Reich* (New York: Simon & Schuster, 1960). When we refer to "cost" we typically mean the cost of information. The cost of information accompanies choice—the decisions to trade one desire, need or goal for another. These choices in turn define and transform production probabilities. To understand the reasons for the cost difference between standardized and nonstandardized information, we need only reflect on what makes information more or less costly in a social institution. Information is less costly (in financial or other terms) to the degree that it (1) successfully connects cause and effect, (2) yields a sense of certainty, (3) exhibits clear utility, (4) complements profitable activities, (5) uses relatively fewer resources to ascertain its costs and benefits, (6) increases legibility, verification and enforcement, and (7) is comparatively easy to acquire, process, reproduce and transmit. Information tends to be more costly when it does not possesses these qualities. See Rodriguez et al., *Cost of Institutions*, pp. 15-30.

[15]Charles Taylor, *A Secular Age* (Cambridge: Belknap Press, 2007).

from Scripture that the Lord is the standard of all activity (cf. Ps 139). So what happens when a social institution intentionally or unintentionally conflicts with divine standards for human development and flourishing? What is traded off?

One thing that is traded off is the holistic development of the human being. Jewish existentialist Martin Buber, a professor of social philosophy at several universities in Europe and Israel, described the ethical situation that schooling and higher education ought to create. Buber believed that a founding presupposition of education ought to be the development of the creative powers of the human being; genuine education is made possible by this presupposition.

> The world, that is the whole environment, nature and society, "educates" the human being: it draws out his powers, and makes him grasp and penetrate its objections. What we term education, conscious and willed, means *a selection by man of the effective world:* it means to give decisive effective power to a selection of the world which is concentrated and manifested in the educator. The relation in education is lifted out of the purposelessly streaming education by all things, and is marked off as purpose. In this way, through the educator, the world for the first time becomes the true subject of its effect.[16]

In addition to the realization of individual capacities, Buber is concerned with the institutional environment—the "space" in which education is procured. Good education entails dialogue in relation. Briefly, Buber suggests three principal forms of the dialogical relation in education: first, the mutual experience of inclusion, where "each is aware of the other's full legitimacy," recognition of the truth of existence as spiritual persons; second, the paradoxical medium of education where the student "cannot experience the educating of the educator" but the educator "experiences both ends of the common situation"; and third, friendship in the form of dialogical relation—the "true inclusion of one another by human souls."[17] The existential complexity of the educative experience is vital to the good.

---

[16]Martin Buber, *Between Man and Man* (New York: Macmillan, 1968), p. 89.
[17]Ibid., pp. 98-101.

Developing a student's capacities, teaching for communion as opposed to compulsion, creating an atmosphere of genuine inclusion between educator and student—all of these have become problematic in today's technical model of education.[18] The institutional structure and environment does not easily support the development of capacity in communion. One question of contemporary importance is whether the *scale* (sheer size) of the larger institution or its organizations, as for example the scale of urban and suburban schools (e.g., 1,000 to 5,000 students) or universities (e.g., 5,000-plus) and their technical orientation, have capacity to extend to their participants the I-Thou situation at the heart of Buber's concern.[19] The I-Thou situation arguably makes

---

[18]We will be referring to a "technical framework" or "technical model." Both are rather loaded terms. Let us briefly unpack them a bit. "[The] growth of scale creates within itself a momentum towards a technical model of production. We can think of this gravitation toward the technical model as the path of least cost, or a process of substitution: universal in place of particular information, abstract and general forms as opposed to concrete and specific forms, more unity and less variety; it is the rise of impersonal factors and relations instead of personal distinctions; it is the physical and sense bound over things which cannot be sensuously comprehended; it is rational organization in place of creative and imaginative power; it is numbers in place of morals. In its strong or extreme form the technical approach embodies its own vision of reality: one of efficient means and universal ends, of belief in the unbreakable link between cause and effect, of a symmetrical set of rules and wholly explicable laws, whose categories are the categories of abstraction, of mathematical reasoning and language in terms of causal uniformities. It is a view in which all real statements about the world must be reducible to generalization and capable of calculation. In its developing form, the technical model is a summarizer and a collector of similarities. Its aim and purpose is to unify measures of the good, to codify a common understanding of good work and commercial propriety, and to remove barriers to consolidation and control. As the institution expands, it reacts to the competition for scarce resources by arranging itself in opposition to the unique and particular. This opens the way to a more streamlined structure of production, which advances on the grounds of its ability to: (1) sustain accumulation and handle large volumes of information, (2) integrate units of production, (3) lower the costs of decision making, (4) decrease the unpredictability of events, and (5) create a system of reliable expectations. The model derives its legitimacy from the growth of scale and the higher returns to capital that it tends to generate. Expansion of output and trade is the prime mover toward the technical model. And the repeated satisfactions of moving production in this direction reinforce the previous decisions and provide decision makers with incentives to stay the course....What this pattern serves to bring out is that the drive to expand inclines the institution to select and use more controllable forms of information. As it does this, it pressures the institutional framework to subtract details, to create a simpler structure of production, and to relegate individual will, values, and beliefs to positions of less significance. Expansion inclines the institution to magnify the ideas of uniformity and of continuing progress toward harmonizing conflicting interests. In a sense, it compels the institution to become a protest against exception, an opponent of distinction, and to lay insufficient stress on the importance of the human component in production" (Rodriguez et al., *The Cost of Institutions*, pp. 23-26).

[19]Martin Buber, *I and Thou* (New York: Simon & Schuster, 1970).

more probable that "rich" ethical relations of ideal humanity exist among and between persons who foreswear treating other persons (and one's self) as mere utility during processes of learning.[20] It means not using people as a means to an end; it means what Jesus said about relating to all people as our neighbors (Mk 12:31) and to help the least able among us (Mt 5; 25); it means what Paul said about speaking truth to one's neighbor (Eph 4:25); it means to *value* and *do* justice (Mic 6:8), and to make justice a sacrifice (Ps 4); it means practicing the virtue of humility (Phil 2).[21] Finally, it means to discover and strive for a social equilibrium between oneself, others and the ecosystem, one informed by the moral sphere and divine purpose. While care ethicist Nel Noddings describes this phenomenon as "a displacement of interest from my own reality to the reality of the other,"[22] the Christian view does not entail a displacement but an equilibrium and relationship of earnest reciprocity taught by Jesus.

THE IRREDUCIBLE VALUE OF PARTICULAR INFORMATION TO EDUCATION

For I-Thou situations to subsist or to thrive within any human institution (e.g., education, health care, law, prison systems), there are two necessary information conditions that must exist: micro and macro.[23] First, particular information, that is, information of a local or individual concern, is a necessary condition for the I-Thou situation because to be known as *I* or as *Thou* one must in either case be known individually

---

[20]C. S. Lewis referred to Buber's argument in his classic education work, *The Abolition of Man* (San Francisco: HarperOne, 2001), p. 79.

[21]Concerning the intellectual virtue of humility, see Robert Roberts and Jay Wood, "Humility and Epistemic Goods," in *Intellectual Virtue: Perspectives from Ethics and Epistemology*, ed. Michael DePaul and Linda Zabzebski (Oxford: Oxford University Press, 2003).

[22]Nel Noddings, *Caring: A Feminine Approach to Ethics and Moral Education* (Berkeley: University of California Press, 1984), p. 86.

[23]Economists Jacob Marschak and George Stigler formally launched the field of information analysis. See Jacob Marschak, "Remarks on the Economics of Information," in *Contributions to Scientific Research in Management* (Los Angeles: Western Data Processing Center, UCLA, 1959), pp. 79-98, and George Stigler, "The Economics of Information," *The Journal of Political Economy* 69, no. 3 (1961): 213-25. Stigler's basic argument is that information is asymmetrical between people and their decision making in economic life. Rodriguez et al. show how information divides such that particular information is traded off for universal information. This division of information threatens individual liberty and local culture.

and uniquely. Particular information then is that depth, width and range of information that is associated with the local, the situational and the individual. As Rodriguez, Loomis and Weeres suggest, it

> refers to data that is mostly qualitative in nature; it consists of properties that are inherently variable, irregular, uncertain, and hard to measure. In general, it is the kind of information that cannot yield precise definitions, which has no exact boundaries to measure, and is unpredictable. Particular information pertains mainly to the non-linear types of behavior, to the unique, dynamic elements of living or physical systems; it is perhaps most applicable to complex social phenomena and the field of human relations where extensive variation tends to dominate the component parts of the data. This information finds expression in personal distinctions, in independence, emotion, feelings, improvisation, value judgments, moral principles, acts of will—all the essential aspects and distinct individualities that make up human personality and the intricacies of human interaction.[24]

The splendor and diversity of individual uniqueness and identity found in particularity is more likely to be retained within a *human* scale, a scale whose context, structure and information economy does no harm to human development, a scale where the contest for scarce resources does not bias the tradeoffs of information. This is in contrast to the aggregated, large-scale organizations (e.g., an individual school) or institution (the whole framework and rules of education) whose information economy must deplete particularity (trade it off) during the intensification of scarcity. Deeper forms of ethical and caring relationships between a teacher and a student or school and family depend on the condition of particular information.[25] This is what high quality educators are trying to preserve in the hyper-homogenizing world of education.

Genuine human community depends on this information. While human beings share a common nature, which informs us as to a range of species-specific knowledge, we are known by others and know our-

---

[24]Rodriguez et al., *Cost of Institutions*, p. 3.
[25]Thomas Toch, *High Schools on a Human Scale: How Small Schools Can Transform American Education* (Boston: Beacon Press, 2003).

selves in the deepest sense individually and existentially, not as mere
extensions of a class, race or members of aggregated groups, where it is
very difficult to account for particular information and individual identity. Nothing here suggests that group affiliation is not a significant
part of human identity. But *I* and *Thou* is the most basic form or starting point of human identity and relationship. Theologian Colin Gunton shows the relationship between the person and particular information in these terms:

> At the heart of the matter, and of immense importance, is the concept
> of the person. The centrality of the personal is explicit in what has been
> written above about the fact that persons have spirit and thus their dis-
> tinctively relational being in the image of God. Indeed, it is the loss of
> the centrality of particular personality. . . . The chief affirmation to be
> made here is that is persons' are, like the persons of the Trinity and by
> virtue of their creation in the image of the triune God, hypostases, con-
> crete and particular, then their particularity too is central to their being.
> . . . The destruction of forces making for homogeneity can be achieved
> by finding ways of allowing persons to be particular, particular in rela-
> tion indeed, but made by that very relationality unique and free.[26]

THE THREAT OF STANDARDIZED INFORMATION
TO HIGH-QUALITY EDUCATION

However, knowing and living at this personal and existential level is
often too costly for an expanding institution to bear. This particular
information does not survive within the technical institution and its
information framework. Scale and scarcity are key factors here. Is
there an inherently different information dynamic in a classroom
where the teacher-student ratio is 1:10, 1:20, 1:30, 1:40, 1:50? At each
amplification of scale, the variables it introduces affect the classroom
ecology and economy in nontrivial ways: in planning, exchange, decision making, relations, resources, space, choice of assessments and so
on. Anyone who has taught knows that scale affects the distribution
of information. Like the individual classroom or school or college, as

---

[26]Colin Gunton, *The One, the Three and the Many* (Cambridge: Cambridge University Press,
1993), p. 196.

the larger institution of education scales up (expands), the presence of very real scarcities (time, resources, etc.) requires that the institution and its participating organizations (individual schools and colleges) increasingly rely on legible or universal information.[27] The institution lurches in the direction of seeing people in uniform ways through an integrated network of central rules. These are "correct" rules thought to move production toward zero or nominal costs. As Nobel economist Kenneth Arrow suggests, "These rules tend to be broad and not very applicable to particulars. They don't take account of the individual case."[28]

The moral and economic problem concerning the scope and application of rules is seen, for example, in public education systems in many sectors of the United States and internationally. Scaling-up classrooms and schools in size (e.g., the bureaucratic practices of mass education in urban and suburban areas) tend to eliminate student individuality (the particulars) by using a lens of sameness in the means and ends of education. The lens acts as a synthesizer. Participants—individual human beings and individual organizations—follow the technical framework, filtering their decision making through the sieve of standardized information. Very little differentiation is allowed to exist because all production activity follows an instrumental logic and rational path. For example, a colleague of ours helped to bring home schooling in California under the technical framework, believing it would advance the ends of

---

[27]"Universal information" refers to "data that is mostly quantitative in nature; it consists of properties that tend to be constant, common, linear, and measurable. In the realm of universal information we can expect to find categories that correspond to standardization, consolidation, and integration; it is fundamentally compatible with a capacity for generating order and stability, prediction, fixed patterns of logical structures, and precise planning and control. In rules, laws, norms, customs, language, values, ideas, and so forth, universal information tends to deal with instances of the type (i.e., abstract and general forms) not the particular or individual. When we speak of the universalizing trend that parallels expanding markets we also mean the social construction of this information. That is to say, as trade grows outside the purview of the existing rule structure, the arena of institutional rules must enlarge and embrace the new circle of trade. This requires a reformulation of the rules—substituting more universal information for particular information. In other words, the rules must become more universal—conform to collective interests—before they can animate plans for further expansion. As the new set of rules organize around the larger market, the old rule set, which once was seen as universal information, now becomes seen as particular information" (Rodriguez et al., *Cost of Institutions*, pp. 3-4).

[28]Kenneth Arrow, "The Economy of Trust," *Religion and Liberty* 16, no. 3 (2006): 13.

education and legitimate an alternative educational model. External legitimation to a market or government entity is thought to give rational form to the activity. (In reality, it signals a deep insecurity about and within the profession of education.) All private schools operate within the technical framework in various ways, including what curricula counts for entrance into the state university system (e.g., the University of California). All Title I programming is standardized under the technical framework. All special education is becoming tightly uniform, just the opposite of its original set of aims. All alternative schools (probation, juvenile hall, community schools and others) are being homogenized, which is exactly opposite of what is needed. More often than not, the alternative-school student has already demonstrated an inability to successfully negotiate the rule structure or demands of the mainstream school. Yet the very environment which was a principal cause of frustration for the alternative-school student now follows him or her to the alternative school: one-size-fits-all standardization originating from, for example, accrediting agencies like the Western Association of Schools and Colleges (WASC). Let us also mention that the National Council for Accreditation of Teacher Education (NCATE) is a major culprit in bringing departments and schools of education within the technical umbrella. NCATE's accreditation regime moves departments and schools of education into the zone of universal information, into the proximity of technical procedures, thus shifting the knowledge base in a manner that scales back the ability to generate the depth and breadth of information necessary to examine and solve complex institutional problems (e.g., human capital, social inequalities, questions of leadership, gaps in student learning). Moreover, George W. Bush's second Secretary of Education, Margaret Spellings, tried in 2006 to bring higher education under this same uniform framework.[29]

Is the standardization of complex production activity a good thing or a bad thing? When we research the phenomenon carefully, the all-reconciling system really is just a technological adjustment of people. It operates within the tradition of matching the person to the machine. It

---

[29]Margaret Spellings, *A Test of Leadership: Charting the Future of U.S. Higher Education* (Washington, D.C.: U.S. Department of Education, 2006).

stabilizes the institution of education through classification, prediction and control over educational events. It essentially solves problems of institutional risk by controlling the parameters of belief and action, confining participants to a statistical space of probability.[30] The answer to the question of standardization, at least in part, depends on where decision making should lie. Because the technical model is highly rational, bureaucratization begins to substitute an unvarying kind of information that channels relations and practices between participants toward New Essentialism.[31] Decision making must not conflict with the logic of this framework. Since it is generally true that the specific kind of education received affects the outlook of individuals, alters individual perceptions about the world and generally determines whether individual life chances are enhanced or diminished, the efficacy of a model of education in means and ends is of paramount concern.

All of this leads us to conclude that rigid standardization in education tends to lead to the I-It condition. This is its cost against the social welfare; this is what makes it a bad thing. The I-It condition is everything that the I-Thou condition is not. Results of technical rationality affect human relationships, making them poorer in quality. It is apropos to cite the social theorist Max Weber in this milieu:

> [The calculability of decision making] is more fully realized the more bureaucracy "depersonalizes" itself, i.e., the more completely it succeeds in achieving the exclusion of love, hatred, and every purely personal, especially irrational and incalculable, feeling from the execution of official tasks. In the place of the old-type ruler who is moved by sympathy, favor, grace and gratitude, modern culture requires for its sustaining external apparatus the emotionally detached, and hence rigorously "professional" expert.[32]

---

[30]Hacking, *Taming of Chance*, pp. 1-10.

[31]For an unparalleled account of the depersonalizing process of this form of schooling, see Samuel Bowles and Herbert Gintis, *Schooling in Capitalist America: Educational Reform and the Contradictions of Economic Life* (New York: Basic Books, 1976), and their follow-up study, "Schooling in Capitalist America Revisited" (2002). Many left-leaning philosophers of education are joining libertarian economists such as Milton Friedman in embracing public-private school choice arguments in order to make available for poor kids an escape from the I-It condition across much of urban schooling.

[32]Max Weber, quoted in Lewis Coser, *Masters of Sociological Thought*, 2nd ed. (New York: Har-

All of this activity and direction is predicated on the price of information brought about by an array of substitutions, abstractions and reductions. It simply costs less for an expanding social institution to impose a standardized grid onto participants. Picture the cost differences in health care between a health maintenance organization (HMO) and a preferred provider organization (PPO). In the HMO the physician's average time with patient is significantly less than in a PPO. In a PPO the patient has "bought" more time and access to a greater range of physicians, including specialists and their enhanced knowledge. Physician time, like a teacher's time, is a scarcity; there is a cost to it. Anyone familiar with these health care organizations intuitively recognizes that patients' are treated differently, perhaps not in every instance, but overall. That difference is often located in the quantity and quality of time, the availability and depth of information, and direct physician access, which is predicated on cost. (We should note that this health care pattern was *designed* this way.)[33]

In education, especially in large-scale urban schools, a similar situation occurs. Teachers are less able to account for the necessary information needed for quality education. In Los Angeles, for example, the LAUSD uses "teacher-proof" curricula originated by Open Court Publishing that regulates production down to the minutes used for transparencies. In larger classes, say 1:30 or 1:40, efficiency of production (planning and exchange) is at a premium. Most teachers in urban education are intimately familiar with certain absurdities undermining teachers' professional work. For those unfamiliar with such issues, see Richard Ingersol's fair analysis in *Who Controls' Teachers Work?* (2003).

In general, relations between people within the technical model of education are often depleted of love, care, duty and justice; relations

---

court Brace Jovanovich, 1977), pp. 230-31.

[33]Kenneth Arrow helps us see why this is so. "The underlying point is that if individuals are free to spend as they will with the assurance that the insurance company will pay, the resulting resource allocation will certainly not be socially optimal. This makes perfectly reasonable the idea that an insurance company can improve the allocation of resources to all concerned by a policy which rations the amount of medical services it will support under the insurance policy" (Kenneth Arrow, "The Economics of Moral Hazard: A Further Comment," in *Collected Papers of Kenneth J. Arrow: The Economics of Information* [Cambridge, Mass.: Belknap, 1984], p. 103).

become transient, utilitarian, nonenduring, nontruth seeking. C. S. Lewis identifies the problem as the difference between membership in a collective, where particular information is depleted, and membership in a community, where particular information is retained.[34] French philosopher Jacques Ellul, also a Christian, described this phenomenon during the postwar period in *The Technological Society*. Ellul suggested that "education, even in France, is becoming oriented toward the specialized end of producing technicians; and, as a consequence, toward the creation of individuals useful only as members of a technical group, on the basis of the criteria of utility—individuals who conform to the structure and the needs of the technical group."[35] Both philosophers understood that social institutions cannot, at the same time, sustain both a technical framework of social reality and genuine human development and flourishing.

The impersonal effects prevalent in the technical model contrasts with the teaching model presented by Jesus of Nazareth, who taught in both large- and small-scale settings but never lost the personal, human side of the connection. In the Gospel of Mark we find that Jesus understood and practiced the I-Thou relationship. We might even say he originated the I-Thou ideal when he spoke of the neighbor—with the uneducated (Mk 1:16-20), the underdeveloped (Mk 1:21-22), sinners (Mk 2:17), the disabled (Mk 3:1-6), the possessed (Mk 5:1-20), the sick (Mk 5:25-32), the self-righteous (Mk 7:1-8), the hearing-impaired (Mk 7:31-37), the slow learners (Mk 8:17-19), the blind (Mk 8:22-26), the wealthy (Mk 10:17-22), teachers who are mistaken about reality (Mk 12:18-27) and the poor (Mk 12:41-44). At each encounter the Lord was an educator and was (and still is) prepared to meet people as individuals with unique problems and particular challenges to their learning. Ultimately, of course, the personal sacrifice of Jesus is the greatest example of his care and concern for humanity. It is the ultimate example for all educators. God of course does not suffer from problems of scale and scarcity. Notwithstanding this real-

---

[34]C. S. Lewis, "Membership," *The Weight of Glory* (New York: HarperCollins, 2001), pp. 158-76.
[35]Jacques Ellul, *The Technological Society*, trans. John Wilkenson (New York: Vintage, 1964), p. 349.

142 EDUCATION FOR HUMAN FLOURISHING

ity, educational structures and strategies could benefit from applying an integrated analysis of the problem of human capital and the work that schools do in the context of institutional thought. In other words, Christian educators would do well to understand the institutional barriers that reduce the opportunities to teach on the intellectual, social and moral principles exemplified by Jesus.

UNIVERSAL KNOWLEDGE

A second condition of information relies on a universal set of knowledge (true belief with a passable degree of warrant) drawn from transcendent reality.[36] One candidate here might be the moral or natural law, that is, C. S. Lewis's Tao.[37] Natural law as a property of reality is a universal because it applies to all human persons. Paul, for example, identified the law of nature in his book to the Romans (e.g., Rom 1–2). Natural law, in the one sense, liberates individuals to move toward the I-Thou situation by carving out morally dutiful and inviolable conditions among the community of persons irrespective of the competing worldviews or technical and utility factors that arise from any given institution. Put simply, natural law as a supernatural institution exists to prevent people from using other people as mere instruments of commerce, as commodities and mere furniture in the economy or political system. There are other recognizable universals: there is a common human nature; there are universal laws of logic and physics; and there are universal ways people should approach each other.

When working in concert with the faculty of conscience, universal knowledge (e.g., the first principles of essentials of practical reason, which we all ought to know) guides the relations and values between persons, and between persons and institutions. For schools this means

---

[36]Universals can be regarded as properties of a fundamental substance, event or relation. For a thorough treatment of universals in contemporary philosophy, see J. P. Moreland, *Universals* (Montreal: McGill-Queen's University Press, 2001).

[37]Natural law is roughly the condition of the moral sphere that intuitively and through reason becomes known to the faculty of conscience whereby a person secures basic moral knowledge. Some scholars view natural law in political or ideological terms. Indeed, political liberals have begun to join others on the ideological right in affirming natural law as a basis for the social contract. See for example, Christopher Wolfe, *Natural Law Liberalism* (Cambridge: Cambridge University Press, 2006).

each student and teacher reciprocate dignity and respect during the mission of learning; both classes of persons coming to understand by separate degrees and, perhaps, by different paths the intrinsic value of the I-Thou condition. For schools to be truly effective, this true and universal condition must be present and operative throughout a school's climate and culture, in policy as in leadership. For example, Ms. Morrison, a middle school teacher, is exercising both particular and universal moral knowledge when she is teaching students Jill and Paul in a way that is focused on three principles: (1) discovering who Jill and Paul are as individual human beings (their interests, talents, gifts, cultural backgrounds, histories, etc.), (2) what they need by way of an education to help make them into knowledgeable and morally competent persons, and (3) what the community (or state) requires the curriculum to cover, the relevant knowledge and skills of the democratic citizen. The technical model undermines 1 through 3.

In a second sense, natural law is capable of setting objective but not necessarily rigid or bureaucratic standards for human relations that are arguably more reliable than standards presently used by and within most educational organizations. Someone might raise the following objection: Whose justice and which rationality will guide the institution of education? An institutional theorist might respond with the counter question, Whose justice and which rationality is guiding the institution now?

New Essentialism has redefined the productive base of education, which splits or divides it from education's first principles and deeper senses of the good. For example, rational choice theory, a basis for behaviorism and neoclassical economic thought, tends to trivialize justice and rationality by subordinating them to a concept used by economists and political theorists called "utility maximization" (self-interest in wants and needs; doing what works only for *me;* getting the best value for the least cost). Those arguments will not be rehearsed here. We pause only to note that some form of a universal will ground the institution of education and its productive base—what happens *in* education. And (Skinnerian) behaviorism, (Rawlsian) distributive liberalism, and (Habermasian) collectivism are inferior sources because of the types of information those theories eliminate from the information economy of education. As overarching views of social reality, they eliminate vital aspects of reality, important approaches, methods and sources of inquiry. In an authentically pluralistic institution the question Who decides among contested notions of the good? is answered by noting that *we all do*, including Christians who hold *public* convictions about education goods and the ontology of social institutions.

Active moral theorists and practitioners (e.g., Rev. Martin Luther King Jr. and C. S. Lewis) have always recognized that natural law creates a justifiable constraint on arbitrary action against other persons, whether by another individual, a collective or a social institution. As a nonnatural institution (all social institutions are nonnatural entities), the purpose of natural law is to constrain individuals by means of the perceptible and felt effects of conscience, which affects beliefs and their formation, which affects the will and action. When a person's conscience is left underdeveloped, it becomes much more open to corruption and is no longer a reliable instrument to guide dispositions and actions. Other social institutions become necessary to constrain injustices and keep people on the path of just action. (Recall that Madison said in *The Federalist* 51 that if all men were angels, government would not be necessary.) In this regard schools used to be institutions that heightened moral awareness; as Lewis said, inculcating just sentiments. But due to the information economy today, schools no longer have the capacity to act as a trustworthy guide in the development of moral dispositions and actions. In other words, the school itself may generate conditions of opacity that prevent the necessary conditions for deeper senses of human development. Our hope is that there may be a way to reverse these institutional effects by constructing a better institutional architecture, which will rely on a new information economy.

WHAT IS AN INFORMATION ECONOMY?

Readers familiar with Plato's *Republic* and Lewis's *The Silver Chair* (from the Chronicles of Narnia series), or even viewers of *The Matrix* movie series, will immediately be aware of one of the central problems with certain human institutions: information. (It is also a problem of knowledge, but for the moment we will discuss the crisis as one of information.) In chapter seven of the *Republic* the great educator of Greece tells the story of an underground cave where humans are chained in such a way that their vision is limited to projections of shadows on a wall cast by a fire at the rear of the cave. The prisoners believe that the shadows comprise reality itself; they have known nothing else. One of the prisoners secures his freedom and begins an arduous journey up and out of the cave, where he encounters the bright light of multidimensional reality. The sun represents the good by which everything else is lit and may be seen. The newly freed prisoner encounters not illusion or a lesser form of reality (a facsimile), but a deeper sense of reality.[38]

One of the central lessons to take away from the parable of the cave is that more information exists outside of the cave than inside it. Knowledge about concrete and immaterial things and values are denied to prisoners in the cave, where they are kept ignorant in order, we might suppose, to administrate affairs without controversy, without cost. In his ascent the liberated prisoner discovers that self-knowledge, knowledge of others, knowledge of the world, knowledge of the eternal and knowledge of goods and purposes are more likely to occur in an environment where wide ranges of information are accessible to persons. However, the prisoner is not content with securing his own liberty; he realizes his duty to help liberate the others in the cave. Thus he travels back down, having this greater knowledge of reality originating from a richer information environment. Good educators are like that. They go back and suffer the toil of battling ignorance in order help fellow human beings (and society) toward proper function.

The cave, *The Silver Chair* and *The Matrix* are literary metaphors for philosophical realities where information is restricted, where diverse kinds of information necessary for knowledge acquisition and flourishing are limited and stand in need of correction. By narrowing the information base and limiting the capacity for inquiry, people predictably sink to the level of their surroundings; decision-making capacities as

---

[38]It amuses me (Steven) to watch the family cat, Rascal, seeming to prefer watching the shadows of a bird moving around as projected onto a window shade rather than watching the actual bird itself through a clear pane of glass. When teachers prefer the shadows to clearer articulations of reality, I become concerned.

well as the exercise of moral agency tend to constrict in direct proportion to the information environment. A similar problem exists for Christian educators where social institutions like education operate in a cave, drawn and quartered from the deeper semblances of reality.

What John Dewey said in 1936 remains true today: "The problem as to the *direction* in which we shall seek for order and clarity is the most important question facing educators today."[39] The direction of any social institution lies in the orientation of information maintained by that institution. And the direction of information within an institution often depends on the cost or price of that information. Yet this is not well-understood terrain in the field of education. It's not as if teachers, professors, administrators and leaders have not given enough attention to the informational direction within education, they have not given any attention to it. Many have pointed out the various effects of the information deficit, noting for example that it is unjust for a child not to receive a quality education, that inequities exist in educational services, that there are curricular wars and the like, but overall they have confused effects for causes. We believe that before an effective reform agenda ensues, particularly one informed by Christocentric lenses, Christian educationists must consider where the institution of education is today *informationally*, which will require comprehending the nature of an information economy.

Put simply, an information economy is how participants within a social institution like education acquire and use information, how they make decisions, how they act on information, and how that information is affected by the formal and informal rules of the game. In this sense an information economy is a property of the institutional environment (this is its ontological status). Information has direction, breadth and depth; it has quantitative and qualitative, theoretical and applied attributes. There is a fundamental, law-like principle of information in the complex good of education: *education goods tend to exchange in proper proportion to their information content.*[40]

---

[39]John Dewey, "Rationality in Education," *The Social Frontier* 3, no. 21 (December 1936): 73.

[40]This is a new value theory of information. See Jacob Rodriguez and Steven Loomis, "A New View of Institutions, Human Capital and Market Standardization," *Education, Knowledge &*

Studies by anthropologist Dean Simonton and social scientist Charles Murray suggest that the information environment for maximizing human development requires space for creativity, complexity, diversity, richness and multicultural understandings; it provides ample room for the exercise of reasonable degrees of liberty and autonomy, all in an environment that fosters thoughtful purpose and whose aim is proper function (development and flourishing).[41] For example, if a school is rich in information, then it is more likely that the education good generated by participants (e.g., teachers and students) at that school is likewise rich.[42] Alternatively, if a school is information poor, that is, if it doesn't optimize information content, then it is likely that the good being developed by that school is underdeveloped and poorer in quality.

The quality of the information environment has multiple variables but is without question influenced by a big one: leadership. A high-quality educational leader will consciously foster a rich information environment. Consider the great think tanks of recent history: the RAND Corporation, the Institute for Advanced Study, the Cowles Foundation, the Hoover Institution, the Brookings Institution or the Max Planck Society. Although most operate from a firm set of philosophical presuppositions about social reality, each of these requires a very broad, liberal information environment for the production of ideas and knowledge. Likewise, the best schools avoid too much rigidity in the information environment, whether in curriculum and cocurricular activities, in conduct, or in running the organization. Wheaton Academy in Illinois is a spectacular example of a school optimizing information in its production activities. Driving onto the campus we are met by a sign regulating speed: 9½ miles per hour. Not 10, not 8 mph, but 9½ mph. What does this signal to the observer? We have entered a creative community. It signals a lack of rigidity. It mocks the rules while continuing

---

Economy 1, no. 1 (2007): 93-105.

[41]Dean Simonton, "Sociocultural Context of Individual Creativity: A Transhistorical Time-series Analysis," *Genius and Creativity: Selected Papers* (Greenwich, Conn.: Ablex, 1997), pp. 3-28; and Charles Murray, *Human Accomplishment* (New York: HarperCollins, 2003), pp. 360-61.

[42]A forthcoming book by Gene Frost, the headmaster of Wheaton Academy in Illinois, nicely captures certain necessary conditions for preserving rich information within a quality school.

to have them. It suggests the Academy is a place of creative learning. And, indeed, since 1853 it has been a place for developing young scholars and creative artists. Effective leaders and creative participants of think tanks, universities and schools operate with a common logic on the fundamental principles of information: they try to optimize it in order to facilitate a complex education good: learning, knowledge, skills, wisdom and understanding.

Contrast the information environment fostered by the high-quality, ethical leader with the environment created by an efficient but cruel leader. Robert Service wrote a brilliant biography of one of the most proficient leaders in the twentieth century: Joseph Stalin. Service writes that Stalin was in many ways both an ordinary and extraordinary man: he was a common man yet a sort of genius, an effective bureaucrat and an even more efficient murderer, a writer and editor, a theorist and a poet, a family man and a charmer. In short, like many leaders, Stalin was a complex figure, not the simple-minded murderer that his name evokes. Some of the characteristics that come out in Service's biography of Stalin are important for the new educator to understand, chiefly because these are signals that result in greater central control and a threat to professional decision making. Notice the manner in which Stalin controlled the information agenda.

- Disorder must always be the diagnosis of the problem.

- Order through more central control must always be the solution; every issue is turned into a prescription for more control.

- We must oppose principles of federalism, decentralization, localism. (Too much variation is problematic.)

- We must eliminate tendencies that restrict or rival central command.

- People who hold on too tight to what was yesterday are a problem.

- The practical results of order count more than unnecessary squabbles over freedom.

- We must embrace, not deny, our unusual capacity for not being bored with administrative work.

- We must be good infighters, masters at bureaucratic manipulation.

- We will want to crush and humiliate the enemy (resisters to uniformity).

- We must fixate primarily on strategy, less on tactics. (We're in it to win the war.)

- We must sacrifice vanity for power.

- We can gain support from followers by conferring status (appeal to the ego).

- Cultivate jealousy among subordinates. Where constant bickering exists one person alone is allowed to arbitrate. (This was one of Stalin's most important methods.)

This informational agenda is not unique to Stalin or to nation-state dictators. Dispositions such as these find their operation in the effective bureaucrat, the assistant principal, the district superintendent, the dean of a school of education, a college provost or president, and even a Secretary of Education (obviously without extending commitments to the evil of murdering people). This is one type of personality in leadership. New educators would do well to navigate, as much as possible, around a person with this type of personality. They must learn to read informational signals properly. It takes an experienced educator to manage this kind of person.

Our larger point, however, is that a healthy school or college will be led well and will be small enough in scale (a key factor) that particular information vital to successful human exchange is not diminished or overshadowed by excessive standardization. Yet it also retains in equilibrium certain kinds of universal information (e.g., knowledge, curricular standards, academic traditions) necessary to guide generally the multifaceted enterprise of learning. In any case, information is vital to the production, acquisition and use of knowledge. The kind, quality, depth and breadth of information are vital to the education enterprise.

An important research question for scholars today is how to avoid information tradeoffs that negatively affect the learning environment.

Changing the direction of educational institutions and implementing serious, lasting reforms relies on maximizing the quality and quantity of information, both in terms of its direction and in terms of its flow through the institutions. In fact, the central problems of education today have less to do with money (though it includes money) than with its economy of information, principally the exclusion of certain types of information fundamental to educational production and the complex development of human beings. Indeed, information is one central variable in the generation of educational and social inequality, and it receives almost no attention from reformers because to our knowledge only a few within education are using an institutional lens of analysis.[43]

Few Christian scholars today, including those faculties in schools and departments of education, are aware of the primary causal mechanisms subsidizing the present direction of education in the United States and internationally. There are far more resources dedicated to the perpetuation and accommodation of the present direction of education (facilitating expansion, school-university alignment, standardization, central control, testing, assessment, accreditation, accountability rationales, etc.) than are allocated to its reform. In this regard, many Christian scholars may have lost the capacity to comment on the existing rule structure of education. If they were aware of the causal mechanisms, then they would also be aware that these information mechanisms are contributing to dangerous disparities in social inequality (e.g., expanding inequalities between whites and Latinos).[44] And to be aware of this and not do anything about it in one's scholarship and policy advocacy is tantamount to complicity. We trust that our colleagues are not intentionally complicit in the

---

[43]Some economists are applying institutional analysis to education. See, for example, Richard Nelson, "Factors Behind the Asian Miracle: Entrepreneurship, Education, and Finance," in *Finance, Research, Education and Growth*, ed. L. Paganeto and E. Phelps (New York: Palgrave Macmillan, 2003).

[44]For several relevant studies, see the *Latino Scorecard 2003: Grading the American Dream* (Los Angeles: United Way of Greater Los Angeles, 2003); *National Survey of Latinos: Education* (Washington, D.C.: Pew Hispanic Center/Kaiser Family Foundation, 2004); R. Kochlar, *Latino Labor Report, 2004* (Washington, D.C.: Pew Hispanic Center, 2005); and Rick Fry, *The High Schools Hispanics Attend: Size and Other Key Characteristics* (Washington, D.C.: Pew Hispanic Research Center, 2005).

furtherance of social inequality, because this would put them in direct conflict with Jesus' social gospel.[45] In any case, it is long past time to take the information economy of education seriously.

LEFT-RIGHT IDEOLOGY IS BLIND TO
DEEPER INSTITUTIONAL REALITIES

What often stands in the way of seeing deeper reality is ideology. Ideology can come from the politics of a guild. For example, the left-right lens of political ideology often obscures the intricate ontological dimensions of the information problem. The approach encompasses the view that "If only our party was in political power, we'd get it right." In reality, nearly all political ideologies today want to expand the size of the state and its manager, the government, that is, until the other political party seizes power. And the assignment of intentionality is fundamental to this form of analysis. Yet there is another way to view of the information problem. What if there were less intentionality than imagined? What if there were fewer devils than might be supposed? What if social structures operated as hidden persuaders, not determining human choices but influencing them in profound ways?

Intentionality often underwriting political or guild ideology is less of an operative force at the institutional level of analysis. There are two extreme positions operating within the broader framework of guild ideology. On the one hand are the system cheerleaders who circle the wagons at the smallest threat to the common school or public school orthodoxy.[46] These are the true believers who view government-funded-and-provided schooling as necessary to the body politic. They defend state schooling with religious fervor. On the other hand, the system crashers want to tear it down and shift focus to alternative education markets.[47] Here, advo-

---

[45]Alasdair MacIntyre suggests that moral responsibility within the social sphere holds where (1) the acts of moral agents are intentional, (2) the incidental aspects of those actions ought to have been known by the moral agent, and (3) the reasonably predictable effects of actions also ought to have been known by the moral agent. See MacIntyre, "Social Structures and their Threats to Moral Agency," *Philosophy* 74 (1999): 311-29.

[46]Linda Darling Hammond, *A Good Teacher in Every Classroom: Preparing the Highly Qualified Teachers Our Children Deserve* (New York: Jossey-Bass, 2005).

[47]William Cox, *Tyranny Through Public Education: The Case Against Government Control of Edu-*

cates seek privatization on market terms, dislodging the state and its government from directly providing schooling services, but allowing for the funding of such services. In some ways both views have in common a larger regulatory state, and for varying reasons both sides offer compelling arguments and evidences.

However, before engaging the political or ideological questions, there are the much deeper institutional or structural issues, for example, the recurring cost-generating inequalities and opacity applied against institutional participants that have ontological priority to questions of the guild. These are the ontological questions of institutional reality that new educators should be aware.

While many academics do indeed notice the effects of the technical direction of education (they typically cite authors like Jonathan Kozol, Alphie Kohn, Debra Meirer and Linda-Darling Hammond), it is less recognized that increased system standardization is a generator of *informational* inequality, in effect producing social and developmental costs. The loss of diversity, the loss of freedom, the loss of ingenuity and creative capacities, the refusal to let one thousand flowers bloom, and the quickly reduced ability to recognize and incorporate knowledge created outside of the evolving rule set conditioned by institutional uniformity—all contribute to costs raised against the social welfare. Social costs are the immeasurable, counterfactual conditions of human underdevelopment, as well as the measurable effects of forgone production by otherwise (potentially) productive people.[48]

A particular advantage for new educators is to study the social choice question. The problem of social choice is that there are liberty tensions arising from the claims, dispositions, actions and goods pursued by individuals and those allowable by collectives. From any given social environment emerges the complex challenge of aggregating diverse individual preferences by the social order. The social choice problem seeks to understand and reconcile individual convictions and preferences

---

cation (Fairfax, Va.: Allegiance Press, 2003).
[48]See Henry M. Levin's work at Columbia University, including a working paper from Levin's symposium "The Social Costs of Inadequate Education," October 24-25, 2005. See http://www.schoolfunding.info/resource_center/research/2005symposium.pdf (accessed 6/1/2009).

largely by showing a rational direction across the social sphere, showing a path for all participants to follow. To be rational means reading the institutional signals correctly, going along with the prevailing direction of education, accommodating it, abiding the rules, not offending the collective order and its leaders. For the new educator this means practicing one's profession according to the rules, not independent of them. This is the sole criterion of rationality.

Social institutions, like education, mediate the content of the signal in the form of rules and other information. Contract theories of society and the state, predicated on philosophies of the public sphere, help to resolve the inherent cultural tensions between competing interests, such as individuals or small groups pursuing their own ends, as well as a society's ordering of scarce resources and collective goods like schooling and higher education. The social contract stipulates that certain rights and obligations be recognized throughout society and culture. Stipulations are either formal (e.g., constitutions, statutes) or informal (e.g., customs, traditions, myths, ceremonies). So, for example, forming a viable education system in a society involves a series of questions and procedures concerning the means and ends of the activity, and ultimately on who decides, what principles and criteria ground those decisions, as well as the nature of the tradeoffs made under conditions of scarcity (i.e., limited resources for a near limitless set of human demands and wants).

Kenneth Arrow's impressive work in the area of social choice recognizes what perhaps is the core problem of civil society, that is, how to reconcile individual and collective preferences within the limits of human cooperation. As Arrow says, "the true grounds for disagreement [in social choice] are the conditions which it is reasonable to impose on the aggregation procedure."[49] The imposition principle can be achieved coercively, as through Arrow's dictator or C. S. Lewis's "conditioners," where one individual or a small group makes decisions for the rest, constraining forms of freedom in radical ways. However, the individual-collective problem raised by social choice theory may also be achieved with a minimum of coercion, as through the stable informational environment of

[49]Kenneth Arrow, *Social Choice & Individual Values*, 2nd ed. (New Haven, Conn.: Yale University Press, 1963), p. 103.

expanding institutions. Logically antecedent to *how* the social choice set is constituted are philosophies of life, models of thought and worldviews, and how these account for reality, being, relations, knowledge, values, action, and the nature and purpose of social institutions themselves, divine or human.

We should recognize that our professional inclination in education lies with not rocking the boat. Many Christian educators have interpreted Romans 13, Titus 3, and 1 Peter 3 in a narrow sense of not resisting any authority. It is, of course, far easier for institutional participants and leaders to comply with the prevailing institutional direction than muster the courage to resist or change it and bear the significant temporal costs of not joining up with the dominant group. For example, an academic leader at a highly competitive liberal arts college in the Midwest was reported to have said in the college newspaper "that there is a push in academia to have external objective measures to show that students are learning, such as using more standardized tests" which that college "will probably implement."[50] Paraphrasing political philosopher James Scott, rather than bearing the cost of leadership in resisting technical trends that threaten human forms of education, accommodating leaders are quick to discount educational means and ends that are not assimilable to institutionally prized (and priced) information.[51] It reflects a model of leadership far less amiable to diverse sources of information, much less capable of protecting freedom in higher learning, and couples education itself to central rules (e.g., formal assessment procedures) making all participants, faculty and students alike, submissive to the thin simplifications of measures and outcomes imposed by well-meaning externalities. Consequently, complex education at all levels tends to adapt to the logic and simplistic forms of the institutional machinery, which is its information base.

---

[50]The obvious question is, if a little standardization is a good thing, wouldn't a lot of standardization under a central authority be even better? Leaders in Christian higher education need to think strategically in order to originate a coherent approach to the pressing issues surrounding central control and standardization.

[51]James Scott, *Seeing Like a State: How Certain Schemes to Improve the Human Condition Have Failed* (New Haven, Conn.: Yale University Press, 1998), esp. pp. 264-65.

CHRISTIAN EDUCATORS AND THE PROFESSIONAL OBLIGATION

It is a promising development that Christian theorists and philosophers, such as Dallas Willard, have recently begun to recognize and report on these significant informational barriers within the larger institution of education. Willard is apposite here: "Education as now understood—the actual social practice—*cannot* come to grips with the realities of the human self. It is not just a matter of 'separation of church and state' and all that has come to mean. Rather, education (the institution) has now adopted values, attitudes, and practices that make any rigorous understanding of the human self and life impossible."[52] Willard's observation is correct in the institutional sense. What has occurred is the obscuring of what a human being is, its ultimate purpose and so forth, which in turn obscures the very nature and purpose of *all* production activities in education, higher or lower in form.

What we have argued should be a little frightening. It is an unarguable axiom that human development and social systems depend for their health on the vigor and ethic of their institutions of education. Thorstein Veblen believed that "nothing more irretrievably shameful could overtake modern civilization than the miscarriage . . . of learning, which is the most valued spiritual asset of civilized mankind."[53] Many philosophers (e.g., Plato) and economists (e.g., Adam Smith) have understood that the vigor and ethic of the institution of education likewise depends on its information economy. The multifaceted connection between a first-rate institution of education, the justice of the *polis* (society as a political community) and the human flourishing of the *demos* (the complex nexus between the common people) is without serious dispute.[54]

For example, following principles first introduced in Aristotle's *Nicomachean Ethics*, political philosopher John Rawls suggests that complex social institutions work best when "human beings enjoy the exercise of

---

[52]Dallas Willard, *Rennovation of the Heart: Putting on the Character of Christ* (Colorado Springs: NavPress, 2002), p. 47.
[53]Thorstein Veblen, *The Higher Learning in America* (New York: Cosimo Classics, 2005), p. 8. The publishing house Hill and Wang first published this work in 1918.
[54]See, for example, the collection of essays edited by Bradley Watson, *Civic Education and Culture* (Wilmington, Del.: ISI Books, 2005).

their realized capacities (their innate or trained abilities), and this enjoyment increases the more the capacity is realized, or the greater its complexity."[55] Creativity depends for its lifeblood on certain informational conditions inherent to the individual student.[56] It is the set of information that the individual student as an educational participant brings to the complex process of education. Entrepreneurship, a role fundamental to a healthy economy, requires skills of information development that lean heavily on the individual.[57] Human accomplishment requires particular principles and conditions that permit and foster purpose, autonomy, single-mindedness and certain aspects of individualism (in the best sense) in order to produce transcendental goods in a variety of fields. Yet the standardization of education today in the United States too often removes the capacity to consider these necessary conditions. In short, they cannot reach agenda primarily due to their cost.

Educators now face a decision. Will we proceed further into the technical direction that ultimately leads to human opacity and the I-It condition? Will we permit the information economy of education to slide further into banal uniformity and standardization? As C. S. Lewis queried, will we continue to pursue the abolition of man? Or will we see this as an opportunity to fulfill the mandate by Jesus Christ to salt institutions with better ways of structuring and doing education? Is there a civil-rights opportunity before educators concerned with justice? Will Christian educators institute new theories and practices that will match contemporary or future challenges? It is plausible to believe that many insiders and outsiders in our audience will continue to choose the path of least cost, either not seeing a problem at all or recognizing then ignoring it. Our hope is that at least a few educators will begin to work on this problem.

Even skeptics will admit that an incremental civil-rights reform and renewal of the schools and higher education over the next twenty to

---

[55]John Rawls, *A Theory of Justice* (Cambridge, Mass.: Harvard University Press, 1971), p. 476. Rawls undercuts his own argument at other points within the text.

[56]Mihaly Csikszentmihalyi, *Creativity: Flow and the Psychology of Discovery and Invention* (New York: HarperCollins, 1996).

[57]Joseph Schumpeter, *Capitalism, Socialism and Democracy*, 3rd ed. (New York: HarperCollins, 1950).

thirty years could have important effects for the field of education. Not least, we could develop new (or older) theoretical understandings of equilibrium points between pupils and teachers in the schools, between colleges and universities and their constituents. Ideally, these long-term effects would center on reconfiguring educational philosophy and on reorienting the frames, categories and paradigms of educational theory and practice in order to liberalize for Christ an increasingly illiberal sector of education, to bring Christocentric understandings and knowledge in teaching, research, agenda, and solving important educational problems of our day.[58] This does not mean that public education will become Christian. What is interesting is that Jesus Christ did not enter the material realm and die to make us Christians. Christ died to make us fully human; being Christian is the means to be fully human. Being fully human means relating with the Creator on his terms, not our own. This recognition would of course require a new way to research and examine the institution of education.

We propose to you that responsibility for understanding the informational dynamics within education is a professional obligation. Christian educators have a double duty to approach the broad field of education intelligently, integratively and transcending present informational constraints, and unified in Christ's passion for human beings and their full and complex development (cf. Mt 22:37; Rom 12:2). In its most basic form Christian civil-rights movements of the past had at least five stages: (1) ending denial, (2) facing reality truthfully, (3) mustering up the courage to engage consistent with Christ-ordered incentives, (4) setting out new theory and practice that leads to institutional reform, and (5) willingly bearing the sometimes significant costs of opposition. The civil-rights movement we speak of here requires a sophisticated (not sophistical) strategy for institutional reform; it operates on principles of maximizing information for human development and is ultimately grounded in the mission of Christ

---

[58]This claim is based on our knowledge of the field, overviews of seven widely read teacher education journals, the organizational structures of Council for Christian Colleges and Universities colleges and universities, and the self-evident lack of Christian-influenced theories of education penetrating the broader institution.

himself, not as a religious figure but as an ontological being-in-fact. The two—human development and the mission of Christ—cannot be separated; one entails the other.

On one level it is a well-known fact that the institution of education is marginalizing or eliminating sources of information. As two important examples, institutional secularization over the years and the contemporary processes of standardization has removed a lot of information. We all know this. Yet it is from our perspective more than a little troubling that the humanity of Jesus Christ (and particularly as Lord of the universe) does not publicly inform any area of theory or policy in American public education. Let us not pass over this point too quickly. The most intelligent man who ever walked the earth—the sage of Nazareth, studied and followed by millions and millions of people, arguably having more influence than any other intellectual in history—informs no part of educational theory or practice. The greatest teacher who ever taught has little or no voice at the table of teacher preparation or educational policy. Plato, Aristotle, Karl Marx (e.g., through the critical pedagogues) and Charles Darwin (e.g., through the psychological behaviorists) have more residual influence over American education agenda than does Jesus.

We would be entirely misunderstood if the interpretation of what we are saying here led to the belief that we advocate some Christian-influenced political agenda, such as those of the recent past (1980s and Jerry Falwell, or the 1990s and Pat Robertson, etc.). We are not doing politics here. Instead, we are doing applied ontology and social philosophy necessary for successful education. The redemption of reason in the schools and higher education is not concerned with ideology or politics, or reducing reality to the sense-perceptible world or to some proclamation about cultural relativism and diversity. It transcends those things. We are suggesting that Jesus Christ's influence in the Christian educator's life is not merely a private affair; it is very much a public one. In this sense we are aligned with J. E. Schwartz, who advocated that Christian teachers within the public schools manifest Christ's influence in their lives naturally, neither adopting a burly evangelistic position nor assuming the privatized position, but as "golden-rule truth-seekers" who "exercise religious liberty while at the same time extending that same liberty to others."[59] To our minds this makes sense and fits well with the Augustinian position and our understandings of the Christian Scriptures. Christian educators in the secular environment, public or private, can simply operate without fear of sanction or reprisal.

Inasmuch as the formal teachings of Jesus and his disciples form no part of theory, policy or practice in U.S. education today, it ought not to be surprising then that there are no Christian educators at the fore of educational reform and renewal, and clearly none at the theoretical level. Unlike fields such as history, philosophy or economics, where prominent scholars such as Mark Noll and George Marsden in history, Alvin Plantinga, J. P. Moreland and William Craig in philosophy, and P. J. Hill in economics help to steward the direction of ideas and theory in those fields, there are no go-to Christian scholars in the field of education.[60] If stewardship means actively caring for and governing institutional direction, we regret to say that many Christian educationists have not been active and integrative stewards over educational practice and theory.[61] Why is that? If education is one of the largest institutions in the economy (it is) and certainly a foremost cultural area for idea production and belief formation, why are Christians underrepresented in the vital area of theoretical work? What are the institutional and informational factors at work that motivate U.S. Christian educators to compartmentalize religious faith? As we suggested earlier, these matters are too often examined through the lens of left-right politics and ideology. We suggest that they should be viewed through deeper lenses of analysis, that is, through theology, ontology and institutional (economic) thought.

---

[59]J. E. Schwartz, "Christians Teaching in the Public Schools: What Are Some Options?" *Christian Scholar's Review* 26, no. 3 (1997): 305.

[60]The exception may be Nicholas Wolterstorff, who has written a great deal on the field of education, but his following tends to be narrow and has not penetrated the larger institution. The writings of Alasdair MacIntyre have provoked some thought among British and European philosophers of education. See Joseph Dunne and Padraig Hogan, eds., *Education and Practice: Upholding the Integrity of Teaching and Learning* (Oxford: Blackwell, 2004).

[61]For a fine discussion concerning educational stewardship, please see Chris Golde and George Walker, *Envisioning the Future of Doctoral Education: Preparing Stewards of the Discipline: Carnegie Essays on the Doctorate* (San Francisco: Jossey-Bass, 2006).

We may take some courage that the abolition and civil-rights movements, both *public* in scope and argument, were well represented by thoughtful Christian educators willing and knowledgeable about how to integrate their faith commitments with the intractable institutional problems of their day. They were engaged in both the theory and practice for problem resolution. In classrooms, in the schools, on college campuses, in the streets and in the centers of power, Christians as public intellectuals were engaged in advocacy on behalf of the poor, the disabled and the disenfranchised. Certainly, the church and its adherents once had the wherewithal to outthink their critics. This is our heritage. Nevertheless, the clear absence of Christian theorists within the broader market of education, particularly in the public sector, may suggest an unwillingness and inability to integrate their faith commitments. There does not appear to be an active, high-level apologetic for Christocentric knowledge informing the greater institution of education in the United States and worldwide. Christian educators, it seems, do not care to bear the cost in self-development toward this end, nor do we care to take social risks. We see little wrong done by a state or an accrediting firm,[62] or if we do, we do not know how to steward the institution in a different direction so that a healthier informational equilibrium exists.

INFORMATION AS TECHNICAL POLICIES AND RULES
THE COMMUNITY KILLER

A healthier informational equilibrium for schools must operate on a proper conception of rules. Teachers in school districts and faculty members in colleges and universities across the United States are today witnessing the deprofessionalization of their vocations, though many are unaware of the actual mechanisms because the causes are so hidden and the effects so incremental.[63] Let us begin by observing that if edu-

---

[62]As Kenneth Young, Charles Chambers and H. R. Kells note, "Accreditation is highly vulnerable to misuse and abuse by those who wish to turn it to other purposes." These authors go on to suggest that a presence of "countervailing forces [exists] . . . to offset perversions of the process or power plays" (p. x). We find the ready and hopeful presence of "countervailing forces" wishful thinking at the moment. See *Understanding Accreditation: Contemporary Perspectives on Issues and Practices in Evaluating Educational Quality* (San Francisco: Jossey-Bass, 1983).

[63]See the excellent study by Richard Ingersoll, *Who Controls Teachers' Work* (Cambridge, Mass.: Harvard University Press, 2003).

cation is a liberal art (or the locus of the liberal arts), then we might expect that certain conditions ought to obtain within the informational environment of a school or college. Among these are opportunities for dissenting views, openness and transparency, valuing diversity of methodological inquiry and practice, minimal emphasis on specific rules and maximal emphasis on general values, and optimization of the flow of information (more specifically, knowledge) into the learning environment and exchange processes.[64]

Within any society there are generally two sources of information regulating educational development and production. First, there are the centuries-old *informal* traditions of academic disciplines and teaching, which, like medicine, make education a professional art and which loosely guide its practice. Second, there are the formal policy- and rule-making functions of bureaucratic structures, such as those articulated by social theorist Max Weber and others, making education and its management a science. Ideally, these two approaches to educational production should function in some rough equilibrium. One in which education as an art exists as improvisational exchange in the complex, multivariable, never repeatable environment of actual exchange between participants, and where the science of education generates some useful and predictable range of measurement, classification and decision patterns in planning and production.

Unfortunately, at nearly every level of education in the United States, the reality is that the former is giving way to the latter. The science of education (it is thought) makes things more efficient and reduces production costs; the art and improvisation of education (it is thought) makes things more variable and raises production costs. Consider the so-called Taylor system of scientific management first applied to schooling in 1912. Note the parallels with the contemporary work of schoolteachers in large-scale urban school districts: "Each worker received an instruction card which described in minute detail 'not only what is to be done, but how it is to be done and the exact time allowed

---

[64]For an example of these principles, please see the work by Whitworth College president William Robinson, *Leading People from the Middle: The Universal Mission of Heart and Mind* (Provo, Utah: Executive Excellence, 2002).

for doing it.' The task for an individual worker was theoretically regulated to get the maximum output from a man without injuring his
health."[65] Fredrick Taylor's principles of scientific management were
handy at a time when industry dictated educational production.[66] Soon
after their application schools began to look and function like Henry
Ford's automobile factory, which had also applied the Taylor system.
The Taylor system engendered four general principles, which can be
linked to our contemporary system of teacher training and professional
teaching performance:

1. Replace rule-of-thumb work methods with methods based on a scientific study of the tasks.

2. Scientifically select, train, teach and develop the most suitable person for each job, rather than leaving individuals to passively learn the
   craft on their own.

3. Managers must provide detailed instructions and supervision to each
   worker to ensure that the work is done in a scientific (efficient) way.

4. Divide work between managers and workers. The managers apply
   scientific management principles to planning and supervising the
   work, and the workers carry out the tasks.

After machines were adjusted to the efficient industry of humans, humans would then be adjusted to the efficient industry of the machine.[67] In
similar manner, formal rules once again are becoming more important,
more central to production concerns than the informal educational traditions and rule-of-thumb human judgment "on the scene" of context-bound
human activity. Due to the competition for scarce resources, "scientific"
approaches to education are—and will continue to be for some time—the
rational way to proceed. For compatibilists between the art and science of
education there is a general tendency to deny that production scarcities
exist thereby assuming that the science and art of education can neatly
coexist. This in spite of the disparate cost differences between their bases

---

[65]Raymond Callahan, *Education and the Cult of Efficiency* (Chicago: University of Chicago
   Press, 1962), p. 31.

[66]Fredrick Taylor, *Principles of Scientific Management* (New York: Harper, 1911).

[67]Daniel Bell, "The Study of Man: Adjusting Men to Machines: Social Scientists Explore the
   World of the Factory," *Commentary*, January 1947, pp. 79-88.

of information. In agreeing with the view held by Adam Smith, Nobel economist R. H. Coase said, "The extent to which we follow any course of action depends on its cost."[68]

John Dewey answers the compatibilist's challenge in these unequivocally positivist terms:

> Here lies the heart of our present social problem. Science has hardly been used to modify men's fundamental acts and attitudes in social matters. It has been used to extend enormously the scope and power of interests and values which anteceded its rise. Here is the contradiction in our civilization. The potentiality of science as the most powerful instrument of control which has ever existed puts to mankind its one outstanding present challenge. . . .
>
> We no longer regard plagues, famine, and disease as visitations of necessary "natural law" or of a power beyond nature. By preventative means of medicine and public hygiene as well as by various remedial measures we have an idea, if not in fact, placed technique in the stead of magic and chance. . . .
>
> [T]he physical and mathematical technique upon which a planned control of social results depends has made in the meantime incalculable progress. The conclusion is inevitable. The outer arena of life has been transformed by science. The effectively working mind and character of man have hardly been touched.[69]

Rules emerge from the predictability work of social science. As philosopher Ian Hacking suggests, "the idea of human nature was displaced by a model of normal people with laws of dispersion."[70] Hacking shows that the development of statistical laws increased the surveillance capacity of the state, and this information environment, we argue, informed the rule-making functions of nation-states, "developed for purposes of social control."[71] Uniform rules lift certain responsibilities from local decision-makers. A clever illustration is when social critic

---

[68]R. H. Coase, *Essays on Economics and Economists* (Chicago: University of Chicago Press, 1994), p. 99.

[69]John Dewey, *The Essential Dewey, Vol. 1: Pragmatism, Education, Democracy*, ed. Larry A. Hickman and Thomas M. Alexander (Bloomington: Indiana University Press, 1998), p. 366.

[70]Hacking, *Taming of Chance*, p. vii.

[71]Ibid., p. 6.

and iconoclast Christopher Hitchens wrote up a piece for *Vanity Fair* describing his rampage of social disobedience by violating many of New York City's (Mayor Bloomberg's) "petty ordinances" such as lifting his feet off of bicycle pedals ($100 fine), sitting on a milk crate ($105 fine) and committing a public nuisance by feeding pigeons in Central Park ($50 fine). These rules emerged from the social science theory called "broken windows," first applied by Mayor Rudolph Giuliani (1994-2001) in New York and continued, even enhanced, by Bloomberg.[72] The question Hitchens raises is appropriate here: "Why are the people of America's most cosmopolitan city being treated like backward children?"[73] Under political, social or educational behaviorism, humans are often treated as though they are backward children.

When we work with new and veteran educators, one of the key areas is rule making for the individual classroom and the school. We try to get the new educator to see that there are generally two types of rules and that students require different rules at different stages of their development. Rules in the second-grade classroom will have different characteristics (and seek unique ends) than rules in the eleventh grade. At the lower stage of development the rule may have to perform more modeling. This means that when a teacher in the second grade develops classroom rules, he or she will make them more specific and also will want to provide exemplars for the rules. That is less the case for the eleventh-grade classroom, where rules tend to be fewer, are framed in more general terms and (hopefully) need fewer specific exemplars of the virtue entailed by the rule. The school is designed to progressively elevate a student's response to cooperation on general principles (virtues, duties, purposes) and attenuate reliance on specific rules. However, this idea depends for its success on the schools developing proper sentiments and higher reason. C. S. Lewis addresses this problem specifically in the *Abolition of Man*. We can no longer take for granted, Lewis suggests, that the schools are able to reliably inculcate virtue.

---

[72]See, for example, George Kelling and James Q. Wilson, "Broken Windows," *The Atlantic Monthly*, March 1982.
[73]Christopher Hitchens, "I Fought the Law," *Vanity Fair*, February 2004, pp. 70-75.

If we look deeper, the problem with the New York situation does not lie with Mayor Bloomberg's alleged pettiness. There will always be such personalities in positions of authority. Rather, what Hitchens and others do not seem to realize is that many people *want* to adjust their beliefs and actions under prevailing circumstances to the principle of least action. Many trade off their liberty for order. Many people are resigned to being treated like "backward children" because they value order more than personal responsibility. People often assent to central and formal rules on the basis of bringing about greater certainty in social relations (lessening personal risk), which tends to reduce conflict. Rather than being my brother's keeper and being kept by him (i.e., self-regulation and local community regulation), I trade off this responsibility to a central authority that regulates people efficiently from a distance through an impersonal bureaucracy. A weak will makes this the easier path. The instruments of control are the formal rules, usually originating from a central authority who is attempting to bring perceptible and legible order over a complex and seemingly chaotic human sphere (e.g., a social institution). Under forces of standardization the individual decision maker, who might be a local principal, teacher, student or a college professor or administrator, has less information, not more, from which to make a decision. The rule constrains individual capacity by failing to deal with context and denying exceptions. Consequently, the loss of information (e.g., the loss of context) denied to the decision maker by the uniform rule necessarily constrains his or her options and choices, thus depleting the need for wisdom *(sophia)* and practical judgment *(metis)*.[74]

The two vital areas of human responsibility—wisdom and practical judgment—are effectively subverted by uniformity. For example, zero

---

[74]With reference to schools, political theorists John Chubb and Terry Moe make the public-choice argument that a central problem of public schools is the organizational constraints on decision making of local educational leaders. Decision making in such contexts, they argue, would benefit from a competitive environment offered by market forces. See John Chubb and Terry Moe, "Politics, Markets, and the Organization of Schools," *American Political Science Review* 82 (1988): 1065-87. This paper was later expanded in the book by Chubb and Moe, *Politics, Markets, and America's Schools* (Washington, D.C.: Brookings Institution, 1990). As we might expect, independent or nongovernment schools tend to preserve marginally more decision making within the individual school. See Martha Alt and Katharin Peter, *Private Schools: A Brief Portrait* (Washington, D.C.: National Center for Education Statistics 2002).

tolerance rules applied in many schools are meant to equalize the application of rules without exceptions. Managers and elites see exceptions as rule breakers, a violation of fairness, which is usually defined
on terms of sameness. Many educational managers think that making
exceptions to rules raises prospects of discrimination. Of course it
does, but not in the manner in which many educational leaders typically mean. Sitting on committees, one will hear the familiar, "Does
an exception to our rules here establish a precedent?" To an audience
that is interested in risk reduction, there is little use in explaining the
differences between exceptions or exemptions to a rule and the prece-
dents that establish a new application of a rule.

The process of adhering to strict uniformity allows the school manager to mitigate his or her risk (lawsuits, suspension, firing, etc.) in rule
application by ignoring context. The kid who forgets to remove his father's pocketknife from his lunch pail after a Saturday fishing trip and
inadvertently brings the knife to school is punished (*must* be punished)
in the same manner and to the same degree as the kid who is an active
gang member and deliberately brings a knife to school to commit an
assault. This is an injustice because the school manager, who has lost
the practice of knowing how and when to apply judgment in a concrete
situation, is prevented by the rules from adjudicating and discriminat-
ing context; wisdom and practical judgment are thereby subverted. The
leader transforms into a mere manager of the rules.

There are many causal forces in this press toward uniformity and standardization, too many to account for in a project of this nature. Part of
the reason includes a change in educational leadership, itself an effect of
the changing incentive structures of educational management. Sometime
between the 1960s and 1980s, following a decided shift in the orientation
of information, educational leaders evolved from leaders of virtue to
managers of demand.[75] Perhaps the most glaring example of this shift
was Allan Bloom's biting account of the spinelessness of university leaders during the most radical incidents of student unrest during the 1960s.[76]

---

[75]See, for example, David Tyack and Elisabeth Hansot, *Managers of Virtue: Public School Leadership in America 1820-1980* (New York: Basic Books, 1986).
[76]Allan Bloom, *The Closing of the American Mind* (New York: Simon & Schuster, 1987).

In one sense it became too costly to "lead," as that term was once understood. In times past, a leader of virtue was a school principal or superintendent, or a college provost or president concerned with complex inputs into the development of human beings, the achievement of their capacities and excellences (moral and intellectual virtues), whether in schools or in higher education. They were more concerned with the individual organization and its capacity to produce the educational good than political correctness emanating from the broader institution. This leader was also concerned with the direction of society by focusing on the deeper ethical and cognitive development of the individual human beings comprising it. Schools and colleges were to develop liberal thinking and ethically responsible students in order to move them toward ethical and responsible autonomy (active, responsible citizenship), a condition for viable democracy. Schools and colleges under the leaders of virtue model recognized the inherent value of particular information and took an active interest in its preservation.[77] The leader understood the educational environment the way a riverboat pilot understood the complex ebb-and-flow environment of a river—in which *metis* knowledge resists standardization because "the environments in which it is exercised are so complex and nonrepeatable that formal procedures of rational decision making are impossible to apply."[78]

The manager of demand today is a bureaucratic "quantity adjuster" (to borrow Friedrich Hayek's phrase) in the schools and higher education. His or her primary concern is reduced to managing the demand for education, increasing the number of participants, increasing the number of rules and procedures, regulating uniformity arising from the technical framework, posturing assent to political correctness (another form of rules), and focusing on the conditioning of individuals as a

---

[77]For example, apart from Nathan Hatch, Notre Dame's former provost and Wake Forrest's current president, there are no Fred Terman's in Christian higher education today. Fred Terman was the bold provost at Stanford University who, between 1955-1965, set out using certain principles of leadership to help make Stanford University into what it is today, perhaps the highest-quality university in the world. Terman understood the key element of quality higher education: marry the very best faculty to the best students and research resources and get out of the way. See Stewart Gillmor's, *Fred Terman at Stanford: Building a Discipline, a University, and Silicon Valley* (Stanford, Calif.: Stanford University Press, 2004).

[78]Scott, *Seeing Like a State*, p. 316.

means for bringing regulative order to society (often the highest value). For reasons having to do with information and incentives, the manager of demand is perceived as the rational prototype in education "leadership" today. The prototype is rational because such a manager responds to the logic of incentives involved with growing and expanding the institution (helping to lower its costs), a process of scaling up (making bigger) organizations. On the level of their aptitude, they tend to see themselves as planners and engineers of society—conditioning participants to obey rules and policies for the "greater good." While education leaders once had the capacity and willingness to lead and take responsibility for their own decisions, and at the same time being comfortable to allow diversity on nonessentials, genuine leadership in education is becoming increasingly rare.

New educators are especially prone to dissatisfaction in this environment. They come to the schools for jobs and soon discover that schools are becoming illiberal environments. New educators often feel handcuffed by their inability to exercise their profession as they had imagined.

CONCLUSION

The information economy of a social institution like education is subject to forces of scale and scarcity. Scale and scarcity set limits on the kind, volume, breadth and depth of information used in production. The information that is associated with the local and individual is traded off for that which can be standardized and governed efficiently by the few from a distance. This in turn affects the decision-making environment for professionals like teachers, professors, managers and leaders, reducing variation and the diversity of thought and practice. While the information economy for a complex good like education should look different than the information economy for a simple good (e.g., steel, widgets, hamburgers), there is enormous pressure today to underwrite the educational enterprise on terms of less expensive information, on terms of efficiency, standardization and so-called accountability (greater central control). Few Christian educationists are aware of the phenomenon, and fewer still have written about it. To bring about change will require a new (and at the same time old) way of looking at education, which will take some serious theoretical work and developing an ability to call into question the institution and its direction. But by entering the profession with eyes wide open, the new educator will be better equipped to navigate the rough (for the good educator) institutional terrain of education. He or she will be better positioned to influence that terrain in positive ways at the classroom and school levels, preserving the informational environment necessary for quality education.

5

Social Ethics and
the Institution of Education

In essence, we have been discussing what happens when education as a large institution and as a process is reduced to a utility function. Don't let this language intimidate or confuse you; it is a relatively simple but important concept used by social scientists to try to quantify the "value added" in receiving (in this case) an education. The value-added approach to education is the coming trend and relies on a cost-benefit analysis of the outputs of schooling and higher education. Its genesis originates in business models and their so-called production functions (the economic relation of inputs to outputs). A positivist and empiricist commitment to verification is at its core.

Christian educators do well to understand *why* these models, concerned with the production of simple goods like widgets, chairs and gardening tools, are being applied to a complex good like education, which is focused on the dissemination and acquisition of knowledge and skills. Because educational decisions are increasingly made on a cost-benefit analysis, principles of efficiency today mirror the "cult of efficiency movement" in U.S. public education from 1900 to 1930. Raymond Callahan's work is preeminent in the efficiency movement.

> My investigation revealed that [the] adoption [of business values and practices in educational administration] had started about 1900 and had reached the point, by 1930, that, among other things, school administrators perceived themselves as business managers, or, as they would say, "school executives" rather than as scholars and educational philosophers. The question which now became significant was *why* had school ad-

ministrators adopted business values and practices and assumed the posture of the business executive? Education is not a business. The school is not a factory.

What was unexpected was the extent, not only of the power of the business-industrial groups, but the strength of the business ideology in the American culture on the one hand and the extreme weakness and vulnerability of schoolmen, especially school administrators, on the other. I had expected more professional autonomy and I was completely unprepared for the extent and degree of capitulation by administrators to whatever demands were made upon them. I was surprised and then dismayed to learn how many decisions they made or were forced to make, not on educational grounds, but as a means of appeasing their critics in order to maintain their positions in the school.[1]

Appeasement is a cost-lowering set of decisions. One of the core problems with the cult-of-efficiency movement, in the early twentieth century, as now, is a role confusion induced by confusion over the nature and complexity of the education good. Basically, society and education participants lose sight of the first aims of education. There are professors of education today who do not know what the education good is or what the first aims of education are. It is a problem of not taking a proper teleological account of education. Thus, teaching and leadership became intimately tied up with management schemes from industry: the rational, the measurable and the calculable. Teachers and managers come to be regarded more as instruments of efficiency than as educators or leaders. The tenuous relationship between business principles and education belies the reality of teaching and leadership as complex intellectual work. Hage and Powers (1992) illustrate the distinction between industrial and postindustrial roles, which, for our purposes, sheds some light on the misapplication of industrial expectations to roles occupied and performed by educators (see fig. 5.1).

We saw in chapter four how decision making and leadership in education is often predicated on utility and self-interest (basically, on cost),

---

[1]Raymond Callahan, *Education and the Cult of Efficiency: A Study of the Social Forces That Have Shaped the Administration of the Public Schools* (Chicago: University of Chicago Press, 1962), pp. vii-viii.

Ideal-Type Characteristics of Industrial Roles	Ideal-Type Characteristics of Postindustrial Roles
1. physical activity	1. mental activity
2. transformation of material objects	2. information gathering and problem solving
3. roles defined in terms of a narrow range of prescribed tasks and routine activities for which goals and procedures are clearly specified	3. roles defined by goals for which no certain procedure can be specified, consequently involving a relatively wide range of nonroutine tasks
4. time and place for role performance are tightly constrained and there is freedom from role-related concerns when outside that place in time and place	4. the time and place for role activity are not tightly constrained, and people have difficulty insulating one social domain (e.g., family or work) from worries or demands emanating from other domains
5. humans as appendages of machines; machines determine how the work is to be done, how long it will take, and what the finished product will look like	5. people determine how work will be done, how much time will be spent and what the finished product will look like; machines are tools
6. satisfactory job performance produces a sense of completion	6. satisfactory job performance produces a sense of mastery
7. nonephemeral aspects of role resist change	7. roles are frequently and substantially redefined via negotiation and even conflict
8. low interaction rates, even for managers; that is, the role-set is small and contained	8. high interaction rates; that is, the role set is large and demanding

Figure 5.1. Contrast between the nature of work in industrial and postindustrial society*

*Jerald Hage and Charles H. Powers, *Post-Industrial Lives: Roles and Relationships in the 21ˢᵗ Century* (Newbury Park, Calif.: Sage, 1992), p. 13.

as well as on the technical outlook. Information and decision making are costly in two ways: in what gets produced and in what doesn't get produced in the processes of education. Pragmatism and utilitarianism are two ethical streams of thought that help to reduce that cost. No one understood this better than John Dewey. Note how Dewey subordinates purpose to the equivocal, sense-perceptible moment: "The category of purpose is *a* category, not the only one, and it is a category which, like any other, has its own specific conditions and function within experience; it is not a priori and externally determinative."[2] This

[2]See Dewey's book review of F. C. S. Schiller's *Humanism: Philosophical Essays* (London: Macmillan, 1903), in *The Middle Works of John Dewey, 1899-1924*, vol. 3: *1903-1906*, ed. Jo Ann Boydston (Carbondale: Southern Illinois University Press, 2008), p. 318.

position is antithetical to our discussion in chapter one. That is why, as ethical systems, pragmatism and utilitarianism tend to dominate educational production today, just as they did between 1900 and 1930. We've come full circle.

For example, two members of Harvard's business-school faculty created the Balanced Scorecard, which is a performance assessment tool that examines profits and share prices, while also measuring the operations businesses feel are essential to achieving success.[3] It is an heir to Fredrick Taylor's principles of scientific management (see chap. 4). Education managers in Georgia, Delaware, Indiana and California have begun to apply it to the schools, and it is the latest in a series of business applications imposed on educational production in order to achieve optimal efficiency.[4]

It is of utmost importance, however, to recognize that education and its processes are not reducible to a utility function. While education does have utility, many educators believe that any utility derivable from education is secondary to higher and nobler ends. We live for truth, goodness, beauty and the achievement of proper conceptions of freedom. We also live for deeper relationships with others and a sustainable one with the created universe. We also live to know and understand God. Yes, choosing a vocation and getting a job are important byproducts of education. Yet the aim of a liberal education is "to develop the mind and character in making choices between truth and error, between right and wrong."[5] A liberal education liberates.

However, the quantification of educational choices exposes an underlying ontology which holds that all public conceptions of social reality are mind dependent and reducible to preferences and their quantitative orderings. The idea is that truth and error, right and wrong are *mere* preferences; they are neither good nor bad, proper nor improper, true nor

---

[3]Robert Kaplan and David Norton, *The Balanced Scorecard: Translating Strategy into Action* (Cambridge, Mass.: Harvard Business School Press, 1996).

[4]Jeff Archer, "Districts Tracking Goals with 'Balanced Scorecards,' " *Education Week*, February 21, 2007, p. 10.

[5]Richard Weaver, "Education and the Individual," *The Intercollegiate Review* (Wilmington, Del.: Intercollegiate Studies Institute, 2008), p. 13. This essay was originally published in 1959 and then again in 1965.

false. The artificial division of fact from value has made this neutrality plausible in the minds of many (perhaps most) social scientists; and this thinking, through its close association with education, heavily influences education.[6] Daniel Bell keenly noted in 1947, at a time of rapid increase in postwar social and economic activity, certain implications that we live with today. Social science professors

> have an ideology geared to the need. Being [social] scientists, they are concerned with "what is" and are not inclined to involve themselves in questions of moral values or larger social issues. They operate as technicians, approaching the problem as it is given to them and keeping within the framework set by those who hire them. Many conceive of themselves as "human engineers;" counterparts to the industrial engineers: where the industrial engineer plans a flow of work in order to assure greater mechanical efficiency, the "human engineer" tries to "adjust" the worker to his job so that the human equation will match the industrial equation. To effect this, the sociologists seek "laws" of human behavior analogous to the laws of the physical world, and by and large they give little thought to the fact that they are *not* operating in the physical world. And almost none among them seem to be interested in the possibility that one of the functions of social science may be to explore *alternative* (and better, i.e., more human) modes of human combinations, not merely to make more effective those that already exist.[7]

Utility of course means the relative satisfaction or pleasure of consuming goods, services and the performance of various types of work. A *function* is the means by which to achieve one's satisfaction or pleasure relative to those goods and so forth. Thus, a *utility function* is roughly a mathematical (economic) expression of a person's preferences with respect to alternative goods, services and work. The utility function "is a function assigning to every alternative . . . a number, in such a way that the utility of one [alternative] is greater than the utility of another" alternative, that is, if the first alternative is preferred to the

---

[6]The modern fact-value dichotomy gains saliency from the thought of Scottish philosopher David Hume (1711-1776).
[7]Daniel Bell, "The Study of Man: Adjusting Men to Machines: Social Scientists Explore the World of the Factory," *Commentary*, January 1947, p. 80.

others.[8] The utility function of education becomes the "objective of maximizing both economic and social returns to education. Economic returns are, for example, earnings, while social returns include the preservation of existing peer groups and social networks."[9] This line of thought has been around for a long time, dating back to the work of Jeremy Bentham, Adam Smith, David Hume and John Stuart Mill.

For example, Bentham believed that things (e.g., goods) and actions (e.g., work) ought to be predicated on their (1) usefulness to the agent or society, and (2) the production of the greatest *amount* of happiness for the greatest *number* of people. Bentham said, "By the principle of utility is meant that principle which approves or disapproves of every action whatsoever, according to the tendency which it appears to have to augment or diminish the happiness of the party whose interest is in question: or, what is the same thing in other words, to promote or to oppose that happiness."[10] Notice that Bentham and his philosophy, utilitarianism, implicitly favor terms of quantification: *number* and *amount*. These are the sort of terms and concepts most favored by a technical model of a social institution. They help participants in a social institution to adopt a basic method by which to calculate decisions. Decision making, including decisions concerning the allocation of scarce resources or how to treat people, becomes a rational and calculable enterprise. Thus the process of deriving a utility function leads to an ethics of accountancy.[11]

The notion of education as a utility function is likely to be unfamiliar to most education students. Many educators, of course, appreciate the economic and sociological benefits children receive for obtaining a

---

[8]Kenneth Arrow, "Utility and Expectation in Economic Behavior," in *Collected Papers of Kenneth J. Arrow:* vol. 3: *Individual Choice Under Certainty and Uncertainty* (Cambridge, Mass.: Belknap, 1984), p. 118.

[9]Mads Meier Jaeger, "Economic and Social Returns to Education," *Rationality and Society* 19, no. 4 (2007): 451.

[10]Jeremy Bentham, *An Introduction to the Principles of Morals and Legislation* (Mineola, N.Y.: Dover, 2007), p. 2.

[11]We can understand why historically this has happened when we understand how ethics shifted from transcendent sources to a mixture of utilitarian and pragmatic thought. Economist Richard Tawney describes the shift in these terms: "Religion has been converted from the keystone which holds together the social edifice into one department within it, and the idea of a rule of right is replaced by economic expediency as the arbiter of policy and the criterion of conduct" (*Religion and the Rise of Capitalism* [New York: Mentor, 1954], p. 228).

good education. It is not absent from our minds that participating in an economy and a society is, in some significant degree, a byproduct of education. Knowledge, skills and experiences are acquired through an education. But the utilitarian nature of education and schooling is not foremost in mind when good educators are educating students. It is a secondary consideration; perhaps a necessary one but in no way near sufficient to what education really means or constitutes. This is particularly true for Christian educators who operate on the principle that truth, goodness and beauty are central aims of learning; these, and the corollary skills of the liberal arts, are foci of schooling and, among several other aims, define the proper ends of education. It is the idea of becoming a better person through the development of knowledge, skills, sentiments, virtues and wisdom. The aim (loosely) is the properly functioning human being, where processes of development and flourishing account for universal and particular information. For centuries this has been the goal of liberal arts. However, there is an obvious problem for the quantity adjuster and social engineer. How do we *measure* a value? On what *scale* do we weigh a sentiment? What *cost* variables are assigned to beauty and happiness? Under what *quantitative* criterion is spiritual growth assessed? How do we get sound ethics or moral education out of *utility* functions?

Our focus in this chapter concerns Christian educators, the public schools, social ethics and moral education. Here, within the public sector of the education market—by far the largest market sector and whose information environment has become heavily regulated by central authorities—the Christian educator will require significant knowledge and skill to bring about a healthier and saltier (Mt 5:13-16) institution on behalf of schoolchildren. In some ways this type of intellectual work calls on the educator to have a transformative impact on three levels: (1) modeling a sense of hope for a truer way of living, (2) offering acute critical resistance and, where needed, being a transformative influence in what C. S. Lewis called "enemy occupied territory," and (3) presenting a time-tested architecture of moral thought.[12] This is important for reasons raised by James

---

[12]C. S. Lewis, *Mere Christianity* (New York: HarperCollins, 2001), pp. 45-46.

Davison Hunter on the insufficiency of contemporary social ethics and moral education programs.

> We say we want a renewal of character in our day but we don't really know what we ask for. To have a renewal of character is to have a renewal of a creedal order that constrains, limits, binds, obligates and compels. *This price is too high for us to pay.* We want character but without conviction; we want strong morality but without particular moral justifications that invariably offend; we want good without having to name evil; we want decency without the authority to insist upon it; we want moral community without any limitations to personal freedom. In short, we want what we cannot possibly have on the terms that we want it.[13]

SCIENTIFIC DETERMINISM

Learning how to offer Christocentric critique and resistance to the technical model of education begins with understanding the basics of the moral sphere and its relationship to the aims of education. The technical direction that has captured the agenda in schooling and higher education leaves the Christian educationist in a lurch when the important issue of moral education arises. Because of the logic of its commitments, the technical framework of education today has little ability to sufficiently justify or reliably ground moral education in anything or any source that is transcendent. This was not always so and suggests that a conscious institutional tradeoff has been made as regards the source(s) that will ground the moral purposes of public schools.

The insufficiency of morality only parallels the tradeoff made by the state itself. As it became increasingly secular within important sectors of government, naturally so did its schools. We need only to recall the dramatic rise of what Elmer Wilds called "scientific determinism"[14] in

---

[13]James D. Hunter, *The Death of Character* (New York: Basic Books, 2000), p. xv, emphasis added.

[14]Wilds suggests that the "scientific determinist has insisted that *all* educational problems be approached in a scientific attitude, that *all* educational practices and procedures be determined by investigations conducted in the scientific spirit and by means of the scientific method. . . . This is the method that the educational scientists would use in determining such matters as educational aims, educational content, educational agencies, educational organization, and

the period 1870 to 1930 to understand why and how moral education within public schools loosened from its transcendent moorings. Consider, for example, these influential doctrines offered in 1922 by Edward Thorndike follower William McCall:

- Whatever exists at all, exists in some amount.

- Anything that exists in amount can be measured.

- Measurement in education is in general the same as measurement in the physical sciences.

- To the extent that the pupil's initial abilities or capabilities are unmeasurable, a knowledge of him is impossible.

- To the extent that any goal of education is intangible, it is worthless.

- Measurement will not mechanize education or educators.

- Measurement will not produce a deadly uniformity.[15]

These question-begging sentiments and dimwitted predictions pervaded the information economy of public schools, schools of education and normal schools where superintendents, principals and teachers received their training. As Jacques Maritain observes, the institution came to hold a scientific view of human beings, whose consequences excluded competing views and diverse sources of information; the scientific view narrowed, rather than enlarged, the information base to good research and practice in education.

> The purely scientific idea of man tends only to link together measurable and observable data taken as such, and is determined from the very start not to consider anything like being or essence, not to answer any question like: Is there a soul or isn't there? Does the spirit exist or only matter? Is there freedom or determinism? Purpose or chance? Value or simple fact? For such questions are out of the realm of science. The purely scientific idea of man is, and must be, a phenomenalized idea without reference to ultimate reality, . . . for education needs primarily to know what

educational methods" (Elmer Wilds, "The Scientific Movement in Education: Scientific Determinism," in *The Foundations of Modern Education* [New York: Rinehart, 1942], pp. 507-8; emphasis added).

[15]William McCall, *How to Measure in Education* (New York: Macmillan, 1922), pp. 3-18.

man *is*, what is the nature of man and the scale of values it essentially involves; and the purely scientific idea of man, because it ignores "being-as-such," does not know such things, but only what emerges from the human being in the realm of sense observation and measurement.[16]

We cannot doubt the secular and naturalistic influence within the institution of education; history is formidable in its evidence. But where do we go from here? In order to answer this pressing question we once again must understand the powerful allied forces underwriting secularity and their historical and philosophical convergence. Doing so will enable the Christian educator going forward to faithfully and intelligently stand in the gap for a healthier, just institution.

In brief, the twentieth century horrors of strict scientific determinism gave way to the broader project of secular pluralism, which moderated a version of scientism that added other sources of information and sensibilities about human flourishing. It is important to note that pluralism is an *effect* and not the cause of the institutional tradeoff discussed here. State secularity was a consistent outgrowth of the demand for its services after the social and economic traumas of the 1930s and 1940s in the United States. By expanding its scope in the affairs of the public, the state and its institutions had to offer its own moral direction and ground that purposely substituted for religious sources of morality. Optimistic faith in scientific naturalism was an engine for this new humanistic direction.[17] It was the age of science, and it was widely believed that human progress depended on a scientific approach to all areas of human concerns, including moral ones. It would be roughly within the span of forty years (1930s to 1970s) before the full force of this secular agenda thoroughly (and legally) controlled institutional information and agenda in public education.

THE STATE AND THE POVERTY OF PLURALISM

For example, normative institutional pressures coerced the self-interest

---

[16]Jacques Maritain, *Education at the Crossroads* (New Haven, Conn.: Yale University Press, 1943), pp. 4-5.

[17]A brief review of the Humanist Manifesto I (1933) and II (1973) verify the organic optimism of their respective eras, having had wide appeal among secularists.

of school managers to strip out religious notions of morality.[18] Rationality shifted to secular sources of morality. Mere convention (e.g., a "bag of virtues" program), communitarianism or some legible versions of tolerance and diversity are the usual sources of present-day moral education programs. Conventionalism means commonly used moral sentiments whose agreement is not based on ultimate reality and the objective moral sphere, but on principles of the agreement itself (e.g., a social contract of some sort). Conventionalism is a powerful way to bind people together on traditional ways of doing things, that is, until those traditions are regarded as too costly for a society to bear. At that point the conventionalism can evolve into a new agreement on a denial of those traditions. This denial can be ethical (e.g., the rejection of Jim Crow laws) or unethical (e.g., the denial of the sanctity of human life). So conventionalism needs something more stable than itself to bring about the reliable moral situation.

Communitarianism is thought by some to be a plausible candidate for a society and its schools. In one sense it represents those ethical ideals arising from particular moral traditions (e.g., see the work of Alasdair MacIntyre). While bringing to the school sensitivity toward traditions, some of those traditions may be suspect to some people. Perhaps tolerance is the answer. The second-order virtue of tolerance gains legs when the state assigns it weight and legibiligy (e.g., in curricula and moral education programs) such that it becomes a first-order virtue (or good) from which all other virtues and moral programs become defined and evaluated. Legibility here means the intentional arrangement of codified information that signals to all participants what a state or state entity, such as a public education system, values by way of information. Legibility orders rules and information that structure specific types of educational exchange on specific types of information platforms.

School leaders choose such programs because they cause the least friction and possess the greatest surface range of social assent; thus they

---

[18]For a thorough discussion of this decision-making phenomenon in organizations, see Paul DiMaggio and Walter Powell, "The Iron Cage Revisited: Institutional Isomorphism and Collective Rationality in Organizational Fields," *American Sociological Review* 48, no. 2 (1983): 147-60.

incite efficiency without suffering the cost of conflict. For example, the new National Curriculum in the United Kingdom suggests that schools should no longer teach objective values (right and wrong, etc.) in order to assuage pluralistic sentiments.[19] Educational policy in the United States is not quite as bold but perhaps as ineffective in construing a direction for moral education. Moral education programs often give the appearance of morality and ethics being taught to young people, but usually adjoining it on the lowest common denominator. They are in reality facsimiles of morality and ethics. The condition of making adult educators and leaders feel plausibly virtuous is achieved without having to endure the very difficult work (and accompanying cost) of teaching what is legitimately and robustly moral and the various ways in which one may reliably discover it and live it. A satisfactory answer, one that avoids problems of regress or relativism, is almost never provided to the public school student who asks, When all is said and done, teacher, why should *I* (or *we*) be moral?

In contrast to its implied meaning, pluralism as a worldview demands only certain types of information and excludes other types by force of institutional rules.[20] This is in contrast to the demonstrably false but widely held belief that pluralism as a cosmopolitan view or structure of reality sanctions the entry of all sorts of information irrespective of its nature. In reality the practice of pluralism in a secular environment by definition *sorts out* or depletes information that possesses transcendent rigidity or strength, while at the same occurrence accepting information that has secular rigidity. This view of course meets certain condi-

---

[19]David Charter, "Schools Told It's No Longer Necessary to Teach Right from Wrong," (London) *TimesOnline*, July 31, 2006 <www.timesonline.co.uk/tol/life_and_style/education/article695140.ece>. See the Department for Education and Skills, United Kingdom for further information on the National Curriculum.

[20]The Latin for pluralism is *pluralis*, meaning more than one. The *Oxford English Dictionary* defines pluralism in its philosophical connotation as "a theory or system of thought which recognizes more than one ultimate principal" (*The Compact Oxford English Dictionary*, 2nd ed. [New York: Oxford University Press, 1998], p. 1370). Robert Roberts defines *moral* pluralism as "the situation in which some moral disagreements stem from fundamental differences of moral outlook and so are not resolvable by argument. Moral pluralism is the 'normal' situation of humanity, but it is more obvious in pluralistic societies like those of Europe and North America" ("Pluralism and Christian Morality," Wheaton College Faith and Learning Seminars for New Faculty, unpublished).

tions of naturalism influencing public policy, as for example the diverse views of John Rawls (whose influence emerges from Aristotle and Henry Sidgwick) and Jürgen Habermas (whose influence is neo-Kantian). One example of this sorting process is occurring in Europe in the construction of the European Union (EU) Constitution, where secular pluralists have worked hard to prevent Christian references throughout the text. This is a passive-aggressive feature of secular pluralism, one that allows for a healthy critique of Christianity yet resists critiques of its own hegemonic naturalistic presuppositions about social reality.

Three more examples draw out what we mean. In the 2006 fall semester, Wheaton College's education department hosted an Illinois-wide teacher education meeting (the Illinois Association for Colleges with Teacher Education [IACTE]). At this meeting were representatives from religious and secular colleges. Two representatives (we will call them Gertrude and Matilda) from secular Chicago-area colleges surreptitiously distributed fliers titled "Accredit Love Not Condemnation," whose contents alleged that the Wheaton College teacher-preparation program and its candidates "condemn" individuals who choose to practice homosexual behavior. The claim in their words: "We believe that IACTE should not legitimize with its presence any institution that dehumanizes and devalues lesbian, gay, bisexual, and transgendered people."[21] Wheaton's education department raised a formal objection and over several months exchanged letters with Gertrude and Matilda. In February 2007, Gertrude and Matilda arranged a discussion opportunity at Chicago's famous Hull House whose topic was titled "Anti-Gay Pledges and Teacher Education: A Dialogue About the Tensions Between Private Beliefs and the Public Good." By closely examining the political agenda, one can see how Gertrude and Matilda and their followers attempted to employ against Wheaton College the passive-aggressive tolerance trick. For example, note how the topic as constructed allegedly occupies at the outset the "advanced," "enlightened" and "rational" position. The respective claims, topic and questions were carefully designed to occupy, a priori, the rational position

[21]See the blog titled "Who Would Jesus Tattle On?" *The Other Eye*, May 17, 2007 <http://therese-othereye.blogspot.com/2007/01/who-would-jesus-tattle-on.html>.

and shift the epistemic burden of proof to the respondent, Wheaton College, who is presumed to hold the irrational and untenable position. The moves by Gertrude and Matilda presuppose that Christian educators would need to self-censor, privatize or eliminate certain beliefs and worldview commitments in order to teach public school students, particularly "lesbian-gay-bisexual-transgender-queer" youth. Absent the tradeoff of certain knowledge preferences, so the claim goes, Christian colleges cannot legitimately prepare teachers for the public arena. (We will have more to say in other venues about this example. Gertrude and Matilda have rejected the opportunity for a debate, but there are larger activist pressures that will need to be formally debated.)

The second example also draws on a policy preference by critics to the Christian position. *The American Economic Review* (an American Economic Association journal) had until very recently refused to publish advertisements for economics faculty positions at Christian colleges such as Wheaton. The argument of the AEA was that it did not permit in its advertisements discrimination on the basis of religion even if the employer is eligible to discriminate on the basis of religion under provisions of the Civil Rights Act of 1964. The AEA was willing to passively embrace discrimination in the one sense (in its own policy preferences) and to aggressively fight discrimination in the other sense. As the twenty-first century unfolds, Christian higher learning will see much more in the way of passive-aggressive strategies against its knowledge preferences. This is the way to signal to Christian educationists in all academic disciplines that there will be a cost raised against our work (or against our Christian worldview) if we really believe and integrate what we say we believe. Fortunately in this case, economist P. J. Hill challenged the logic of AEA's position and AEA modified its position.

The third example is similar and another expression of an activist homosexual agenda of raising information costs against Christian colleges and universities and their orthodox knowledge and moral traditions. A group of philosophers has petitioned the American Philosophical Association (APA) to sanction colleges and universities that prohibit faculty, students and staff from engaging in homosexual acts. The petition seeks to prevent those colleges and universities from advertising in APA venues or "mark institutions with these policies as institutions that violate our anti-discrimination policy."[22] Fortunately, another group of philosophers offered a counter petition, arguing "the present policies of the APA prohibit discrimination based on religion or political convictions. But the policy recommended attempts to segregate and penalize religious institutions for abiding by their long-standing and coherent ethical norms. Moreover, this policy would foster an environment that would encourage discrimination against philosophers whose religious, political, or philosophical convictions lead them to disapprove of homosexual acts."[23] It would seem that both groups of philosophers are focused on the prohibition of behaviors and not beliefs or dispositions about behaviors. One question that will be too costly to debate is whether discussions about this form of discrimination, homosexual behavior, will ever occur on the terms of belief and disposition, that is, on the terms of biblical sexual orientation and whether someone can be discriminated against for holding an unbiblical sexual orientation even where the person in question is abstinent. Political correctness will prevent the freedom for such discussions.

Once having had a reasonable architecture, pluralism as a view today is a tool by which a state (or super-state, as for example the EU) or market can remove competition for the control of language and concepts that might otherwise impede state or market expansion and influence. In other words, like postmodernism, pluralism is a closed model of reality akin to the technical model we have discussed. It would seem important for the Christian educator to consider the corruption of legitimate pluralism as one cause of *information loss* in society and its social institutions. Yet pluralism itself is also an effect of mass culture, which, in turn, is a result of technological flatteners and communication integration (or networking), that is, the ability to deliver a common set of messages and programs to a mass audience.[24] This analysis seems to imply that pluralism is not really pluralism at all but

---

[22]See www.petitiononline.com/cmh3866/petition.html (accessed on April 15, 2009).

[23]See www.ipetitions.com/petition/apa/index.html (accessed on April 15, 2009).

[24]Thomas Friedman's popular work *The World Is Flat: A Brief History of the Twenty-First Century* (New York: Farrar, Straus & Giroux, 2005) is an excellent example of the communication flatteners occurring across the world.

a very poor reproduction. By its very nature real pluralism is corruptible; it has no internal defense mechanism against its corruption. It is not grounded in anything more substantive than itself. Legitimate pluralism requires a set of reliable and true standards of human existence (a real reality) by which tolerance is operable.[25] Whatever good real pluralism harbors for political systems, its moral strength is readily drained away through pernicious relativism. Once objective standards (e.g., natural law) are removed from view, the view from nowhere is the governing alternative. This is the necessary stage before capricious power enters to fill the void. The state and its institutions must assert their authority to preserve order, creating isomorphic homogeneity across institutions like education. In doing so they must play informational favorites; because the state is not neutral, it must bias certain informational content and sources.

THE NEW PUBLIC

By some accounts a free-wheeling economic system supported by expanding state apparatuses fed mass consumerism in the United States during the 1950s and 1960s, shifting the locus of cultural power away from earlier civic and religious traditions and institutions (civic progressives in the mold of Jane Addams and Hull House, the church, etc.). Social power was lodged within new and accessible forms of media and persuasion. During the period of media expansion, the small town and its particular values in the fabric of American life gave way to mass society and its new universal values.[26] Social solidarities were defined around television events (e.g., the space programs), advertising (e.g., the proliferation of billboards, TV commercials, political ads) and various "canned" news programs (e.g., newsreaders like Walter Cronkite and others), televised sports (e.g., the Super Bowl) and televised war (e.g., Vietnam). Children began to watch three to seven hours of commercial television daily, the effects of which help to condition appetites, dispositions, values and beliefs.[27]

---

[25]On the question of tolerance and its likewise corruptible attributes, see S. D. Gaede, *When Tolerance Is No Virtue* (Downers Grove, Ill.: InterVarsity Press, 1993).

[26]See Arthur Vidich and Joseph Bensman, *Small Town in Mass Society: Class, Power, and Religion in a Rural Community* (Princeton, N.J.: Princeton University Press, 1958).

[27]See the policy report by the American Academy of Pediatrics' Committee on Public Education, "Children, Adolescents, and Television" in *Pediatrics* 107, no. 2 (2001): 423-26.

Table 5.1. U.S. Juvenile Arrest and Delinquency Statistics 1950-2000[a]

	Arrests Total	Arrests for Violent Offenses	Arrests for Aggravated Assault	Arrests for Murder	Delinquency & Court Cases	Del. Rate per 1,000 youth ages 10-17
1950	35,000	3,300	1,250	186	55,000	5.0
1955	195,626	12,000	2,100	207	197,000	10.0
1960	527,000	28,000	6,100	380	510,000	20.1
1965	1,074,000	30,000	13,000	635	697,000	23.6
1970	1,661,000	55,000	21,000	1,350	1,052,000	32.3
1975	2,078,000	77,000	32,000	1,370	1,317,000	38.8
1980	2,000,000	77,000	34,000	1,500	1,445,000	46.4
1985	1,763,000	75,000	37,000	1,380	1,112,000	42.2
1990	1,850,000	97,000	55,000	2,700	1,299,000	51.0
1995	2,089,000	115,000	66,000	2,800	1,714,000	60.7
2000	2,369,000	99,000	66,300	1,200	1,757,000	59.1
2003	2,220,000	92,000	61,500	1,130	1,615,000	51.5

Table 5.2. Historical Living Arrangements of Children in U.S. 1950-2000[b] (in percentages)

	1950	1960	1970	1980	1990	2000
Two Parents	86.8	86.5	85.2	76.7	72.5	64.0
One Parent	8.9	10.3	11.9	19.7	24.7	31.7

[a]Sources: FBI, Department of Justice, Bureau of the Census. See particularly the Census Bureau's bicentennial edition: "Historical Statistics of the United States, Colonial Times to 1970." Numbers are rounded to nearest thousandth or tenth. Violent offenses are crimes of murder, forcible rape, robbery, and aggravated assault (in earlier data, general assaults). Delinquent acts are defined as juvenile-initiated crimes against persons, property, drug offenses and against public order. Delinquency cases and rates are estimated figures based upon figures provided by the Office of Juvenile Justice and Delinquency Prevention, Department of Justice.
[b]Source: U.S. Census Bureau (1990; 2001; 2004).

These new social solidarities began to create what Leon Mayhew calls "the new public," which can be widely manipulated without the need for repressive coercion.[28] Increasing social and geographic mobility increased the transience of the American family, with many people moving to Western states, especially to California. Complicating social matters, juvenile delinquency rates tripled between 1960 and 1995. The juvenile violent crime index alone rose about 65 percent between 1980 and 1995. And living arrangements of children in two-parent households demonstrated a significant decline between years 1950 to 2000. While we are not assigning specific causal factors here, a correlation and convergence of macrosocial events from the 1950s foreword suggests that something significant was happening within the fabric of American life. The beneficial side of statistics helps us to see this.

In this postwar social climate, moral education in many U.S. schools during the latter half of the twentieth century became ambivalent. During the expansion of the state, its regulative rules and services resulted in an increasingly central role in education, a clear transition occurred, one where theistic sources of knowledge that had once informed school curriculum and character development within the framework of local communities shifted to secular-sourced knowledge informing curriculum and character development. These competing sources of information left in doubt a unity of educational purpose, particularly within the ethics of school organizations and programmatic moral education.

For example, on the one hand there was the residual Christianity (the old universal) and its assertion that morality and moral education must at some stage address the human will in conflict with a holy God. Yet, on the other hand many Christian educators over the last forty years have been conditioned institutionally to privatize their faith in their vocational service to Jesus Christ, as a consequence privatizing (in our view) the ultimate provision of moral education. Privatization oc-

---

[28]Leon Mayhew, *The New Public: Professional Communication and the Means of Social Influence* (Cambridge: Cambridge University Press, 1997). For particularly biting accounts of these phenomena of popular culture, see the work of Herbert Marcuse, e.g., *One Dimensional Man: Studies in the Ideology of Advanced Industrial Society*, 2nd ed. (Boston: Beacon, 1991), and Theodor Adorno, *The Culture Industry: Selected Essays on Mass Culture* (London: Routledge, 1991).

curred during a time and in a cultural environment where the declared thought of the day by elites and persuaders was fiercely secular. This thought and its direction received formal sanction by the U.S. Supreme Court in the early 1960s through a jurisprudential direction that had already been established as far back as the 1930's Hugo Black court.

THE RETURN OF POSITIVISM

Positivism had already worked to loosen the ties that had somewhat bound most Americans around realist conceptions of morality, reducing these ties to emotivism, subjectivism, cultural relativism and conventionalism.[29] As a matter of public policy, state institutions now viewed human beings as physical-temporal beings whose destiny was no longer timeless; ascertainable actuarial tables of social insurance programs substituted for things eternal.[30] There is some irony here in the seemingly odd link between positivism and pluralism. It verifies that periodic shifts within culture often create ingenious tensions between seemingly incongruent systems of thought. The positivist quest for certainty and precision helped to manufacture universal doubt. This process was nudged along by an advanced stage of pluralism on a range

---

[29]Positivism is a branch of empiricist philosophy arising from the work of the Vienna Circle, of which A. J. Ayer was a significant student (A. J. Ayer, *Language, Truth & Logic*, 2nd ed. [New York: Dover, 1952]). The essential reason that logical positivism failed was its inability to meet with its own criterion of verifiability. For a brief review of the varieties of positivism in education or various disciplines, see D. C. Phillips, "After the Wake: Postpositivistic Educational Thought," *Educational Researcher* 12, no. 5 (1983): 4-12, and Owen Fiss, "The Varieties of Positivism," *The Yale Law Journal* 90, no. 5 (1981): 1007-16. Michael Polanyi wrote in 1951 what is even further along today: "Justice, morality, custom and law now appear as mere sets of conventions, charged with emotional approval, which are the proper study of sociology. Conscience is identified with the fear of breaking socially approved conventions and its investigation is assigned to psychology. Aesthetic values are related to an equilibrium of opposed impulses in the nervous system of the beholder. In the positivist theory, man is a system responding regularly to a certain range of stimuli" ("Scientific Convictions," in *The Logic of Liberty* [1951; reprint, Indianapolis: Liberty Fund, 1998], p. 10).

[30]At a 1940 inter-faith conference held by U.S. religious intellectuals, a hyperbolic but probably sincere Mortimer Adler presented a paper that held "the most serious threat to democracy is the positivism of the professors which dominates every aspect of modern education and is the central corruption of modern culture" (Mortimer Adler, "God and the Professors," in *Science, Philosophy and Religion: A Symposium* [New York: Conference on Science, Philosophy, and Religion, 1940], pp. 120-49). Adler went on to compare the positivist movement embraced by academics as a greater threat than Nazism (hence the hyperbole).

of views, including reality, human nature, ethics and the human will.[31] This social phenomenon inevitably led to an effect called moral relativism, which challenges human confidence in being right and certain on some moral matters. During this same time the certainties and doubts of science substituted for the certainties, questions and mysteries of Christianity.[32] These theories left a huge gap in moral knowledge and skills in the schools.

It is said that positivism is dead in philosophy proper and so it seems, for good reason. Yet forms of positivism are alive and well within an assortment of social institutions, including education, regrettably, especially in large-scale public school systems where many children and their families lack the education and social capital to raise objections to it. It is alive and thriving for a variety of reasons that were discussed in chapter four. These reasons mostly center on two important benefits (both simplifications) that positivism brings to the institutional table. First, positivism, when wedded to its various philosophical allies, controls the factors of human production efficiently through an ontological abstraction and economic reduction of humans, their work and their purpose. This entails looking on the teacher as a technician and the student as a commodity or product, essentially the raw material that is acted on and conditioned in behavioristic fashion. Here, it would seem, lie some of the more immediate tangible economic payoffs in the technical processes of human capital development, where climbing the ladder of educational attainment takes the place of acquiring deeper forms of knowledge, skills, understandings and wisdoms.

Second, positivism basically substitutes for the certainties of belief and faith in God, the competing Protagorean certainties ("man is the measure of all things") of alternative conceptions and measures of real-

---

[31]Maritain argues that the principle aim of education, under a philosophical-religious conception of the human being, is the "conquest of internal and spiritual freedom to be achieved by the individual person, . . . his liberation through knowledge and wisdom, good will, and love" (*Education at the Crossroads*, p. 11). Since this view of the human being had been called into question by positivism and thereby substituted for a secular view, pluralism responded by shutting out a whole range of views on these subjects, including the most basic questions and aims of education.

[32]Steven Loomis and Jake Rodriguez, "Sympathy for Warranted Certainty: Universals and the Institution of Education," *Journal of Education and Christian Belief* 9, no. 1 (2005): 47-70.

ity. The payoff here is that state bureaucracies—any state—and market firms (e.g., the Educational Testing Service, accrediting agencies, textbook companies) do not have to compete formally or informally with the church or large-scale private foundations and civic institutions in setting larger institutional agenda. There is no knowledge competition; it was settled in the secular direction. By publicly marginalizing the church and its adherents, the state and other secular institutions pacified perhaps the only institution that could match scale, whose information economy might otherwise threaten state monopoly over information in educational production (especially its rule-making functions).[33] Michael Polanyi was one of those few who understood the deep threat that positivist ideas could have on the human condition. In the early 1950s he wrote:

> The philosophy-to-end-all-philosophy may be designated, if somewhat loosely, as Positivism. It continued in the nineteenth and twentieth centuries the rebellion against the authority of the Christian Churches, first started in the days of Montaigne, Bacon and Descartes; but it set out not only to liberate reason from enslavement by authority, but also to dispose of all traditionally guiding ideas, so far as they were not demonstrable by science. Thus, in the positivist sense truth became identified with scientific truth and the latter defined—by a positivist critique of science—as a mere ordering of experience.[34]

In preparing the Christian educator to understand what precisely is at stake in the vital fields of social ethics and moral education, we suggest a framework from which intentional and effective character development might aim. We show how Christian educators and leaders might integrate some form of Christocentric moral knowledge into their practice. The framework we have in mind possesses ideas substantive enough

---

[33]Due to the Blaine Amendment and immigration trends, the Catholic school movement beginning in the 1870s successfully organized and nearly matched the scale of public schools of the day. A replication of that movement today might initially challenge public school orthodoxy (i.e., bring about effects from competition), but it would remain difficult for a system of schools to operate legitimately outside of the existing institutional framework. For a well-written history of the Catholic school movement, see the study by Anthony Bryk, Valerie Lee and Peter Holland, *Catholic Schools and the Common Good* (Cambridge, Mass.: Harvard University Press, 1993).

[34]Polanyi, *Logic of Liberty*, p. 10.

to avoid vulgar relativism as well as to match the authority and complexities contained within the transcendent moral sphere.[35] Ultimately, every social-ethics and moral-education program must answer questions on the origin, nature and destiny of humanity.[36]

THE NATURE OF CHARACTER AND MORAL EDUCATION

The prelude to this section shows why James Davison Hunter is prescient when he observes that people want what they cannot possibly have, in terms of social ethics and morality, on the terms that they want it: "This price is too high for us to pay." But it is not a new criticism. C. S. Lewis famously wrote: "In a sort of ghastly simplicity we remove the organ and demand the function. We make men without chests and expect of them virtue and enterprise. We laugh at honour and are shocked to find traitors in our midst. We castrate and bid the geldings be fruitful."[37] This leads to the opportunity for Christian educators to become public intellectuals and shows why the alternative price is too high to pay: the loss of sound ethics and morality places a significant cost against individual human beings and society and its institutions. In other words Christian educators can learn to demonstrate to new generations of students, to colleagues and to policy makers what good social ethics and moral education is, how they are properly grounded and why they are important to the social welfare. We will try to do some of that preparation presently.

The philosophical study of morality, a discipline called ethics, has existed for several millennia. Ethos, the Greek root for ethics, is also a Greek term for character. An ethic is one's character, and character is one's ethic. As a byproduct of ethics, moral education is rooted in

---

[35]Relativism has both a constructive and destructive effect. Its most vulgar and destructive effect is nihilism, the idea or view that there is no objective morality, no *real* good, no meaningful purpose toward which human beings are disposed. Relativism at its most constructive is the view that in spite of the many sources that people use to ground their private morality, this relativism is possible when unity exists in principles guiding public morality.

[36]Herman Horne suggests that all philosophies of education must answer these questions. Positivism and pluralism allow these questions to be avoided because of the potential cost of conflict among competing positions. See Horne, *The Philosophy of Education* (New York: Macmillan, 1927), pp. 263-84.

[37]C. S. Lewis, *The Abolition of Man* (San Francisco: HarperOne, 2001), p. 26.

sacred and secular traditions, ancient, medieval, modern and post-modern civilizations, within Eastern and Western cultures, in northern and southern hemispheres, and serves as a basis of character development. Such traditions are important for investigation because, among other reasons, what communities value as moral often finds its target in the intentional development of its members' character.

There are at least two dimensions from which character may be discussed: in a collective (or collectivist) sense and with respect to an individual. In addition to a society or culture having certain characteristics (e.g., a national character), character also fits into the moral sphere on an individual level, character as a faculty of being and location of action; character is possessed by individual human beings. In this sense it is not a collective, societal or cultural possession—though these realms are among the sources that help to shape individual character.[38] But character as a faculty is always first and foremost exemplified on the individual level; it is one of the necessary faculties that makes a human being a moral person, one made in the image and likeness of God.

Character is associated with the will. The sum total of a person's beliefs or worldview necessarily affects that person's character and will as well as their specific orientation to life. Beliefs about the world tend to guide dispositions, actions and habits. The historical record is quite clear on this point. For example, the dispositions, actions and habits of saints have brought much good into the world. In contrast, the dispositions, actions and habits of villains have brought much evil into the world. Propaganda and indoctrination are powerful allies to authoritarian personalities. This is why belief formation, when based in truth, understanding and wisdom,[39] is a critical component of education, and is why philosopher Herbert Spencer said the following:

Education has for its object the formation of character. To curb restive

---

[38]Social groups and cultures are not thinking, sensing, rational organisms—they are amorphous. But, as Plato implied, society is the individual writ large. It is the case that societies and cultures, large or small, possess general *character*istics, while clearly not possessing a character in the sense of a faculty. Tocqueville, for example, spoke of certain American characteristics when writing *Democracy in America* in the 1830s.

[39]Regarding what truth *is*, see William Alston, *A Realist Conception of Truth* (Ithaca, N.Y.: Cornell University Press, 1996).

propensities, to awaken dormant sentiments, to strengthen the perceptions, and cultivate the tastes, to encourage this feeling and repress that, so as finally to develop the child into a man of well proportioned and harmonious nature—this is alike the aim of parent and teacher.[40]

Spencer was only saying what Aristotle and others recognized long ago: character must find its target between extremes. Courage, for example, is the mean between being cowardly or foolhardy. Discovering the mean between extremes requires willing and knowledgeable parents, teachers, community elders, coaches and other social and political institutions to guide youth in the appropriate directions. Education is concerned with developing moral character irrespective of the academic or vocational subject or skill taught. All educators are educators of character. For Christian educators the ultimate exemplar is the life of Jesus Christ.[41]

From about 1870 through to today the information economy of education in the United States underwent a gradual technical-epistemic shift that substituted ontological questions for epistemological ones.[42] It had been some time since Alexis de Tocqueville observed that "liberty cannot be established without morality, nor morality without faith" was a widely held view.[43] The shift relegated God and religious traditions to second-order curricular status and, then, as things moved along, to a status of virtual privatization, unreliability, irrelevance and irrationality.[44] God, the father of facthood, shifted in status—that is, as humans count status—from a mind-

---

[40]Herbert Spencer, *Social Statics: or, The Conditions Essential to Happiness Specified, and the First of Them Developed* (1851; reprint, New York: Robert Schalkenbach Foundation, 1995), p. 180.

[41]If Jesus Christ is who he said he was (is), both human and divine, the Lord over everything that has ever existed or that will exist, then would he not be among the most important persons who ever existed? Further, if the reports of his work and teachings were reliable accounts of his life, then wouldn't these qualify as possessing some level of transcendent authority? If accounts of his life are true, shouldn't this knowledge receive some room on the moral education agenda? If so, why isn't Jesus Christ a relevant figure for discussions involving morality, ethics and programs of moral education?

[42]Christian Smith, *The Secular Revolution: Power, Interests, and Conflict in the Secularization of American Public Life* (Berkeley: University of California Press, 2003).

[43]Alexis de Tocqueville, *Democracy in America* (New York: Gateway, 2002), p. 11.

[44]Michael Ariens and Robert Destro, *Religious Liberty in a Pluralistic Society* (Durham, N.C.: Carolina Academic Press, 1996).

independent being to mind-dependent being, reducible to mere belief. This knowledge had obstructed the new uniformity aligned with
high-modernist (secular) sensibilities. After Darwin, scientific for-
mulas to recondition human character through the reordering of institutions found favor with a new, secular class of institutional entrepreneurs (C. S. Lewis's "conditioners"). As we shall soon see,
innovative life paths attempted to replace old ways of living and dying. Character and its education became a field of battle. The fight
over how character would be defined in practice and purpose would
consume the institution of education for the last fifty years or so.

If character is located within an individual person, what specifically
is character itself? Although offering a set of necessary and sufficient
conditions for character is elusive, we can define character generally as
that (relatively fixed, relatively malleable) person-dependent (material-
immaterial) faculty which contributes to human identity and agency,
and otherwise includes such things as behavior, habits, capacities, dispositions, values and thought patterns that originate from a person's
identity, genetic makeup, social environment, spiritual condition, and
individual experience and effort.[45] The faculty of character is not simply a result of our genetic makeup, as many sociobiologists and psychologists hold.[46] Nor is character the sole product of socially constructed experience and environment, that is, the blank-slate argument,
as many people in the social and behavioral sciences believe.[47] Neither
is character something entirely spiritual, unaffected by genetic or sociocultural influences.[48] Character is influenced by and takes initial form
quite early from all four of these domains—biology, environment, intellect and soul/spirit.

Character is often confused with *mere* intellect, personality or social
acumen. This is a fundamental misunderstanding made by many con-

---

[45]As to the role of experience, see John Dewey, *Experience and Education* (New York: Touchstone, 1938).
[46]See Steven Pinker, *The Blank Slate: The Modern Denial of Human Nature* (New York: Viking,
2002).
[47]See John Locke, *An Essay Concerning Human Understanding* (Chicago: Great Books, 1952).
[48]Dallas Willard, *The Divine Conspiracy* (San Francisco: Harper, 1998); Nel Noddings, "Long-
ing for the Sacred in Schools: A Conversation with Nel Noddings," *Educational Leadership* 56,
no. 4 (1999).

temporary educators and school psychologists. However, simple attention to cognitive, psychological or social skills is not sufficient ground for character education. Many bright, mentally healthy and socially skilled people can appear to act rationally yet have false beliefs and be immoral agents. They can harm people and appear to be quite psychologically actualized and socially adjusted.[49] Instead, the education of character requires a deeper, more profound grounding—it requires the formation of true beliefs and habits of will that serve as a basis of moral dispositions and acts. In philosophical terms, character education seeks as its end an ontological inclination toward (at minimum) finite and (where religion is concerned) infinite goods.[50]

A young person is more likely to successfully reach an ethical and not merely psychological conception of happiness *(eudaimonia)* and purpose *(telos)* when taught to recognize and desire finite goods (moral virtues—known intuitively by introspection and through instruction), as well as to avoid acting on desires for vice. There are no guarantees that this will be the case, but the tendency exists for it to be so. The nature of the good life is a life of deeper well-being than the instrumental goods of economic materialism or political involvement can provide. When character is successfully tutored toward an intrinsically valuable end, a substantial spillover effect tends to accidently or circumstantially produce spiritual, economic, social and political goods for one's self, family, community and nation.

Since a person's character is the faculty that interacts with the moral sphere in every moment of every day, then bringing the character into proper alignment with the moral sphere is a central role of moral education.[51] The causation of this alignment is complex and occurs on the

---

[49]In the forthcoming *Stalin's Challenge to Modern Leadership*, Joseph Weeres, Jacob Rodriguez and Steven Loomis show the managerial logic and rationality of a megalomaniac.

[50]See Robert Adams, *Finite and Infinite Goods: A Framework for Ethics* (Oxford: Oxford University Press, 1999). When we speak of "goods" in this chapter, we are referring to intrinsically valuable aims and dispositions of character. An intrinsic good is that which is desired for its own sake. In contrast, instrumental goods are those desired in order to obtain another good.

[51]Character education is one facet, a very important facet, of moral education. The moral sphere is designed to tutor a person's character and does so with or without formal effort through the faculty of conscience. Yet the moral sphere contains rules, virtues, reasons, dispositions and moral properties just as real as physical properties. This view is called "moral realism" and is dealt with in greater detail later.

natural level as well as on the supernatural (or spiritual) level. At least five compelling purposes exist for moral education:

1. to keep society from falling apart and returning to a state of nature

2. to ameliorate human suffering

3. to promote life and human flourishing as dignified ends

4. to resolve conflicts in just ways

5. to ensure civil discourse in a plurality of private moralities

On this much, at least reasonable and moral people can universally agree. While clearly necessary, these penultimate purposes are ultimately insufficient for a transcendent moral conception of education. In the ontological sense a person coming into an affirmative relationship with Jesus Christ (abiding in his Word in sanctifying ways) is the ultimate destination for moral education. Moral education, particularly within monotheism and especially within Christianity, has among its chief ends the attentive recognition of God's existence, the necessity of orienting one's being toward a loving relationship with God, and alignment with God's eternal, divine and natural laws, including those that require treating other persons with dignity and justice (Is 1; Mic 6:8).[52] Morality begins, ends and is grounded in God's (ontologically necessary) existence and nature. In the final analysis most Christian educators will view moral education as a value problem, with the human will in conflict with God's love and holiness (Rom 6–7). It is a problem of sin and a sin nature.

The value problem is overcome on two dimensions: on the natural level, through the proper tutoring of the character using the assortment

---

[52]It is important to distinguish between these various types of law. Eternal law is God's providential ordering of natures to their ends, e.g., human beings were designed to fellowship with God, eyeballs are designed to see, a tree's nature is to help regulate the ecosystem (and provide a base for the ink on this page). Natures are discovered inductively, through the routines of reason and observation. Divine laws are those specific commands from God in time, including the Decalogue and the commands of Jesus of Nazareth. Natural law arises from God's eternal law concerning the nature of things and is grounded in this higher reality. Natural law is known deductively, e.g., we deduce that human beings are intrinsically valuable beings, therefore rape of women and the torture of infants for amusement is wrong. Positive law includes all human-based law, including, convention, civil, public, common and state law. Traditionally, positive law largely has been grounded on principles emerging from divine and natural law. Indeed, the founding American documents presuppose and directly appeal to natural law.

of dimensions from the moral sphere, and on the supernatural level with an existential turn toward God. Religious communities see the answer to the value problem in a proper equilibrium between developing responsible human autonomy in freedom (being able to resist the crowd if required by divine/natural law or conscience) and of civil and divine heteronomy (recognizing particular components of society and most especially God as legitimate moral authorities). These moral authorities urge the striving for certain types of goods—for example, *agapē* (love) or *civitas* (civic virtue)—and place certain kinds of obligations upon us—for example, *dikaiosynē* (be just, do justice).

In addition to the five purposes of moral education already mentioned, other reasons exist for moral education. These include reaching a state of self-actualization, reducing pathology and advancing civilization through the strengthening of the social contract.[53] The nature of how an individual classroom or school is run has direct implications for how participants view or will come to view the social contract. The school as an institution helps prepare future citizens for this social compact.

Reasons, too, are often grounded in a spirit of pragmatism. The Protagorean spirit—in short, humans are the measure of all things—captures the overarching principle girding human-centered morality.[54] In contrast to their religious counterparts, secular humanists tend to view moral education as a technical problem: with the correct (therapeutic) inputs or right political rules, society can condition or construct a psychologically healthy person, which produces an increasingly rational, *ergo* moral, person. In this sense morality is not transcendent but is conventional, even antirealist in that it denies the moral sphere is anything but a convention of culture or social construction. Morality is ultimately subject to the relative caprice of a person, institution or culture. Under the technical framework of education, the inductivity of secular psychology replaces the deductive metaphysics of Christian philosophy and theology.[55]

---

[53]See Paul Kurtz, *Humanist Manifestos I and II* (Buffalo, N.Y.: Prometheus, 1973).

[54]Protagoras (485-420 B.C.) was an early Greek sophist and antagonist of Socrates. See Plato's *Protagoras* (New York: Penguin, 1956).

[55]Two versions of secular humanism exist: one that values autonomy (with roots in genetics and psychology) and the other valuing heteronomy (with roots in anthropology and sociology).

Moral education as such has over the centuries traversed this dichotomy between God-centered and human-centered morality. Some argue that for anything to get done in the area of moral education, it is critical to begin the framework of a public morality and moral education with areas of near universal agreement. In other words, consensus on several of the essentials must precede diversity on the particulars. At some point all educators will be served by a greater, more rigorous understanding of the philosophical presuppositions that ground and guide every sense and version of moral education program. Christian educators perhaps have more responsibility in developing the ability to convey why a particular moral rule or virtue is right. Without such knowledge and the ability carry it off, Christian educators may fail to adequately have their colleagues and their students appreciate the greater depths of human capacities, faculties, potentialities, pathways and purposes that are necessary before real and long-term changes can take place within human beings and, as a consequence, within society.

In order to be salt and light (Mt 5:13-16), Christian educators should also consider practicing the ministry of presence, that is, physically being in particular space and time for Jesus, in thoughtful prayer and contemplation (praying for love in the face of rejection, contemplating how to live and inspire for Christ) with an apologetic ability to discuss and argue (in its constructive form) truth in winsome ways. Morality and moral education exemplify at the same time both simple and complex components. As with any form of knowledge and skills, Christian educators would do well to seek to understand both the simple and complex aspects of morality in order to more successfully exchange this valuable knowledge with youth and colleagues. To the continuous question, Why be moral? community elders and Christian educators should be prepared to offer a satisfactory justification that not only avoids problems of regress and relativism, but more importantly inspires a child (or adult) to *be* a moral person, and an institution to likewise be moral.[56]

---

[56]A regress problem occurs whenever a first cause or principle is absent in a chain. For a chain to exist, a first link must exist. To the question, Why be moral? an antirealist will likely say that the social contract depends on a pragmatic principle of reliability. But this may not be an

MORAL EDUCATION, REALITY, HUMAN NATURE AND THE WILL

Many ethicists say morality is largely driven by our worldview, that each moral education program is driven by a view of the world and a specific conception of how human beings ought to fit into it. If we believe the material universe is the sum total of reality, certain other beliefs, including ethical ones, logically follow. This is also true for theism and other worldviews with varying accounts of metaphysics. Philosopher Ronald Nash identifies a worldview as "a conceptual scheme by which we consciously or unconsciously place or fit every-thing we believe and by which we interpret and judge reality."[57] Put simply: theories about the nature of reality and being drive views of human nature and activity. To see how our respective views of human nature affect our ideas of appropriate human ends, consider this important statement from logician Leslie Stevenson:

> Different conceptions of human nature lead to different views about what we ought to do and how we can do it. If an all-powerful and supremely good God made us, then it is His purpose that defines what we can be and what we ought to be, and we must look to Him for help. If, on the other hand, we are the products of society, and if we find our lives are unsatisfactory, then there can be no real solution until human society is transformed. If we are radically free and can never escape the necessity of individual choice, then we have to accept this and make our choices with full awareness of what we are doing. If our biological nature predisposes or determines us to think, feel, and act in certain ways, then we must take realistic account of that.[58]

---

adequate answer. Why should we be moral for that reason (ad infinitum)? Ultimately, an anti-realist will reply that the survival and continuing evolution of the species, including his or her own survival and evolution, depends on most people adopting conventions of morality. At this point morality no longer is justified as objective principles and properties originating in divine nature. Instead, morality regresses to the human instinct for survival. Conventions serve to temper individual aspirations for power and individual advantage and coerce a sense of coop-eration. This is the nature of the increasingly popular movement called evolutionary ethics. See the writings of Thomas Hobbes, Karl Marx, Friedrich Nietzsche and more recently Bryan Skyrms, *Evolution of the Social Contract* (Cambridge: Cambridge University Press, 1996).

[57]Ronald Nash, *World Views in Conflict* (Grand Rapids: Zondervan, 1992), p. 16. See also Robert George, *Clash of Orthodoxies: Law, Religion, and Morality in Crisis* (Wilmington, Del.: ISI Books, 2001).

[58]Leslie Stevenson and David Haberman, *Ten Theories of Human Nature* (Oxford: Oxford University Press, 1998), p. 4.

In order to understand whether or not a social-ethics and moral-education program may succeed, it is important to briefly investigate the nature of how our beliefs about morality form and reform. The essence of social ethics and moral education is the slight, moderate or radical alteration of one's worldview and commitment to the moral sphere.

Presuppositions about reality. While many views of reality exist, there are two common ways in the Western tradition for human beings to view the core of reality: materialist and dualist. As we saw in earlier chapters, popular materialist views of reality called naturalism (or physicalism or materialism) tend to hold that only nature or physical things exists. Another popular view of reality is called metaphysical dualism. Although technically metaphysical dualism can take either secular or sacred form, theistic dualism (the most widely held version of dualism) holds that the universe is a regulated system where human beings are governed by particular laws (e.g., moral and spiritual laws). Human beings have the freedom to reject these laws, but their rejection may entail temporal or eternal consequences.

Many of the information-and-policy controversies in culture and in the schools are traceable to the battle between these two views. The law of noncontradiction eliminates the pluralistic possibility that both views are ultimately correct accounts of reality. The article of faith for scientific naturalism is that a deity does not exist, hence nature is all there is. Yet no instrument of science and nothing within the methodology of naturalistic or social science could ever *disprove* the existence of a deity.[59] Therefore, the nonexistence of a deity must be presupposed—which is to say it is asserted a priori (before experience or theory), after which the view seeks its coherence. Regarding the social power of scientific presuppositions, review this statement from Harvard biologist Richard Lewontin:

> Our willingness to accept scientific claims that are against common sense is the key to an understanding of the real struggle between sci-

---

[59]In other words, it is a category fallacy were one to scientifically search after God, angels or the soul (all nonphysical entities), simply because both the tools and methodologies of science are designed to observe and measure physical entities and forces that affect them, not immaterial ones. Science has nothing and can have nothing final to say on the question of a deity.

ence and the supernatural. We take the side of science *in spite of* the patent absurdity of some of its constructs, *in spite of* its failure to fulfill many of its extravagant promises of health and life, *in spite of* the tolerance of the scientific community for unsubstantiated just-so stories, because we have a prior commitment to materialism. It is not that the methods of science somehow compel us to accept a material explanation of the phenomenal world but, on the contrary, that we are forced by our a priori adherence to material causes to create an apparatus of investigation and a set of concepts that produce material explanations, no matter how counterintuitive, no matter how mystifying to the uninitiated. Moreover that materialism is absolute for we cannot allow a divine foot in the door.[60]

If certain presuppositions of science keep God out of the picture, then the presuppositions of religion—particularly those of Christianity—argue that there would be no picture at all but for God, the First Cause. Nevertheless, Christianity itself is not only a presupposition (see the work of Alvin Plantinga); it also has many evidences and lines of argument that contribute to its truth bearing.[61] When we break down and examine all the relevant parts of moral education, all moral education programs operate with certain a priori beliefs about reality; yet the Christian educator is warranted in holding that his or hers is the best or most complete explanation of the evidence of reality.

Presuppositions about human nature. This book has made it easier now to appreciate basic theories of human beings, to diagnose what is wrong (and right) with humanity, and to offer some reasonable prescriptions for putting it right. When a person has an unreasonable, wrong or even absurd view of reality at the outset, this likely carries over to his or her view of human nature. There are of course several broad traditions in Christian thought about what constitutes human nature. We hold to the dualist position for theological and philosophical reasons. And while Christian ethics may not require dualism (body and soul), there is a strong tradition for taking such a position.

---

[60]Richard Lewontin, "Billions and Billions of Demons," *New York Review of Books*, January 9, 1997, available online at http://www.nybooks.com/articles/article-preview?article_id=1297 (accessed on May 29, 2009).

[61]Alvin Plantinga, *Warrant and Proper Function* (New York: Oxford University Press, 1993).

Given space limitations we cannot fully articulate that tradition here.[62] There are two main positions. The materialist view of reality tends to define the human being as the sum of its physical parts. The brain, for example, is equated with the mind; mental events are said to be the equivalent of brain events.[63] Whereas a dualist view of reality sees human nature as having a unity of identity, but a unity composed of two parts: body and soul (with mind and spirit existing as components of the soul).[64]

Contrast the views of two leading educationists concerning the orientation of human nature. Alfie Kohn's view of human nature, which is rooted in social-psychology (i.e., human nature is largely the product of our social environment, basically a blank slate theory), with the view of William Kilpatrick, whose view is that human nature has a predisposition to rebel (our nature is the product of our will, and our will has a defect in orientation).[65] Kohn believes that children become cognitively and emotionally aware of others when their own psychosocial needs are met. Kilpatrick suggests that a child's will requires deliberate tutoring toward the good, the inculcation of proper sentiments. Given the two divergent views of human nature, it is not surprising that Kohn argues for moral education programs which change the culture of schools into "caring communities" that meet children's needs. In contrast to the feminist ethics and prosocial skills of Kohn, Kilpatrick is more disposed to the masculine ethics of character education by emphasizing time-tested, universalist principles of virtue. Thus, moral education is not only affected by disputes over components of reality, but moral education is also affected by disputes between feminine and masculine conceptions of ethics.[66]

---

[62]For a full discussion, please see J. P. Moreland and William Craig, *Philosophical Foundations for a Christian Worldview* (Downers Grove, Ill.: InterVarsity Press, 2003).

[63]See John Searle, *Minds, Brains, and Science* (Cambridge, Mass.: Harvard University Press, 1984); Steven Pinker, *How the Mind Works* (New York: W. W. Norton, 1997).

[64]See J. P. Moreland and Scott Rae, *Body and Soul: Human Nature and the Crisis of Ethics* (Downers Grove, Ill.: InterVarsity Press, 2000).

[65]Alfie Kohn, *Beyond Discipline: From Compliance to Community* (Alexandria, Va.: Association for Supervision & Curriculum Development, 2006); William Kilpatrick, *Why Johnny Can't Tell Right from Wrong* (New York: Touchstone, 1992).

[66]For an account of feminist ethics, see Carol Gilligan, *In a Different Voice: Psychological Theory and Women's Development* (Cambridge, Mass.: Harvard University Press, 1993). For an ac-

Presuppositions about the will. A significant contest between deterministic and libertarian theories of the will has also been fought over for centuries. Today, everyone but the most ardent and mechanistic behaviorist (e.g., a Watson or Skinner and their followers) would argue that human beings possess some capacity of will that directs agency. Agency might be defined as that quality of power that has first-order causal powers and, in turn, possesses the ability to refrain from action. First-order causal powers are those which, apart from any antecedent condition, I will to act. In other words, a libertarian scheme of agency has the following elements:

1. Student *S* is a substance that has the active power to bring about intentional act *e*.

2. *S* exerts active power as a first mover (an "originator") to bring about *e*.

3. *S* has the categorical ability to refrain from exerting active power to bring about *e*.

4. *S* acts for the sake of a reason, which serves as the final cause or teleological goal for which *S* acts.[67]

In moral education we presume that a child, adolescent or adult has the capacity to act toward the good and refrain from acting with vice, assuming he or she has proper functioning faculties. An expectation exists that children, adolescents and adults have both the capacity and the responsibility to act morally and to refrain from acting immorally. When Stephen or Sophia, for the sake of a reason, repeatedly act of their own volition toward the good, they are increasingly empowered over time to achieve the good and avoid vice.

Alternatively, a deterministic model of the will, such as held by many conceptions of behaviorism and some accounts of economics, denies such freedom (or first-order causal powers) of agency. Instead, social, economic, historical, racial, biological and theological conditions dominate and cloud our powers and capacities thus nullifying our first-

count of "masculinist" ethics, see Harvey Mansfield's *Manliness* (New Haven, Conn.: Yale University Press, 2006).
[67]Adapted from Moreland and Rae, *Body and Soul*, p. 124.

mover abilities. This essentially means that Stephen and Sophia do not act freely to chose *x;* rather one or more of these conditions act on them such that certain forces *make* them choose (force Stephen or prevent Sophia from choosing) *x.* These students become second-order (or even tertiary) movers having secondary, almost reactionary, causal powers— similar to a pool ball colliding randomly with other balls on the table. In the social deterministic view the moral-education programs educators select would need to liberate students from the human plight by deconstructing class and institutional structures that negatively affect or enslave many students.[68] For the Christian educator the truth about the will lies somewhere in the elusive middle: the will has both libertarian agency (which secures first-order causal responsibility for acts) and is influenced in significant ways, particularly with respect to those persons with *akrasia* (weak will), by biological, social, institutional and spiritual forces.

MORAL REALISM AND ANTIREALISM

As a subset of ontological realism, moral realism possesses similar characteristics and is described in the following terms: (1) moral statements are the sorts of statements which are true or false, (2) the truth or falsity of our moral statements is largely independent of our moral opinions, and (3) ordinary canons of moral reasoning constitute, under many circumstances at least, a reliable method for obtaining and improving (approximate) moral knowledge.[69] Moral realism admits that ethical properties, principles, laws and relations exist in reality apart from individual or cultural derivation, with, in certain instances, universal applicability to all human beings. While moral realism is not per se an epistemological scheme, it possesses epistemological implications.[70]

---

[68]See R. G. Peffer, *Marxism, Morality, and Social Justice* (Princeton, N.J.: Princeton University Press, 1990).

[69]Richard Boyd, "How to Be a Moral Realist," *Essays on Moral Realism,* ed. Geoffrey Sayre-McCord (Ithaca, N.Y.: Cornell University Press, 1988), p. 182.

[70]A very brief word about antirealism. While moral realism of the kind described affirms an objective reality where truth conditions for moral claims are independent of (but necessarily concern) human beings, antirealist conceptions of morality are the opposite and nearly always reducible to a different sort of power. Antirealist power is nearly always reducible to that Homeric force whose tendency is to subsume liberty to one's (or one's group) discretion,

Consequently, moral realism is the view that there are brute moral *facts* in the universe that human beings know or can know or cannot *not* know in a properly foundational way.[71] These properties are known most likely by way of some faculty of intuition, conscience or heart, reason, numinous perception, or an as-yet-unidentified physical organ leading to a "moral sense."[72] In the sixth chapter of the *Republic*, Plato lays out an argument for two realms divided by a line: the realm of matter (visible by the physical senses) and the realm of the forms or ideas (intelligible by the mind). The former is less real than the later because they are facsimiles of reality. The realm of matter (i.e., sensible particulars in the temporal realm) ultimately gives way to the eternal realm of forms. Knowledge of the eternal forms is what brings illumination and the truth of reality to the educational enterprise. Within early Greek realist conceptions of education, the ways of knowing include reason, understanding, faith and perception.[73]

One of the central roles educators (e.g., parents, teachers, mentors) have is the responsibility to lead students out of a dark state of ignorance into the light of knowledge. Cognition implies not only the capacity for beliefs but, as Lawrence BonJour has argued, the target of cognition itself is true belief.[74] This role, teaching for cognition, is achieved via a variety of pedagogies. The other principal role an educa-

---

irrespective of one's ideology. In general terms the view holds: (1) there are no normative truths about what one (or one's group) morally ought or ought not to do, (2) there are no normative truths about what is rational to do, (3) there are no normative truths about what it is rational to believe, (4) moral statements are not true or false, they are either instrumental (useful) or not, (5) moral statements amount to mere opinion or emotional claims moral opinions originate from self or culture. Since moral antirealism is ultimately nihilistic and dispossessed of all the qualities that secure moral conditions, we shall not consider it any further.

[71]Where should educators locate the knowledge of moral properties? Four options have dominated moral realism: reason, conscience, community and reliable traditions. A fifth area educators ought to reexamine is moral intuition. Here, G. E. Moore's *Principia Ethica* should be compared with Kant's views on the work of reason.

[72]See respectively, G. E. Moore, *Principia Ethica* (Cambridge: Cambridge University Press, 1903); J. Budziszewski, *Written on the Heart* (Downers Grove, Ill.: InterVarsity Press, 1997), and his *The Revenge of Conscience* (Dallas: Spence, 1999); Lawrence Kohlberg, *Essays on Moral Development: Philosophy of Moral Development* (San Francisco: Harper & Row, 1981); William Alston, *Perceiving God: The Epistemology of Religious Experience* (Ithaca, N.Y.: Cornell University Press, 1991); James Q. Wilson, *The Moral Sense* (New York: Free Press, 1993).

[73]Plato, *The Republic* (Buffalo, N.Y.: Prometheus, 1986), pp. 246-53.

[74]Lawrence BonJour, *The Structure of Empirical Knowledge* (Cambridge, Mass.: Harvard University Press, 1985).

tor has is to do soul work, which is to say, educators *care*fully nourish the appetites of the soul toward the appropriate intellectual and moral virtues. This includes vocational training, the skill-based training requisite to land a job or do work. Each of these three functions of education—cognitive development, virtue development and vocational training—have at their root an associate form of knowledge. For example, teaching for cognitive development, which leads people out of a given state of ignorance, generally involves propositional knowledge, knowledge *that*. Teaching for the development of virtues, in contrast, seeks knowledge of a kind that transforms a person's beliefs, dispositions and actions toward the good (e.g., Christ's conception of "good"). This is *why* knowledge. And finally, education for vocational training is mostly concerned with skill-oriented knowledge, or knowledge *how*. These kinds of knowledge are context dependent, contingent on a particular teleology.

Indoctrination is different than education. The process of education seeks at its end *true* belief with understanding, whereas indoctrination seeks, at its end, *mere* belief of a sort. Education implies learning without coercion; an existentially voluntary, willing and mutual effort on the part of a student and teacher. Indoctrination implies the opposite. Education is usually liberating, with knowledge bringing the opportunity of cognitive, spiritual and economic emancipation. Indoctrination depends on information that tends to seek control of beliefs, attitudes, dispositions and, ultimately, the actions of human beings. Therefore, our understanding of indoctrination is as follows: a person indoctrinates belief(s) *B* if he or she teaches with the intention that the student(s) believe *B* regardless of the evidence, where evidence counts minimally as "anything that has a bearing on the epistemic status of the belief, including reasons (facts known or justifiably believed), experience, or intrinsic features of the proposition believed such as self-evidence."[75]

Whatever the intake of moral knowledge, versions of moral realism are considered cognitive accounts of morality, but not all cognitive ac-

---

[75]William Alston, *A Realist Conception of Truth* (Ithaca, N.Y.: Cornell University Press, 1996), p. 196.

counts of morality are realist. Cognitivism is the idea that moral claims have truth value, where moral properties are superveniently (i.e., imposing themselves on to the human scene) present (in its realist version), and human beings can know the truth claims themselves (except, for example, in skepticism). Forms of cognitive realism include naturalism, nonnaturalism and supernaturalism. Noncognitivism is the general theory that moral claims amount to mere attitudes, dispositions or emotions of the claimant (e.g., the student or teacher).[76]

The general denial of truth obfuscates a transcendent and authoritative realm where moral properties and universals exist. Absent the qualities of transcendence and authority, moral education is at best, and often much worse, mere communitarian window dressing.[77] Although secularism offers versions of moral realism that could be practically effective, there will inevitably be questions related to the ultimate purpose of moral properties, which somehow supervene upon human beings.[78] It may be the case that secular moral realism can never answer the teleological and ontological questions satisfactorily; that is, purpose implies intention, intention implies agent causation, and agent causation implies personality, and personality at this ontological level implies a necessary being, so purpose implies necessary being.

A plausible sacred theory of moral realism could be based on natural law. There are many accounts and versions of natural-law theory. On general terms this theory, which is Aristotelian, Pauline and Thomistic at its roots, holds that principles (or properties) of morality are properly basic to the constitution of humanity such that three things obtain: (1) these moral principles do not *need* to be deduced because they are the kind of principles we human beings cannot not know, (2) these principles cannot be deduced because they are what everything else is deduced from, and (3) in virtue of (1) and (2) any principle that *can* be deduced is not properly basic. Finally, natural laws are said to supervene upon human beings in a way that brings about (1).

---

[76]A. J. Ayer, *Language, Truth, and Logic* (New York: Dover, 1946).
[77]Hunter, *Death of Character*, p. 128.
[78]The de facto question is, Why this state of affairs and not another?

The essence of this supervenience does not appear the result of chance. Because of the nature of principles, relations and properties of the moral kind, these do not appear to arise in an impersonal universe. If they exist in fact, they do not have the "marks" of chance. Therefore, any such moral principles (or properties) may be linked to and terminate in an ontologically necessary being—a cosmic moral lawgiver. Human knowledge of these laws, while not perfect in so-called gray areas or hard cases of moral life, is nevertheless a prima facie duty, and it is reasonable to follow these laws in clear or easy cases. Natural law informs our faculty of intuition directly such that acts (or even dispositions to act) of rape, murder, inflicting pain for pleasure, wanton and malicious mistreatment of the blind, deaf, elderly and senile are morally objectionable. Intuition is a property of the conscience. The conscience lies within the heart. The Hebrew term for heart, *leb*, is identified by the Hebrew Scriptures as the seat of human identity.[79] University of Texas philosopher J. Budziszewski helps the Christian educator as to the paradoxical force of the conscience:

> If the law written on the heart can be repressed, then we cannot count on it to *restrain* us from doing wrong; that much is obvious. I have made the more paradoxical claim that repressing it hurls us into *further* wrong. Holding conscience down does not deprive it of its force; it merely distorts and redirects that force. We are speaking of something less like erosion of an earthen dike so that it fails to hold the water back, than like the compression of a powerful spring so that it buckles to the side. Here is how it works. Guilt, guilty knowledge, and guilty feelings are not the same thing; men and women can have the knowledge without the feelings, and they can have the feelings without the fact. Even when suppressed, however, the knowledge of guilt always produces certain objective needs, which make their own demand for satisfaction irrespective of the state of the feelings. These needs include confession, atonement, reconciliation, and justification.[80]

Where individuals and groups acknowledge principles in accord with natural law, people make vague, imperfect efforts to conform to it.

---

[79]See Robert Saucy, "The Theology of Human Nature," in *Christian Perspectives on Being Human*, ed. J. P. Moreland and David Ciocchi (Grand Rapids: Baker, 1993), pp. 17-54.
[80]Budziszewski, *Written on the Heart*, pp. 27-28.

But in contrast to antirealism, individuals and groups do not *make* these moral laws, which is to say society does not *determine* these laws; people enact (or ought to enact) civil laws and order institutions consistent with them.

The director of Princeton University's James Madison Program in American Ideals and Institutions, Robert George, ties natural law to the moral and civil law of America.

> The concept of "natural law" is central to the Western tradition of thought about morality, politics, and law. Although the Western tradition is not united around a single *theoretical account* of natural law, its principal architects and leading spokesmen—from Aristotle and Thomas Aquinas to Abraham Lincoln and Martin Luther King, Jr.— have shared a fundamental belief that humanly created "positive" law is morally good or bad—just or unjust—depending on its conformity to the standards of a "natural" (viz., moral) law that is no mere human creation. The natural law is, thus, a "higher" law, albeit a law that is in principle accessible to human reason and not dependent on (though entirely compatible with and, indeed, illumined by) divine relation. . . . Thomas Jefferson appeals to "the Laws of Nature and Nature's God" in justifying the American Revolution.[81]

American Christian moralist Martin Luther King Jr. centered his part of the civil-rights movement during the 1950s and 1960s directly within the transcendent strength of natural law. Concerning the law King said:

> What is the difference between a just and unjust law? Well, a just law is a law that squares with moral law. It is a law that squares with that which is right, so that any law that uplifts human personality is a just law. Whereas that law which is out of harmony with the moral law is a law which does not square with the moral law of the universe. It does not square with the law of God, so for that reason it is unjust and any law that degrades the human personality is an unjust law. [82]

---

[81]Robert George, *The Clash of Orthodoxies*, (Wilmington, Del.: ISI Books, 2001), p. 169. See also professor George's more academic work, *In Defense of Natural Law* (Oxford: Clarendon Press, 1999). For a Reformed Protestant account of natural-law theory, see Stephen Grabill's, *Rediscovering the Natural Law in Reformed Theological Ethics* (Grand Rapids: Eerdmans, 2006).

[82]Martin Luther King Jr., "Love, Law, and Civil Disobedience," *A Testament of Hope: The Essen-*

Let us take stock. Some version of moral realism is true and ought to be defended by Christian educators in classrooms, schools, district committees on character education. That version, especially when finding its terminus in Jesus Christ (Col 2:3), is dependent on the idea that moral properties exist, and where they exist they are objective and in many cases universal. They inform human beings about the right dispositions to have, and perhaps more importantly inform us concerning the right ways of acting. Moral realism is authoritative and transcendent, features notably lacking in most moral-education programs in public schools today. However, present attitudes in public school law, management and teaching about God and religion may make attempts to use natural law or any divinity-based morality *de jure* moot. This secularization of the public square and its public school classrooms is a highly regrettable development in American culture, chiefly because it vacates very real and powerful incentives to lead a more complete moral life.

THE MORAL SPHERE

Another way for educators to define and defend morality is to discuss the actual ethical systems of beliefs and judgments concerning right and wrong motives, attitudes and behaviors. Normative ethics "is the philosophical attempt to formulate and defend basic moral principles and virtues governing moral life."[83] Nonnormative ethics is not a prescriptive enterprise: it isn't applied morality. Indirectly, nonnormative ethics sets up a framework from which to have conversations about morality and describe instances of individual and cultural morality. Descriptive ethics "is a factual study of

Ethics Philosophical Morality			
Normative Approaches		Nonnormative Approaches	
Normative Ethics Proper	Applied Ethics	Descriptive Ethics	Metaethics

Figure 5.2. Normative and nonnormative approaches to ethics

---

tial Writings of Martin Luther King, Jr., ed. James Melvin Washington (San Francisco: Harper & Row, 1986), pp. 49, 293. Similar arguments to King's are found in the writings of Reinhold Niebuhr, e.g., *Love and Justice* (Louisville, Ky.: Westminister John Knox Press, 1957).
[83]Tom Beauchamp, *Philosophical Ethics* (New York: McGraw-Hill, 1982), p. 28.

Normative Ethics				
Teleological Schemes Consequence Centered Morality—concerned with *ends* or *the good*			**Deontological Schemes** Duty Centered Morality—concerned with obligation to rules and persons	
Utilitarian: acts are right if they promote more pleasure than pain (Bentham) or greater good for greater number (Mill)	Telos: acts are right if in accord with one's design or purpose or in line with the Good (Plato and Aristotle)	Pragmatism: acts are right if they work for personal satisfaction or reduce group tensions (Dewey)	Formal: acts are right if done from sense of duty to universal standard of good (Kant)	Intuition: acts are guided by a hierarchy of objective moral rules intuited by observer appropriate to situation (Ross)

Example of Blended Scheme Theistic Ethics	
Teleological Acts are right if consequences are in accord with biblical principles	**Deontological** Acts are right if done from duty to love God and neighbor as self (Golden Rule)
When consequences and obligations are thoroughly considered, maximum good for all often sustained	

Figure 5.3. Teleological and deontological schemes of normative ethics

moral attitudes, behaviors, rules, and motives which are embodied in various individuals and cultures."[84] Metaethics focuses its inquiry on the meaning of moral terms such as *justice* and *good*. Applied ethics is the actuating of moral conduct under given schemes of morality and areas of life such as medicine, law, education and business. The target here is a normative one. Figures 5.2 and 5.3 roughly help to orient our direction.

A teleological theory, which focuses on the purpose of morality itself, ties moral education to right or just outcomes. An act is good if target consequences obtain. In contrast, a deontological theory suggests that it is an intrinsic good to do our duty for duty's sake. In this schema moral rules or principles govern our actions. Both teleological and deontological systems offer different grounding to accommodate multiple and varying

[84]J. P. Moreland and Norman Geisler, *The Life and Death Debate: Moral Issues of Our Time* (New York: Praeger, 1990), p. xi.

metaphysics. For example, rules and duties can be grounded in either human conventions (e.g., constitutions, declarations of rights and treaties) or in the divine (e.g., religious moral codes, practices and traditions allegedly from a cosmic moral law giver). Likewise teleological-oriented ethics may also be nontheistic (e.g., care ethics advocated by Nel Noddings and Carol Gilligan) or theistic (e.g., ethics emphasizing human ends in keeping with original design features).[85] Thus neither teleological ethics nor deontological ethics is absolutely beholden to a particular metaphysic. Yet both are intimately concerned with right actions. We have briefly covered the two primary theories of human nature and actions. But what of the human actor (the student)? Is there a way to improve the chances of right actions by focusing on the intrinsic nature of the student's character?

Regarding ethical categories, virtue ethics is distinct from normative ethics. Where normative ethics focuses almost entirely on the *actions* of persons, virtue ethics emphasizes the moral development of the *person* performing those actions. In educational parlance virtue ethics is the summum bonum of character education. Any moral-education theory would be deficient without some attempt to develop the character of human beings. For by attempting to improve the internal dispositions of souls it would seem to logically follow that persons would live more ethically fulfilling lives.[86] Indeed, a public morality should blend aspects of authoritative rules and duties, with the consideration of right and just consequences, along with increasing sanctification of the moral agent. What is "virtue" and how does it interplay with character? And how can human beings develop virtuous character? The answers to these two questions are crucial to understanding what is taking place in contemporary moral education.

In antiquity Augustine defined virtue as the art of right conduct; ordinate affections—loving certain things in the right way, in the right

---

[85]Nel Noddings, *Educating Moral People: A Caring Alternative to Character Education* (New York: Teachers College Press, 2002); John Hare, *Why Bother Being Good? The Place of God in the Moral Life* (Downers Grove, Ill.: InterVarsity Press, 2002).

[86]It would seem many, perhaps most, virtue ethicists presume an immaterial component or substance of the human being. This usually takes the form of a soul. By advocating an internal reorientation of a person's character over time, we are joining Aristotle and Augustine in postulating a method of moral sanctification of one's soul.

degrees. Aquinas defined it further by noting the term *virtue* could be applied to the two chief aspects of the soul: intellect and moral appetites. Thus, there are virtues relevant to intellect and morality.[87] Moral virtues are those habits of action that tend to perfect the species-specific ends of the soul (usually in terms of design by God). Loving one's neighbor, becoming a just person and seeking the rational mean are examples of species-specific ends of the soul.[88] It is a state of moral excellence consistent with the design purposes of the human beings. Aquinas reasoned that there are four chief or cardinal virtues: (1) prudence (which he said is the principal of all virtues), (2) justice, (3) temperance and (4) fortitude. These virtues become properties of the soul over the course of time in cooperation with one's will. Thus the development of appropriate habits and dispositions during childhood becomes a critical pedagogical feature of character and moral education. We believe that it is possible for Christian educators to transcend this problem in our effort to develop a universal public morality.

There are several ways to integrate virtue ethics with teleological and deontological ethical systems.[89] Figure 5.4 will help us to conceptualize options related to virtues and rules.

	Virtues	Rules
Option 1	Virtue ethics are basic	Principles/rules are derivative
	(Virtue drives rules)	
Option 2	Virtues are derivative	Principles/rules are basic
	(Rules drive virtues)	
Option 3	Virtue ethics and moral principles/rules are complementary, equally basic spheres of morality, the former focusing on character traits of persons, the latter on principles	
Option 4	Virtue ethics and moral principles/rules are two different spheres of morality, the former specifying an ethics of supererogation for moral saints and heroes, the latter specifying an ethics of obligation for common morality	

Figure 5.4. Integrating virtue ethics with teleological and deontological ethical systems

---

[87]Robert Roberts and Jay Wood, "Humility and Epistemic Goods," in *Intellectual Virtue: Perspectives from Ethics and Epistemology,* ed. Michael DePaul and Linda Zagzebski (Oxford: Oxford University Press, 2003).
[88]Aristotle *Nicomachean Ethics* (Buffalo, N.Y.: Prometheus, 1986), p. 53.
[89]See Moreland and Geisler, *Life and Death Debate.*

	Duty	Consequence	Virtue
Concern	moral obligations rule-centered	moral consequences result-centered	character development character-centered
Principles	discovered rule determines result	created result determines rule	created virtuous person determines rule and result

Figure 5.5. Three moral dimensions contrasted

As we have suggested, Christian educators seek a comprehensive, thoroughly transcendent, and authoritative public morality for all persons, often independent of situation. It is our notion, then, that option three coupled with the consideration of consequences is an appropriate direction to this investigation. Figure 5.5 illustrates all three of these moral dimensions in contrast.

So, a key approach toward development of a realist moral-education program entails teaching several universal rules or principles and several target virtues, which together will more likely produce outcomes or consequences of an ethical nature. For example:

- Three rules

  1. Caring for—treating well in love and justice—one's neighbor (from Jesus)

  2. Act especially on that maxim you would will as a universal law (modified categorical imperative from Kant)

  3. Always treat human beings as intrinsically valuable ends, never as means (ends principle from Kant)

- Four cardinal virtues

  1. Prudence: the right application of reason

  2. Justice: acting for the sake of a due and righteous end

  3. Temperance: to say and do as we ought

  4. Fortitude: the ability to withstand enticement

If persons seek to violate the spirit of the public morality, then liberty-limiting principles exist to ensure social liberty. Moral philosopher Tom Beauchamp suggests there are historically four liberty-limiting principles. They are

1. *The harm principle:* a person's liberty is justifiably restricted to prevent *harm to others* caused by that person.

2. *The principle of paternalism:* a person's liberty is justifiably restricted to prevent *harm to self* caused by that person.

3. *The principle of legal moralism:* a person's liberty is justifiably restricted to prevent that person's *immoral behavior.*

4. *The offense principle:* a person's liberty is justifiably restricted to prevent *offense to others* caused by that person.[90]

Grades	Agapism/ Care	Duty/Rules	Virtue	Consequences	Telos/ Purpose
K-3	modeling from teacher	limited, fair and just, originating from teacher	stories, fables and songs		
4-6	continuing to motivate behaviors	fair, just and originating from teacher with explanation to student	introduction to moral exemplars and cardinal virtues		
7-9	operating behind the scenes	teacher and student negotiate	exemplars and cardinal virtues	introduction to consequentialist schemes: greater good/ happiness	
10-12	Secondary: Reacquaintance with neighborly love	Tertiary: Duty to rules and principals operate behind the scenes	Primary: Practicing the virtues as center points in self and community	Tertiary: Greater understanding of competing social interests	Secondary: Introduction to human purpose

Figure 5.6. Prospective moral-education matrix

---

[90]Beauchamp, *Philosophical Ethics*, p. 270.

Outside of some constitutional or revolutionary action, there does not seem to be a complimentary set of liberty-limiting principles that an individual may apply against a state or some other form of collective agency and its transgression against the individual.[91]

A PROSPECTIVE MORAL EDUCATION SCHEME

Given what lies within the moral sphere, given the two sources that ground our public morality, given the five purposes of moral education, and given a developmental sequencing strategy, the following moral education matrix (see fig. 5.6) may be one sound way to deliver differentiated moral education to children and adolescents. This one applies to school cultures. Critique it. As an exercise, apply your understandings of child- and adolescent-development theory, biblical understandings and so forth, and construct your own moral-education sequence. How should these areas of the moral sphere interact within an age-appropriate moral-education program?

CONCLUSION

In one sense, the Christian educator today is working at a significant disadvantage within public school systems. The institution and its elites work hard to exclude Christocentric information and have intentionally erected artificial (secular) institutional barriers. This of course denies to moral-education programs four essential characteristics of the moral enterprise: coherence, correspondence, transcendence and comprehensiveness. Thus the secular state must fashion some other way for moral-education programs to achieve coherence. Typically, such efforts are predicated on pluralistic conceptions of ethics, from which three principles soon emerge. First, the *fact* of diversity about morality leads to, second, the *demand* for tolerance among nearly all views, which in turn leads to, third, the *insistence* of respect for persons and their ideas, that is, except for those persons and ideas that file a special claim of being

---

[91]For example, see the Kelo case, where the U.S. Supreme Court expanded the meaning of the Takings Clause (Fifth Amendment) of the U.S. Constitution, thus allowing the state to take private property from an individual citizen under an expanded meaning of "public use" (*Kelo et al. v. City of New London et al.,* Sup. Ct. No. 04-108, February 23, 2005).

transcendent, such as a divine account regarding the moral sphere. All normative information not emphasizing the preeminence of these three principles is typically purged from moral-education programs.

The secular conception of the state is not an informationally neutral conception, as some would like to suppose. A secular state has informational preferences of its own and will sanction some moral education programs over others.[92] Christian educators will do well to offer faith and reason to the complex question of moral education in the public sphere.

---

[92]The secular state cannot answer these questions: How does a proceduralist understanding of the constitutional state (e.g., Kant) achieve autonomous justification and rational assent from the governed? How it is possible to provide a strictly secular, naturalistic justification of political rule? On what ground?

6

Issues and Questions for Educational Practice, Policy and Leadership

In 1964 James Bryant Conant, the former president of Harvard University, authored the careful, multiyear study "The Education of American Teachers," which raised a set of important questions fundamental to the nature of how teachers are educated, trained and certified in the United States (there are some international comparisons as well). Much of the work is relevant to the contemporary problems of educating teachers. What is important for our study is Conant's observation about the insufficiency of mere survey work in the philosophy and history of education, too often thought sufficient within teacher preparation programs. Students of education, Conant argued, require more than the stale survey of philosophical positions. He suggested that the best courses in these areas of education have been taught by "the professor of the philosophy of education [who] train[s] his students to think clearly and critically about educational issues . . . [and who has] tackled the problems [in education] that come under the headings of epistemology and ontology."[1]

We have attempted to come up with a text that does some of this within the context of Christian thought. The first three chapters provide a foundational perspective for education. Chapters four and five provide the education student with an applied ontology of the institution of education as it actually exists today and in the near term (the

---

[1]James Bryant Conant, *The Education of American Teachers* (New York: McGraw Hill, 1964), p. 130.

next twenty years or so), not as we might imagine it to exist. In this chapter we show the student where some further work might yield theoretical and practical fruit.

The ideas that an education student considers while at the university preparing to become a teacher and a public intellectual can have a profound effect over time. We sometimes take for granted that educators at every level are themselves leaders of a sort, and many will become school and university leaders in a formal sense. Being a classroom educator is one of the most important leadership positions in a society. Over time, new educators will influence students, families, communities and leaders and boards of education in important ways. New educators will likely join a union or a professional association of teachers. They will sit on committees and will have a voice on how things are run, how they are organized, and what on the agenda receives emphasis. Within a few years they will have opportunities to become department chairs, curriculum coordinators, grant managers, program managers, master teachers training new educators, and assistant principals. A few years after that some educators will become school principals, assistant superintendents and superintendents, and a few will be called to work as clinical faculty in teacher education and as scholars in schools of education. On what basis will this professional work be done? In what direction will it proceed? What worldview and theoretical framework will ground it? What set of institutional facts and information priorities will the educator influence (and be influenced by) over his or her professional career?

We remind ourselves that educators have a responsibility to be institutional stewards and trustees within their own sphere. This entails, among other things, anticipating and raising questions such as these: What are the important questions of practice? What are the necessary policy and leadership questions for twenty-first-century education? What will the effects of globalization and deculturalization return to the field of education? How can Christian teachers and leaders integrate the Christian worldview in public ways by recasting questions in light of the important realities and pressing truths of Jesus Christ? What are the appropriate means and ends of education? This chapter mentions briefly how present and future opportunities for Christian integration might help to add an important set of ideas to the reform of education.

We recognize that all educators true to the profession have certain attitudes, dispositions and actions in common. For example, they should care deeply about the quality of education a child and adolescent receives. However, this book is written specifically with the *Christian* educator in mind. Although much detail is to be worked out, one answer to the dilemma of practice is to develop several plausible schools of thought that have the rigor and power to help enlighten, reform and redeem the institution of education for the triune God. How that is done is where controversies quickly surface.

This brings us back to several important sources informing this particular project. First, our general editors, J. P. Moreland and Frank Beckwith, laid out in their précis a bold integrative mandate for the Christian Worldview Integration series authors. For example, they write that, "Integration [of Christian thought] is crucial to the current worldview struggle and the contemporary crisis of knowledge. . . . There simply is no established, widely recognized body of ethical or religious knowledge now operative in the institutions of knowledge in our culture." If we are reading this correctly, this implies that Christians should consider developing a body of ethical and religious knowledge that operates within the institutions of knowledge in culture. The field of education is a knowledge institution. Therefore, Christian educators should consider developing a body of ethical and religious knowledge that operates within education. We have taken a step in this direction and have signaled where more work might be done.

Second, noted philosopher Dallas Willard made the equally bold and (we believe) accurate claim that the redemption of reason within the institution of education requires Christian thought.

> I think one of the greatest needs today is to help people to understand the changed situation between reason or understanding and revelation in our time—in particular, to understand that what is in trouble on our campuses today is reason itself. . . . My claim will be only the body of Christian knowledge—I will say this slowly—only the body of Christian knowledge and intellectual method can redeem reason. . . . This is

the fundamental fact of our time, from which reason must be redeemed: the incomprehensibility of reason and knowledge in naturalistic terms. Reason and knowledge are not to be found in the sense-perceptible world. It's just that simple. If you have to understand everything in terms of the sense-perceptible world, reason and knowledge are gone.[2]

This is particularly relevant for educators, new or old, because they are and should consider themselves to be in a knowledge profession. And anything that interferes with the optimal development and transfer of knowledge should be examined.

However, the institution of education, and educational practice specifically, function today largely on the informational priorities and assumptions of the sense-perceptible world. As we have shown, emphasis on the mere utility of the sense-perceptible world can bring the institution to a point of disequilibrium where the informational environment is corrupted, where rationality *(ratio)* is split or divided from reason *(intellectus)*, where the individual and his or her education is sacrificed at the twin altars of the social engineer: uniformity and efficiency. The division of rationality from reason authorizes a lower-cost direction in education and society, because arguments over what direction to proceed are informed by the instrumentality of means and never on the value of ends. Naturalism, scientism and secularism have adjudicated the ends in ways that are no longer open to review. For example, the artificial church-state disputes are the product and not the cause of these lower-cost philosophies. Today, the institution of education functions on a nonteleological account of social reality. This is a problem for ontological reasons covered in this book. Restoration of the proper ends of education in the classroom or school, at the college or university will help to remedy this problem. This seems to be what professor Willard is getting at.

Third, although we did not cover his work in detail, referring to it here or there, the faith integration example of C. S. Lewis was instrumental to our project. We both admire and appropriate his body

---

[2]Dallas Willard, "The Redemption of Reason" (keynote address at the academic symposium "The Christian University in the Next Millennium," Biola University, La Mirada, Calif., February 28, 1998).

of work. Two works are especially important: *The Abolition of Man* and *Miracles*. Educators would do well to read them both.

Fourth, the salting and lighting equilibrium mandate discussed by Jesus Christ (Mt 5:13-16) makes worldview integration relevant to the Christian educator, new or old. This is an ongoing, day-to-day activity, not a one-time thing. It is not enough to try to live in some ideal pie-in-the-sky world or to live as an ostrich and ignore the very real social problems in education. Sustainability of good practice requires that Christian educators connect with the truths of reality, not hide from them.

Justice-seeking, thoughtful educators of whatever faith tradition, or even of no faith tradition, simply must negotiate the hostile effects of certain social structures and institutions on behalf of other human beings. This is what the popular educational phrase *change agency* is meant to imply. In this regard we touched on Alasdair MacIntyre's insightful essay "Social Structures and Their Threats to Moral Agency," and his important maxim "Always ask about your social and cultural order what it needs you and others not to know."[3] There are two general ways to work within social institutions: (1) with the knowledge that institutions are powerful instruments that act as "hidden persuaders" across the social environment, and with the awareness that they influence beliefs and the belief structures of participants, and (2) with no knowledge that social institutions have this power. The exercise of effective moral agency, says MacIntyre, requires the first.

When we direct our comments to a Christocentric approach, we are of course not speaking of a theocratic or heavy-handed sense of Christianity or integration of Christian thought, nor a return to a past golden age, to borrow Marsden's important caution, though we must not neglect rich traditions as informative models.[4] We admire, for example, the truth-bearing work of John Paul II, who intimated during his long life that Christianity (today) does not impose but proposes. We mean that Christian educators simply have the ontological

---

[3] Alasdair MacIntyre, "Social Structures and Their Threats to Moral Agency," *Philosophy* 74, no. 289 (1999): 328.

[4] George Marsden, *The Outrageous Idea of Christian Scholarship* (Oxford: Oxford University Press, 1997), p. 10.

and epistemological right to inform their theory and practice in ways that are Christian, just as critical pedagogues have the right to inform their theory and practice in ways that are Marxian. But a Christian influence varies with context. An educator may cooperate, may withhold cooperation or even resist the social structure. It depends on the nature of the circumstances and the institutional facts at hand; it depends on what the moral law requires.

We see an opportunity going forward for both practitioners and theorists to influence the institution in positive ways by becoming active, critical, constructive and hope-restoring stewards of education; to consider questions few are considering and humbly but boldly propose solutions few today understand or think important. In other words there is an opportunity to affect the agenda of education, to change the code of communication channels within the institution, and to widen the information base of knowledge, and to increase the costs in the development and flourishing of human beings. This is in part what philosophy of education is all about: reasoned, forward-thinking, philosophical stewardship of the institution of education. To paraphrase philosopher Arthur Holmes, when brilliant teaching, liberal learning and first-rank scholarship is offered to God, it becomes an act of worship. "In short, we must return to the liberal arts. We must build community and reintroduce the *paidagogus*. Christian scholarship must be cultivated, and we must focus on the theological foundations of learning."[5]

We have also made the descriptive claim that many Christian educators and leaders in U.S. schools, and in some sectors of higher education, have acted rationally. That is, within one point of view of rationality, they have responded predictably to the institutional incentives set before them. They have read the prevailing institutional signals accurately and have oriented their activities (e.g., their leadership, research, practice, policy) in a direction consistent with institutional standardization. They have become agents of accommodation. By abiding the

---

[5]Arthur Holmes, *Building the Christian Academy* (Grand Rapids: Eerdmans, 2001), p. 118. Holmes was talking about Christian higher education, but his words have value for our broader project.

information channels, they have lowered the costs to their own work, even while costs have risen against the social welfare, particularly to poor children and their families who have little capacity to opt out of the technical institution. Dewey spoke of "waste" in the schools. Well, this is a form of waste in the opportunities lost by educators who lacked the courage to act.

It is fair to say that some leaders and educators have responded to an inferior set of incentives, to lower priced sets and sources of information, to well-meaning but harm-inducing externalities, to an amoral (and possibly immoral) rule structure, and to the wrong theoretical model of education. Some educators have traded off their convictions for preferences, privatized their public worldview and become so comfortable *in* the world as to become *of* the world.[6] Certain principles of the Enlightenment (e.g., epistemological skepticism), modernity (e.g., pragmatism, scientism and behaviorism) and postmodernity (e.g., banal pluralism) have so shaken educators' confidence in what is believed that it has separated them professionally from the rich historical traditions of education and from the power of Christian faith publicly available to them. Finally, in this regard, what central theoretical problems in education, if any, are Christian scholars, educators and leaders trying to solve?

---

[6]We recall the words of the prophet Ezekiel when God advised him to remind the shepherds of Israel the purpose of their calling. "The word of the LORD came to me: Mortal, prophesy against the shepherds of Israel: prophesy, and say to them—to the shepherds: Thus says the Lord GOD: Ah, you shepherds of Israel who have been feeding yourselves! Should not shepherds feed the sheep? You eat the fat, you clothe yourselves with the wool, you slaughter the fatlings; but you do not feed the sheep. You have not strengthened the weak, you have not healed the sick, you have not bound up the injured, you have not brought back the strayed, you have not sought the lost, but with force and harshness you have ruled them. So they were scattered, because there was no shepherd; and scattered, they became food for all the wild animals. My sheep were scattered, they wandered over all the mountains and on every high hill; my sheep were scattered over all the face of the earth, with no one to search or seek for them.

Therefore, you shepherds, hear the word of the LORD: As I live, says the Lord GOD, because my sheep have become a prey, and my sheep have become food for all the wild animals, since there was no shepherd; and because my shepherds have not searched for my sheep, but the shepherds have fed themselves, and have not fed my sheep; therefore, you shepherds, hear the word of the LORD: Thus says the Lord GOD, I am against the shepherds; and I will demand my sheep at their hand, and put a stop to their feeding the sheep; no longer shall the shepherds feed themselves" (Ezek 34:1-10 NRSV). The roles of the steward and shepherd are similar in that a core responsibility is to guide human flourishing in the light of reason and revelation.

Given our analysis, which suggests the displacement of first principles for a subordinate set of second-order and tertiary principles, it
would be academic malpractice not to raise objections and challenge
new and veteran educators to seek an active, more reliable path of theory and practice. If what we have argued in this book is even close to
being a true account of the institution and its direction, then we have
leveled an original critique whose potential implications are important
for the reform agenda of the institution of education worldwide. For
those implications to be realized, a plausible Christian-influenced architecture of thought is called for, one that is consistent with the faith
and learning précis offered by Moreland and Beckwith in the series
preface to this book.

THINKING BROADLY ABOUT EDUCATION

Since we have taken pains to trace some of the vital background presuppositions of education (chaps. 1-3) and to offer a critique of its present direction (chaps. 4-5), it is appropriate now to discuss in broad terms
the possibility for a new institutional direction. In this regard Nobel
economist Douglass North's view of how to effect incremental institutional change is helpful:

> 1. A set of ... entrepreneurs articulate a new set of beliefs in fundamen-
> tal conflict with the existing order—beliefs that are held, at first, by a
> small minority.
> 2. The opponents of these entrepreneurs act in ways [silence, radical
> opposition, etc.] that make these beliefs appear true, thus confirming
> the revolutionary beliefs in the eyes of pivotal players. Thus events be-
> yond the direct control of the new ideas proponents occur that lend
> some credence to these beliefs.
> 3. The result is a spread of the beliefs to some of the pivotal decision
> makers. When the pivotal decision makers accept the radically new be-
> liefs, they provide sufficient political support for radical action.[7]

Therefore, let us for the moment think as entrepreneurs. Borrowing
from North's framework of institutional change, there might be three

---

[7]Doug North, *Understanding the Process of Economic Change* (Princeton, N.J.: Princeton University Press, 2005), pp. 106-7.

plausible remedies or antidotes to the technical model of education. This is certainly not an exhaustive set of remedies, but three that might have an important impact. The extent of that impact will be known through further research.[8]

First, there is a need to optimize the flow and diversity of information into the production processes of education. The technical model of education will not, because by definition it cannot, optimize the flow and diversity of information. As we learned earlier, the technical model feeds off a closed system of standardized, measurable information—it cannot survive long without it. We are calling on educators to place a brake on the technical system by reintroducing some of the previously eliminated particular information. By maximizing the flow or volume of information and the diversity of its direction and sources (particularly information from the local, individual, cultural), the technical model cannot sustain itself. It will no longer be able to aggregate human performance to a mean. It will no longer be able to lock up the means and ends of education in naturalistic forms. While there is some uncertainty and risk about what schooling will look like, human development can be improved by proceeding in the direction of variation. Liberalizing the volume, kinds and sources of information is a more tenable position for knowledge and skills development. In the classroom and the school, this means liberalizing the learning environment in ways that help to optimize the interests, talents and gifts of individual students while balancing the broader interests of society. Liberalization of the environment might include certain democratic practices within the classroom, diverse pedagogical techniques used to reach as many individual children as possible, and various reforms to the curriculum. Professional educators would control the means of education

---

[8]As Kenneth Arrow suggests, nearly every research endeavor entails some uncertainty. "A particularly important class of projects that society may consider are research activities. By definition, research is a venture into the unknown, such as geographic exploration was in the time of Columbus. The outcome of any research project is necessarily uncertain, and the most important results are likely to come from projects whose degree of uncertainty to begin with was greatest. The shifting of risks is thus most needed for what is very likely the most profitable of activities from society's point of view" ("Insurance, Risk, and Resource Allocation," in *Collected Papers of Kenneth Arrow*, vol. 4: *The Economics of Information* [Cambridge, Mass.: Belknap, 1984], p. 81).

and would partner with local communities and states in identifying the ends of production. This direction would involve a plausible equilibrium between the individual and collective within education.

Second, there is a need to loosen governing structures and rein in the span of their control. The technical model enjoys a quasi-hierarchical span of control through narrow rules and an expanding public-private bureaucracy that enforces them. Not only is it increasingly difficult for the private to operate outside of the public, it is difficult to achieve systemic diversity of provision for schooling anywhere, especially within the public and increasingly for the private. By scaling down this model, thus scaling down the span of its central control, the institution is disaggregated and decentralized. This means allowing one thousand flowers to bloom, where decision making has more connection to a local community. It may also mean that schooling may look different in different locations. Individual organizations no longer feel institutional risk about being different. Although small in scale as countries go, New Zealand decentralized their education system (and other institutions) with very promising results, including the creation of "self-managed schools," thus assigning accountability where it belongs: closest to the point of exchange between teacher/professor and student, school and family, college or university and its constituents. More empirical and theoretical research is needed concerning how scale affects information in education.

And third, in order to foster legitimate human development in just ways, an overarching (true) universal is needed in order to prevent the corruption of education by nonbenevolent institutional, organizational or individual forces and actors. Like C. S. Lewis's *Abolition of Man* argument, we would propose that moral law already exists for this purpose, but it may be supplemented elsewhere by other sources available within the moral sphere (e.g., Aristotelian virtues, MacIntyre's communitarian traditions, Kantian duties and obligations, Nodding's care ethics).

These three very brief proposals seek to (1) expand the information base of education while (2) anchoring it to some reliable version of ontological realism. The proposals are sourced from the Hebrew and Christian Scriptures, and are not inconsistent with the equilibrium work offered by Jesus Christ himself. As we suggested, further research is needed in these three areas.

We turn now to a few specific recommendations in three market sectors: public education, Christian education and schools of education. Arguably two of these, public schools and schools of education, are market sectors most shielded from reform, not only because they would probably have the most to lose from a thorough recalibration but because these two sectors of the education market have participated in structuring the rules of the game that favor a technical rationality.

CHRISTIAN EDUCATORS AS PUBLIC INTELLECTUALS

Another critical reform area is the need to see educators (and educators seeing themselves) as public intellectuals. The historian Mark Noll wrote in the 1990s that the evangelical segment of the Christian church lacked a mind.[9] Today, philosopher J. P. Moreland and others see some hope on the horizon for the intellectual engagement of the Protestant side of the church. Moreland writes:

> Signs indicate we are gaining momentum and may well be ready to manifest our Lord's true character in a way appropriate to the crisis of our age. Our Christian schools are already outperforming our secular counterparts. More and more churches are recovering our rightful role in racial reconciliation, in caring for the poor, and in being a presence of light in a dark place. There is growing dissatisfaction with playing church. The Intelligent Design movement cannot be stopped. Christians have substantially recaptured lost ground in the discipline of philosophy in universities around the land.[10]

We desire that Noll's critique evolves into Moreland's hope, that Christian's across broad denominational traditions are taking seriously Jesus' admonition to renew the mind (Mt 25) and Paul's instructions to oppose false beliefs and make one's mental life captive to Christ (2 Cor 10:5). These principles apply to every Christian independent of creed or denomination.

---

[9]Mark Noll, *The Scandal of the Evangelical Mind* (Grand Rapids: Eerdmans, 1995).
[10]J. P. Moreland, *Kingdom Triangle: Recover the Christian Mind, Renovate the Soul, Restore the Spirit's Power* (Grand Rapids: Zondervan, 2007), p. 13.

In his quixotic book *Teachers as Intellectuals*, leading critical pedagogue Henry Giroux offers an ideological rationale for why teachers in
the schools ought to refine their ways of seeing social reality and structure their professional practice in order to assist their students to (1)
deconstruct centers of illegitimate power (e.g., usually class and race,
but Christians can broaden this out) and (2) develop a politics of education that liberates individuals from certain cold vulgarities of behaviorism and capitalism.[11] From what we can tell, the critical perspective is
notably absent from Christian writers on matters of education. There
seems to be a view that maybe we could do with a little less standardization, but everything else in education seems to be working just fine.

We agree with Giroux that schoolteachers ought to be educated in
such a way as to see themselves as intellectuals. We argue that Christian educators ought to consider becoming *public* intellectuals on behalf
of their students and Jesus Christ. Generally, educators who work in
the schools, public or private, are intellectuals to the extent that they
are successfully using their own reason and rationality (their intellect)
as well as engendering in others the struggle for a good education, that
is, the acquisition of relevant knowledge, skills and virtues of the democratic citizen, on behalf of that individual (the self) and on behalf of
the community (us). This work and what it entails is much more complex than that. Indeed, it requires nothing less than the complex gen-
erational renewal of culture, society and their social institutions. While
the critical pedagogue approach to this intellectual work is arguably
much more embedded in the training of educators in the United States
than is specifically Christian approaches, there are aspects of both approaches that are important for the new educator to consider.

Learning how to accurately critique and deconstruct social reality is
important intellectual work. Randall Collins notes the importance of
awareness for the intellectual.

> What [intellectuals] learn that makes them eminent is an awareness of
> not only of the great solutions of the past, the ingredients that they can
> put into their own creations, but also where the action next will be.

---

[11]Henry A. Giroux, *Teachers as Intellectuals* (New York: Bergin & Garvey, 1988).

They need to appropriate the puzzles which have the greatest significance for the future activities of their colleagues. This sense of how to relate to the intellectual field is the most important item of cultural capital individuals take from their teachers.[12]

Educators who have been *critically* trained are often highly effective observers of social reality. They are also idealists looking for a better, more effective set of results that (they believe) can be delivered by a more democratic education system. No less important then is the reconstruction of social reality on basic principles of justice. Critical educators are not mere technicians dispensing prepackaged curricula. Becoming an effective and virtuous educator in the tradition of Jesus requires much more than mere techniques or methods in the classroom, much more than classroom-management strategies for behavioral control, much more than even expertise in the content-area knowledge (though it requires these in some form and measure). The theory and practice of the profession of education requires far more, and yet it includes the indispensable liaison work of becoming (being) a public intellectual.[13]

Most of the work done in professional practice is of a public nature; it is done in front of a small-scale public of students, the next generation of citizens responsible for the stewardship and renewal of civilization. We link the term *public* to the term *intellectual* because there has been an inordinate privatization or compartmentalization of that domain most important to the Christian educator: the truth and reality that Jesus Christ is Lord of all that is, and who has dominion over every square foot of physical reality and every dimension of nonphysical reality, including the intellect. Being a public intellectual for Jesus Christ, being a public intellectual from within any of the orthodox Christian traditions, is just as legitimate as the public intellectuals Giroux and the critical pedagogues are concerned with creating from within the Marxist tradition. Jesus

---

[12]Randall Collins, *The Sociology of Philosophies: A Global Theory of Intellectual Change* (Cambridge, Mass.: Belknap, 1998), p. 33.

[13]On a minimalist view educators who are intellectuals are those who use their intellect (higher reason) throughout their professional practice. This includes both the deconstructive and the reconstructive aspects of the educational enterprise, what Brazilian educator Paulo Freire called pedagogy of the oppressed, pedagogy of hope, pedagogy of love, pedagogy of freedom, etc.

Christ had (and has) more to say about justice, social or otherwise, than any other thinker in history. Christian educators can and should consider adopting a transcendent view of their work, a view whose central virtue is the fearless pursuit and transfer of knowledge. Of course, this requires a new, subtler view of faith and reason as intellectual work.

There are several ways by which Christian educators can inoculate themselves from the social pressures of the institution of education. C. S. Lewis's idea of the scholar is one way that we favor. Lewis preached the essay "Learning in War-Time" at an Evensong service October 22, 1939, at a time when Great Britain was at war with Germany. Its insight on the purpose of becoming learned, becoming a scholar has direct application to our argument in this book. We cite Lewis's argument at an appropriate length.

> [The essential nature of the learned life] has indirect values which are especially important today. If all the world were Christian, it might not matter if all the world were uneducated. But, as it is, a cultural life will exist outside the Church whether it exists inside or not. To be ignorant and simple now—not to meet the enemies on their own ground—would be to throw down our weapons, and to betray our uneducated brethren who have, under God, no defense but us against the intellectual attacks of the heathen. Good philosophy must exist, if for no other reason, because bad philosophy needs to be answered. The cool intellect must work not only against cool intellect on the other side, but against the muddy heathen mysticisms which deny intellect altogether. Most of all, perhaps, we need intimate knowledge of the past. Not that the past has any magic about it, but because we cannot study the future, and yet need something to set against the present, to remind us that the basic assumptions have been quite different in different periods and that much which seems certain to the uneducated is merely temporary fashion.
>
> A man who has lived in many places is not likely to be deceived by the local errors of his native village; the scholar has lived in many times and is therefore in some degree immune from the great cataract of nonsense that pours from the press and the microphone of his own age. The learned life then is, for some, a duty.[14]

---

[14]C. S. Lewis, "Learning in War-Time," in *The Weight of Glory* (New York: HarperCollins, 2001), pp. 58-59.

Intellectual work requires a breadth, depth, width, volume, diversity and complexity of information and knowledge unlike nearly any other work in order to expand the frontiers of learning, in order to preserve knowledge and liberty, and in order to bring nearer optimal states of social welfare.[15]

Academic freedom of course is critical to the intellectual enterprise. The loss of that freedom in any amount necessarily and adversely affects a range of goods. Specifically, it tends to narrow the range of thought, the facility to see diverse options and viable alternatives, the capacity for creative and disciplined thought, the ability to transcend one's present time, the preservation of moral agency in the face of constricting social structures and institutional role playing. It is also in this highly uniform yet competitive institutional environment where important tradeoffs are made;[16] it is imperative to recognize that not all things are compatible.[17]

THE PUBLIC SCHOOLS

We advocate the optimization of information into the learning activities of public schools, which is far less likely to occur in schools and school districts of scale. One approach for future study is to examine the effects of progressively loosening the school curriculum from more uniform curricula in the early grades to less uniform curricula in the

---

[15]See Randall Collins, *The Sociology of Philosophies: A Global Theory of Intellectual Change* (Cambridge, Mass.: Belknap, 1998), and Charles Murray, *Human Accomplishment: The Pursuit of Excellence in the Arts and Sciences, 800 B.C. to 1950* (New York: Harper, 2004).

[16]One of those tradeoffs is freedom. For an excellent statement about liberty in the academic context, see Michael Polanyi, *The Logic of Liberty* (Chicago: University of Chicago Press, 1951).

[17]The more common view is that all things can be compatible. That with enough imagination and mental work, a college or university does not need to divide between its independence and a modern, technical system of production. However, in order to reach this belief there must either be a denial of scarcity, including information scarcities inherent to production, or a narrower definition of the term *independence*. In this line of thought there is often a refusal to see or to understand that a tradeoff is being made as institutional scale builds up pressure for universal information, which necessarily causes the depletion of particular information. Yet the avid belief in compatibility is why versions of Hegel's thought or the John Nash (1950) equilibrium is so appealing among social scientists in education. Social choice problems between the individual and the collective are thought inherently resolvable through discovery or creation of the right set of rules, a process of synthesis, when in reality the aggregation process over time does violence to individual and local production preferences. (See John Nash, "The Bargaining Problem," *Econometrica* 18, no. 2 [April 1950]: 155-62.)

later grades, which may capture information that is more particular to an individual student. As students mature and develop responsible autonomy, as they become engaged political citizens and economic agents, their decision-making capacities may be enlarged by providing greater curricular choice sets nearer entry into higher education or the labor market. There are many ways to achieve this aim. Figure 6.1 suggests that there may be some symmetry achieved between the universal and particular information during key stages of human development.

For example, during the elementary years students could be given six hours of instruction based on the universal, standardized information (let us say core knowledge and essential skills basic to all developing human beings) and two hours of interest and gifting-specific instruction as determined by the students, their parents and the teacher or school. By middle school students would receive four hours of instruction in core knowledge and four hours of interest-based instruction in courses providing for aesthetic, artistic, physical and creative development. Finally, provision in high school would be more interest or gifting-driven instruction, with only two hours of core knowledge being required and six hours of independent study or interest-specific instruction available. There is of course an outside range of curricular choices. As students near adulthood, curricular paths and choices should widen, not narrow, in keeping with a vision of freedom and responsible autonomy of individual human beings.

Academic choices can look differently in different locations but might include applied sciences, humanities, arts and integrated studies, including interest-based vocations in the upper grades (engineering, architecture, landscaping, auto shop, farming, computer hardware, small business entrepreneurship, etc.). This process allows for the richer information conditions that can increase human and social capital, as well as the cultural nuances and needs of a local community. Autonomous decision making shifts from the institution (top-down) to the students, their parents and local schools (bottom-up).[18] Yet we must keep in mind

---

[18]Figures 6.1 and 6.2 are ideas in development and will appear in a forthcoming article with Anna-Marie Powers on school organization based on Hebrew principles of information and organizational structures.

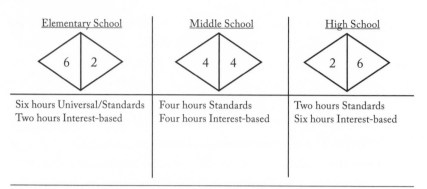

Figure 6.1. Hours of instruction based on level of schooling

that the students are viewed as age-appropriate coproducers of the education good at all stages of their development. As students mature, they assume more liberty and greater responsibility for ownership over the direction of their development.

Decentralized schooling should be viewed in a holistic manner. Students are provided the opportunity to follow through with several particular foci of interest in all years of compulsory education. If the goal of education is in part to produce responsibly critical and ethically creative thinkers who are self-motivated, life-long learners, then a decentralized organizational model will better equip students with basic and choice-driven knowledge, skills and experiences. In our view this model would avoid any particular extremes among educational philosophies, such as progressivism, essentialism and perennialism. It will also help to minimize harms already created by new essentialism. The model carves out structural space for the best content and pedagogical features of each of these philosophies.

Another innovative approach toward information modeling is the Hebraic social-political organization (see fig. 6.2). This model might provide an interesting structure by which to organize some sectors of public schooling. By appropriating a bottom-up organizational model, the individual student becomes the nucleus or core of production activities. At the local level, information is retained in all educational processes and all participants account for complexity. Students increase their autonomy and decision-making responsibility as they move up the educational ladder. The model links the individual student to the local community via the school. The school in a sense becomes, with the family unit, a dynamic point of equilibrium between individual liberty and community responsibility.[19] As we have seen, the school today functions as a mechanism of disequilibrium. It does so by aggregating the individual into the collective, thus failing to preserve or protect legitimate senses of individual (negative) liberty.[20]

The purpose of this model of education is to protect the nucleus of learning—the student—in order to preserve particularity (diversity) while developing a responsible, intelligent community member. Accounting for diverse interests and learning abilities also protects equal opportunity, including the complexities of individual responsibility and choice in learning. Ultimately, too, teachers are accountable to students, parents and peers in a roundtable model of leadership, with little need for a costly hierarchical bureaucracy. The teacher-student relationship changes from an I-It, or a means-end relationship on some utility (e.g.,

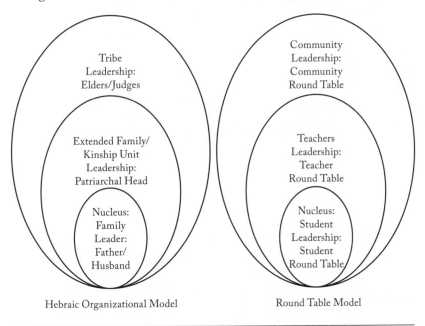

Figure 6.2. Comparison of Hebraic social/political organization to round-table organization

---

[19]See John Dewey, *The School and Society* (Chicago: University of Chicago Press, 1915).
[20]Regarding the differences between negative and positive liberty, see Isaiah Berlin, *Liberty: Incorporating Four Essays on Liberty* (Oxford: Oxford University Press, 2002).

Christian Option	View of Reality and Knowledge	1st Amend-ment Church/ State	Role of the Public School	Response to School Authorities	Highest Values
Agent for Encul-turation	Reality and Knowledge are Split: Secular/ Sacred Public/Private	High Wall of Separation (Neutrality as Separation) Protection of State from Church	Prepare Student for Democratic Role in Society	Passively Obedient	Social Stability
Christian Advocate/ Evangelist	Reality and Knowledge are Split: Sacred higher than Secular Knowledge: No Public/ Private Distinction	Church/God Occupies a Higher Sphere than State Protection of Church from State	Use the School to Further Knowledge about God	Answers to a Higher Authority	Spreading of Christian Public Morality (Foundation of U.S. institutions)
Golden Rule Truth-Seeker	No Split in Reality or Knowledge Sacred and Secular Equally Relevant/ Integrated Spheres of Life	Right to Express Religious Beliefs and Responsibility to Extend Right to Others Non-establishment and Free-exercise Clauses are Naturally Observed (Neutrality as Impartiality)	No Direct Proselytizing Truth and Justice Seeking (if this quest leads to knowledge about God, so be it)	Unafraid to Go Where Truth Leads Compliant Within the Bounds of Academic Freedom	Truth, Justice, Integrity, Intellectual Honesty The Quest for Truth is Ultimately a Quest to know God

Figure 6.3. Options for Christian public school teachers

test scores), to an intrinsically valuable I-Thou situation, where the end of education is human flourishing as guided by knowledgeable, caring adults and a coherent, relatively efficient yet diverse curriculum. The result of compulsory education restores to the arduous (and often boring) acquisition of knowledge, skills and experiences an opportunity for higher interest studies. This decentralized model provides one important bridge from the school to the community such that it provides to each student access to rich informational conditions (diverse sources of knowledge), as well as human and social capital, in order to maximize learning and chances for life success.

Christian educators and leaders within the schools also have several faith-integration models from which to choose. In an important and often-cited article by J. E. Schwartz, three options for Christian public school teachers are presented: (1) the agent for enculturation, (2) the Christian advocate/evangelist and (3) the golden rule truth-seeker. We have roughly captured Schwartz's options in the matrix found in figure 6.3.[21]

It is our view that the Christian teacher who practices in the range of Schwartz's "golden rule truth-seeker," a position consistent with the précis of this book, will be in a superior position to maximize information, thereby maximizing the potential for genuine education. If this idea of what happens to information within expanding institutions is correct, then increasing the flow, depth and diversity of information will help the Christian educator improve the public school learning environment and overcome the information challenge posed by the technical framework.

CHRISTIAN EDUCATION

A key problem in Christian education today is whether to respond to the same information network now controlling the broader institution of education. There is great incentive to do so. There are gains to be secured when Christian schools gauge their activities against the criteria of the technical framework. This is a rational way to think, particularly as students of Christian schools will compete for university admissions with students from the public sector. So the natural thing to do is to align the Christian school curriculum with the cur-

---

[21]Matrix developed from J. E. Schwartz, "Christians Teaching in the Public Schools: What Are Some Options?" *Christian Scholar's Review* 26, no. 3 (1997): 293-305.

riculum required by state university systems. The problem is that state university systems have a particular conception of the curriculum, not to mention a particular a priori commitment to naturalism (through secularism), which emphasizes secular approaches to knowledge. For example, it is an open question whether a science course at a Christian school that formally spent class time on the intelligent design movement would qualify as acceptable credit at any state university system in the country. On the other hand, the opposite problem occurs when a Christian school curriculum fails to measure up to the standards of knowledge appropriate to the academic traditions, including the basic and reasonable commitments of the sciences (physics, chemistry and biology).

The history of Christian education is as old as the first generation of Christians. Today, Christian education offers a variety of foci in education: schooling, church and parachurch ministries, soul care and discipleship, leadership development, and programs in the outdoor education and camp ministries. One of its institutional virtues is that Christian education often looks different at different organizations and within various faith traditions. Christian education in evangelical Christian traditions tends to possess greater curricular and pedagogical freedom than the public schools, though in accordance with broad principles and traditions within Protestant theology. Relative to the larger institution, its information and knowledge base operates at the margins of production. Its knowledge and focus inherently conflict with the broader and mostly secular institution of education.

What do these larger historical developments have to do with Christian education today? As we have suggested, information is a necessary condition for the development and production of knowledge or good in any field. Where the flow of information is restricted, the creative development and production of knowledge and complex goods slows.

Christian education is highly valuable to the institutional church, parachurch organizations and more importantly (though not separately) to the Lord Jesus Christ. However, it is perhaps equally important to the moral, spiritual and intellectual health of society at large. As the

American founders and others, like Tocqueville, remind us, the knowledge base offered to society by Christian schools was once regarded as an active condition—a public good—for the health of American political and social institutions. Because the knowledge itself is of the exclusive and suspiciously *certain* kind, it has a tendency to act as a jamming mechanism in the network of secularly based universal information. Inasmuch as the state represents and governs universal information, it has removed from the public agenda the higher-cost particular information most valued within Christian education (Jesus' brilliant ontic and social theories of equilibrium, spiritual formation, discipleship, Christ-centered morality, higher-cost pedagogical exchanges and the like). Under the present milieu of secularism this information is virtually irrelevant, perhaps even harmfully intolerant, to the production of the education good. Christian education and its now-quirky emphases and particulars come to be seen by the secular mind as obstructions to human progress as advanced by secular human ingenuity. Christian knowledge interferes with a secular kind of social consensus and advancement.[22]

If our theory of what happens to information within expanding institutions is correct, then increasing the flow and depth of information will help Christian education improve its academic position and overcome whatever information challenge it might have (e.g., parochialism). The School of Alexandria during the patristic period provides one important model for Christian education.[23] The first step that Origen reportedly taught his students is aptly described by Gregory of Neocaesarea in these terms:

> [Origen] introduced us to all schools of thought and was determined that we should be ignorant of no type of Greek doctrine. . . . Nothing was forbidden us, nothing was hidden from us, nothing inaccessible to us. We were to learn all manner of doctrine—barbarian or Greek, mystical or political, divine or human. We went into and examined with entire freedom all sorts of ideas, in order to satisfy ourselves and enjoy

---

[22]John Dewey, *A Common Faith* (New Haven, Conn.: Yale University Press, 1960).
[23]Edmund Fuller, ed., *The Christian Idea of Education* (New Haven, Conn.: Yale University Press, 1957).

to the full these goods of the mind. When an ancient thought was true, it belonged to us and was at our disposition with all its marvelous possibilities of delightful contemplation.[24]

Origen's economic move was to maximize the diversity, volume and depth of information into his school in order to produce a complex good: an informed, educated, intellectually virtuous and wise Christian. Obviously, a set of conditions would be required to do this in age-appropriate ways.

Again, our idea is not to list a series of specific solutions. Rather, we wish to demonstrate an opportunity over the next twenty to thirty years to think differently about the provision of schooling and ideas for ensuring genuine education and human development. To do this, we need to enlist the help of Christian universities and their schools of education.

CHRISTIAN UNIVERSITY SCHOOLS OF EDUCATION

Christian universities that have schools of education have not exactly been effective stewards of the field of education. While this is painful for us to admit, the fact is readily apparent when we recognize that no good theoretical work is originating from them. They are not solving important problems in the field of education. As one former dean told us, schools of education in general have become in their research commitments expert at taking the pulse of a dying patient. If theory is the rails on which practice occurs, then we have a bit of a problem. In fact, there have been no significant ideas originating from Christian schools of education for at least several decades. Rather than originating theory or basic research that might steward the institution in a more humane direction—basically the ethical task of theory—Christian schools of education appear resolved to operate within existing theoretical structures developed by the technical model of the secular academy.

Let us consider the case of practice. There are generally two arcs of educational practice within teacher education departments and schools of education. Educational practice when done well has an arc of ascent: it is an ascent of the scholar in which students and society come to bene-

---

[24]Ibid., p. 157.

fit, where education is rich in texture and information, where the good of education is the individual's complex development and flourishing, which contributes bottom-up to social welfare. Practice as an ascent uses the individual student as the fundamental unit of analysis for good practice. Educational practice when not done well has an arc of descent: it is the descent to the technician in which students and society lose, where education is depleted of information and knowledge, where the teacher is a mere quantity adjuster in which the mantra of education becomes, "If I can't see it or measure it, either it doesn't exist or it isn't important." The descent of practice uses aggregates and the statistical curve as the unit of analysis; it is an emphasis on the collective and away from the individual. Teachers or professors caught in the descent tend to look at education as the gathering and analyzing of data in order to make decisions, whereas teachers or professors working within an ascent try to figure out and then realize a world that doesn't yet exist. The former is called "data-driven decision making," but no one will tell you that only quantitative (statistical) data counts in the process. The later is called wisdom, the right use of knowledge and information to make decisions; it is the exercise of the liberally educated person using practical know-how *(mētis)* in order to bring about a richer social environment.

From our knowledge of the field many and perhaps most of the schools of education and teacher education departments in higher education are appropriating an insufficient theoretical framework for their initiatives. An insufficient theoretical framework leads practice toward a descent (a regression) not an ascent (a progression). The descent of practice is the consequence of decisions made by teachers and professors under conditions of scarcity (insufficient resources, including vital sources of information), which control and align schools of education with the technical market of information (basically, the rules) developed under the expanding institution of education and coordinated by the state and quasi-state accrediting firms.

As we have seen, the wider institution of education centralizes the rules in order to deal with a scarcity of resources and resolve diverse interests and disparate claims on those resources. What is not widely recognized is that the centralization of the rules in the technical framework helps schools of education to deny that scarcity as a real condition exists, leading to the corollary belief that all things are compatible, that we can solve everything if we just get the right rules or correct beliefs (dispositions) about education, and that there are no costs in producing education. By adopting this criterion, schools of education help to conceal important tradeoffs: nearly everyone comes to believe that education in the robust and traditional sense is sustainable in the technical framework of thought.

At its core, this descent comes about as a tradeoff of one type of information (particular, individual, local) for another type (universal, collective, standardized) that occurs in educational production and research about production. Most research today supports the technical framework, almost none of it challenges the technical direction. Yet it is this division of information that raises costs in the educational enterprise chiefly by continuously shifting the nature and perception of the education good away from the development of the individual human being (e.g., the unique student in the school, the individual teacher-in-training in higher education) and away from recognizing and tapping dynamic resources from the local environment.[25] Understanding this division requires an improved way (an institutional way) to see information as a scarce resource in education. Theories that use the individual organization as the basic unit of analysis (what economists call the theory of the firm) cannot see or determine the loss of vital information and rising costs in society brought about by that loss. In our assessment of the field of education we are using a fundamentally different unit of analysis by which researchers, leaders, policy makers and teachers-as-scholars can see, reflect on and develop strategic questions regarding the cost of information in education. The institutional work in this book will help readers to acquire these new epistemic lenses.

It is of utmost importance for students and scholars to understand that the descent of practice engulfs the entire spectrum of schools of education and teacher preparation. It is a process of transforming even

---

[25]For a political understanding of this phenomenon, see James Scott, *Seeing Like a State: How Certain Schemes to Improve the Human Condition Have Failed* (New Haven, Conn.: Yale University Press, 1998).

the visions of the education good and the means by which those schools and departments pursue it. We can, for example, anticipate some of the decision making by schools of education coming from shifts in the education market by accrediting agencies and the changes this will bring about in the information base of the institution. As one instance, some people believe that aligning a school of education's productive activities with an accrediting firm like the National Council for Accreditation of Teacher Education (NCATE) ensures the quality of their activities; that it is the rational way to proceed; that it provides for us a reliable common (collectivist) vision of our profession. In reality, this is not the case. Quality only comes of three sources: quality scholars, quality students and quality ideas. It does not emerge from uniform rules of production. Instead, alignment with the accrediting firm only means a descent into the wider rule structure of the market (everyone looks the same, everyone becomes uniform), which means a tremendous loss of information in their productive activities and the eventual diminishment of the professoriate and their students. To our knowledge, only one major figure during the initial stages of the descent had anticipated its result. Harry Judge, of Oxford University's school of education, early on predicted several of the effects created by the descent of practice:

> The Holmes Group is absolutely correct in insisting that the research universities must be closely associated with the formation of the teaching profession, but should recognize that in making such noises they are singing a hymn and not reciting a creed. . . .
>
> At present, or until very recently, such prestigious [universities] distinguished themselves—for good external reasons—by neglecting teaching teachers at the expense of other academic and professional pursuits related more or less peripherally to the diurnal business of the classroom. Changing that world, as the Holmes Group wishes it to be changed, implies a massive shift in objectives, in the criteria for esteem and promotion, in the balance of research, in the exercise of power. Given what the report so clearly says about the centrality of pedagogy, it follows that a new generation of specialists in the relevant fields must shortly rise to prominence. They are not yet in place.

One test, 10 years hence, of whether the Holmes agenda "happened" will take the form of a study of faculty lists in selected institutions. If reform has bitten, there will be fewer economists, sociologists, historians, administrative theorists (above all, them), and even psychologists, and many more specialists in curriculum, teaching, and teacher education.[26]

In order to develop the capacity to transform the institution of education and the conscience of its participants, the church will have to rely on Christian higher education, especially Christian schools of education, to carry the integration mandate.[27] One place to begin is the rule structure of education. For any deep and positive change of the kind discussed in this book, schools of education will need to develop the capacity to call into question the rule system within education, itself a key source of inequalities and the underdevelopment of human beings. To do this requires a change in how educators and scholars see the institution—a change in social epistemology, if you will. In turn this will require the ability to bear the costs of being different, of seeing differently, of seeing the social institution more deeply than others.

For example, schools of education err when they take for granted that information is costless, that scarcity does not exist, that the full potential of human beings can be achieved and maximized under institutional expansion, that there is no consequential tradeoff between efficiencies of education production and the complex information requirements of the good being produced. They err when they take for granted that a compatibility exists between the principles of efficiency (the domain of lower cost) and the complex development of human beings (the domain of higher cost), that persistent problems such as inequality are resolvable with the right collective dispositions or the

---

[26]Harry Judge, "Reforming Education: A View from Abroad," published online by *Education Week* (http://www.edweek.org/ew/articles/1987/06/24/3-39judg.h06.html, accessed May 29, 2009).

[27]When the term *Christocentric* is used, we measure a guess that there is often a reflexive view that entails a *narrowing* not a broadening of investigative pathways. Such a reflexive view is both inconsistent with ancient Christian traditions and with Scripture. Paul informs us that *all* knowledge and wisdom is rooted (grounded) in Jesus Christ (Col 2:3). If this is true, then to have a Christocentric view of anything is to seek the broadest and truest possible view of a matter.

right set of rules. These errors will remain if there is no shift in the information base and epistemological lenses of schools of education.

Taking these matters for granted leads to at least three important problems we see today in nearly all schools of education: (1) a denial of scarcity (e.g., in talent, time, information, knowledge, resources, ideas, problems, modes of inquiry), (2) an unrecognized loss of information in their production activities (e.g., excessive standardization), and (3) an incapacity to address rising levels of social inequality that threaten human development and the social welfare.

We can understand why these problems exist when we understand that schools of education and their departments of teacher education are part of the greater system of production within the institution of education. When they are functioning properly, they are the market sector that helps to set institutional agenda. They educate practitioners, the leaders and the scholars, toward ascent not descent. A few Christian schools of education even contributed (at one time) to theory and institutional policy. Presently, however, most are not functioning properly; many are securing gains from trade by acting as mere suppliers of labor (e.g., teachers, administrators and researchers who study practice as a descent). Arguably, it is not enough to train teachers to fill roles in the schools without educating them in how to steward the institution of education by showing them how to manage their classroom agenda, their school, their school district and their state department or board of education.

Christian schools of education have an opportunity to play an important role in setting the institutional agenda. The question is, will they? For schools of education to make that contribution a conscious shift in emphasis is needed, one where good theoretical work is paramount, where Christian leaders (trustees, presidents, provosts and deans) support and resource new initiatives and innovative research projects that steward theory and improve professional practice. As Kenneth Arrow showed, there is "complementarity between a productive activity and some kinds of information."[28] Theoretical research is a costly activity that requires enormous breadth and depth of informa-

---

[28]Kenneth Arrow, "On the Agenda of Organizations," in *Collected Papers of Kenneth Arrow*, vol. 4: *The Economics of Information* (Cambridge, Mass.: Belknap, 1984), p. 172.

tion, and the time to develop it. Resources have a way of improving the
information environment, as any first-tier university or think tank will
attest. Yet resources are a necessary but insufficient condition for the
productive activity we have in mind. That kind of activity also requires
talented faculty and strong, curious students thinking differently and
boldly about the institution of education.

All of this is difficult to achieve when we recognize that the institution of education over the last sixty-plus years has centered the direction of production securely within collective interests, evident by the
vast numbers of people participating in schooling and higher education
in the United States since 1946. What is not commonly understood is
that both research and practice have tracked this path. This is different
from the orthodox belief that research and practice are inherently ir-
reconcilable; that research and its methods move toward the universal
(it does) and practice move toward the particular (it does not). Practice,
as we have seen, now tracks the standardized information environment
of education. Because research and practice track the same rule structure, this turns out to be a false belief. They both track the technical
model of production, which is to simply recognize that the individual
human being and educational theories and metatheories are no longer
the chief concerns of research.

Most research conducted within schools of education today hold
these properties in common: (1) it is nontheoretical or atheoretical, (2)
it is focused on practice as a descent and not on larger issues or first
principles, and (3) it is almost uniformly biased in a certain direction on
the gradient of social choice, one that emphasizes an expanded state or
market on technical terms.[29] The lack of capacity to accurately take
stock of the existing institution, the lack of desire or inability to critique
its rule structure, is a function of the rules becoming more universal as
the system of education expands. This is so because institutional expansion requires the turnover of the property-rights structure (basically, the rules of access and use) such that old principles connected to
the first set of property rights (e.g., the higher-cost development of

---

[29]Arthur Levine, "Educating Researchers," *The Education School Project* (New York: Columbia
University Press, 2007).

scholars) must give way to the principles associated with the new, more universal property rights (e.g., the lower-cost development of technicians). Both research and practice are subject to these information constraints imposed by institutional growth. So one line of thinking is that theoretical research is the inequality producer; that moving toward technical forms of practice will situate schools of education closer to resolving inequality and other concerns. The fact that two decades of effort have been invested in this direction has not brought research or policy any closer to resolving issues of inequality does not seem to deter schools of education from continuing to focus almost exclusively on technical forms of practice. In other words, the rules that promote expansion become the criterion of rationality for good research and practice. All information and inquiry that cannot be demonstrated to expand the system (or somehow threatens to work against it) is seen as particular or private information. Any research and scholarship that does not line up with the existing information structure loses agenda. As a consequence no Christian school of education is producing bona fide scholars. Consider the alternative reality if five or six Christian universities developed or received resources sufficient to establish small-scale top-level Ph.D. programs. What would the effect be? One possible impact is that higher education would improve and a cadre of Christian scholars would lead in the area of ideas.

This is of course merely a thumbnail sketch of opportunities for Christian schools of education. Yet it fastens the information economy of education to the background presuppositions of Christian truth. In the words of John Paul II:

> The present age is in urgent need of . . . *proclaiming the meaning of truth,* that fundamental value without which freedom, justice and human dignity are extinguished. By means of a kind of universal humanism [Christian higher education] is completely dedicated to the research of all aspects of truth in their essential connection with the supreme Truth, who is God.[30]

---

[30]Inasmuch as Christian purposes of education extend across denominational boundaries, we took the liberty of substituting "Christian higher education" for John Paul II's "Catholic Universities." Emphasis is in the original.

In light of this commitment, one probably shared by all Christian educators, we recommend pursuing deeper understandings of the Christian faith in order to resolve pressing, nearly intractable problems.

CONCLUSION

James, the brother of Jesus and a leader of the early Jerusalem church, signals that people ought to be careful before becoming teachers because teachers will incur a stricter judgment (Jas 3:1). James includes himself as a teacher. This declaration of supreme accountability suggests that because teachers have truth-bearing responsibility as elders in the shepherding of human development through direct teaching and the leading of learning organizations, teachers will be judged more severely. For Christians this assessment occurs at the judgment seat *(bema)* of Christ (Rom 14:10-12; 2 Cor 5:10). This should provoke at least two internal reflections before responding to the high calling of being a Christian educator: a healthy fear and trembling, which appears to be one motive for why James mentions the closer scrutiny; and the honorific responsibility borne by the Christian educator to Christ and all human beings within the educator's orbit of work.

In this regard we leave the reader with an authoritative reflection from Augustine's *The City of God.*

> The Heavenly City, in contrast [to the earthly city, which knows many idols and gods], knows only one God as the object of worship, and decrees, with faithful devotion, that he only is to be served with that service which the Greeks call *latreia*, is due to God alone. . . . While this Heavenly City, therefore, is on pilgrimage in this world, she calls out citizens from all nations and so collects a society of aliens, speaking all languages. She takes no account of any difference in customs, laws, and institutions, by which earthly peace is achieved and preserved— not that she annuls or abolishes any of those, rather, she maintains them and follows them . . . *provided that no hindrance* is presented thereby to the religion which teaches that the one supreme and true God is to be worshipped.[31]

---

[31]Augustine *City of God* 19.19, trans. Henry Bettenson (New York: Penguin, 1972), p. 878, emphasis added.

Index